Recreation and Sport Planning and Design

Second Edition

Jim Daly

Human Kinetics

Library of Congress Cataloging-in-Publication Data

Daly, James W., 1934-
    Recreation and sport planning and design / James W. Daly. -- 2nd
ed.
        p.   cm.
    Includes bibliographical references and index.
    ISBN 0-7360-0345-2
    1. Recreation areas--Australia--Planning.   2. Recreation areas-
-Australia--Design and construction.   3. Sports facilities-
-Australia--Planning.   4. Sports facilities--Australia--Design and
construction.   I. Title.
    GV182.3.D24   2000
    796'.06'94--dc21   99-42475
                                                                        CIP

ISBN 0-7360-0345-2

Managing Editor: Cynthia McEntire
Assistant Editors: John Wentworth and Kim Thoren
Copyeditor: Patsy Fortney
Indexer: James Daly
Graphic Designer: Stuart Cartwright
Graphic Artists: Tara Welsch and Stuart Cartwright
Cover Designer: Jack W. Davis
Photographer (cover): © Michael P. Manheim/The Image Finders
Printer: United Graphics

Printed in the United States of America   10   9   8   7   6   5   4   3   2   1

Human Kinetics
Web site: http://www.humankinetics.com/

United States: Human Kinetics, P.O. Box 5076, Champaign, IL 61825-5076
1-800-747-4457
e-mail: humank@hkusa.com

Canada: Human Kinetics, 475 Devonshire Road Unit 100, Windsor, ON N8Y 2L5
1-800-465-7301 (in Canada only)
e-mail: humank@hkcanada.com

Europe: Human Kinetics, P.O. Box IW14, Leeds LS16 6TR, United Kingdom
+44 (0)113-278 1708
e-mail: humank@hkeurope.com

Australia: Human Kinetics, 57A Price Avenue, Lower Mitcham, South Australia 5062
(08) 82771555
e-mail: liahka@senet.com.au

New Zealand: Human Kinetics, P.O. Box 105-231, Auckland Central
09-523-3462
e-mail: humank@hknewz.com

Contents

Preface

Communities in which we work and play are enhanced by well-planned recreation and sport facilities and services. It is estimated that $566 million worth of work was completed on recreation and sport projects during the 1995–96 financial year, around 20 per cent ($114 million) of which was undertaken by public sector organisations. The types of projects included golf courses, playing fields, stadiums, swimming pools, landscaping and park construction.[1]

This book contributes to encouraging rational planning by suggesting some practical guidelines to assist in not only the planning, but also the design of cost-effective facilities for the community.

I am particularly impressed with the breadth of information in the book commencing with the benefits of recreation and sport, then proceeding on to discussing various planning methodologies, before concentrating on practical planning principles and guidelines for those who have the task of actually bringing projects to fruition.

One major theme that flows through the book is the need for cooperation at all levels. Emphasis is placed on the need for recreation and sport clubs and associations to work closely with local councils, state governments and national organisations to deliver the most effective and efficient recreation and sport facilities and services. It is encouraging to see that guidelines are being suggested as a valuable starting point for the planners and designers of our recreation and sport facilities.

The success of the first edition suggests that there is a growing need for a practical publication dealing with recreation and sport planning. The Office for Recreation and Sport is pleased to hand over the publication of this second edition to Human Kinetics in the knowledge that a wider market can be reached. Our continued interest in this manual will be to encourage its distribution in Australia.

It is appropriate that a book of this nature is available as we set our sights on planning for the next century. I commend this recreation and sport planning and design guidelines publication to you as an important contribution to our knowledge of how best to plan and manage recreation and sport facilities and open spaces in the communities of the future.

Simon Forrest, Executive Director
Office for Recreation and Sport
South Australia

---

[1] Australian Bureau of Statistics [1997] *Sport and Recreation—A Statistical Overview,* cat. no. 4156, p. 78.

Acknowledgments

As with the first edition, many people have contributed to this publication. The support given by the Office for Recreation and Sport in South Australia is most appreciated. At the executive level, I have been supported by Lyn Parnell, Director of Recreation and Sport, who cleared the way for publishing approvals. Team members Mike Schetter and Philip Freeman have offered constructive advice on the contents of various chapters and this has been part of a cooperative learning process for all of us. Other staff members who have contributed to specific sections are Bronte Leak and Leith Hughes on outdoor recreation and trails development. Ray Scheuboek was an excellent research assistant who contributed significantly to the outdoor recreation chapter and updated the dimensions for the sports dimensions in appendix C. Some of the plans of indoor facilities used in the first edition and used again in this edition were produced by Dennis Horne, a former colleague.

The development of chapter 7 on coastal recreation was funded by Environment Australia Marine Group who saw the need to produce planning guidelines for coastal recreation as part of its wider responsibility for the protection of the Australian coastline. Others who helped review this chapter include Damien Moroney, Coordinator, Coast and Green Seas; Peter Swift, Manager, Marine Facilities, South Australia; and the Surf Life Saving Australia staff at the state and national levels.

It is a pleasure to have the enthusiastic input from people who are prepared to share their expertise. Rick Bzowy is a leading Australian sport facilities architect who provided new material on aquatic facilities. Graeme Alder has a wealth of knowledge on management of facilities and his expertise is reflected in much of the management section of chapter 6. Another person with special skills is Simon Reynolds who has contributed his knowledge on skateboarding. Fortunately, Chris Reeves, who was instrumental in designing the first edition, was again able to develop plans, diagrams and tables for this edition. A sincere word of thanks is due to Sandra Romeo who keyed in the text from a variety of notes given to her in a less than orderly manner.

I am constantly surprised by the ready cooperation of people who go out of their way to share information. This applies to those in other states who have provided photos, publications from which I was given permission to quote and other information that has added to the quality of this edition. In particular, I would like to thank Pam Armstrong, Manager, Infrastructure Development Queensland, Tourism, Sport and Racing who shared the enthusiasm of developing a comprehensive information database for facility planning.

Although this edition has had input from many sources, some of whom are acknowledged above, it is incumbent on me to take responsibility for the views expressed, including any errors. I hope the reader will be generous in accepting my limitations and that this publication will assist in furthering recreation and sport planning and design at local, regional and national levels wherever the need for good planning exists.

Introduction

I experienced a great deal of satisfaction from the way in which the first edition of this manual has been accepted as a guide to effective recreation and sport planning. Rather than being a superficial revision, this edition is a sincere attempt to provide entirely new material and updated references.

Of particular interest is a new chapter on coastal recreation, bringing together for the first time planning criteria applicable to the most popular recreation activities occurring along the coast. There is a growing concern for protecting our coast and recreation planning should be considered early in the planning process rather than as an afterthought as seems to be the case at present. Planning criteria for a range of recreation activities are provided taking into account beach safety, tourism and other uses as an integral part of coastal planning and management.

The controversy of how to develop and use appropriate recreation open space standards has not been resolved and to assist in understanding the present thinking, this chapter updates the overview of recreation open space legislation and official planning documents. In addition, I have provided some templates to at least give a starting point for the development of recreation and sport open space at local, district and regional levels.

Another change is the addition of a chapter on facilities and management. Some of this material such as diagrams for indoor centres has been moved from the appendices of the previous edition and a new section on aquatic facilities is now provided. Skateboarding is a growing recreation and sport that has a huge number of participants demanding well-planned facilities at local, district, regional and state levels. Some suggested layouts and planning criteria are provided. Since facility provision is only half of the equation, this chapter concludes with an extensive section on management of facilities.

Photos are a visual way of learning from each other and examples of good practice from each of the Australian states and territories are again provided. I am sure that additional information is available on these projects if readers wish to contact states and territories on these and other facilities. The dimensions for sports have been updated and new ones added. Again, an extensive index is provided for easy reference to specific information.

No author is entirely satisfied with what is produced, and since the previous edition, significant changes have occurred in the expectations of the community to recreation and sport provision of facilities and services. I hope that this publication will stimulate fresh thinking and fewer mistakes in planning and design through lack of knowledge.

CHAPTER 1

Benefits of Recreation and Sport

In this chapter, the benefits of recreation and sport are identified to assist planners by providing practical arguments for justifying recreation and sport open spaces and facilities at state, regional and local levels. The diversity of recreation and sport is first addressed, then benefits are provided under four headings using a summary statement. If more information is required, specific benefits are identified. Finally, evidence of the benefits is given with full references. Disbenefits of recreation and sport are also discussed.

PLANNERS AND THE QUALITY OF LIFE

Planners have a particular responsibility to understand the contribution that recreation and sport makes to enhance the quality of life—both of individuals and communities. The main arguments for advocating the benefits of adequate recreation and sport facilities and services for all ages should be well understood because they are an important part of the planning process.

To some extent everyone is a planner; the term does not only refer to those professionals who draw up policies or strategies for cities and large commercial projects. For effective communities, recreation planning involves many people, including recreation officers, parks managers, community development officers, health workers, education officers, youth workers, community arts officers, tourist officers, private sector developers, marketing experts and volunteers in community organisations. Particularly, the people who will be affected by the results of the planning decisions should also be involved. Therefore, planning is an ongoing process—not just a specific task that has a predetermined beginning and end.

Increasingly, planners are being challenged to place more emphasis on the issues that affect the quality of life. One way to do this is to measure the levels of satisfaction or priorities that people give to various community services and facilities. It is interesting to note that recreation and sport facilities and services rate highly when people are asked to score their community priorities.

DIVERSITY OF RECREATION AND SPORT

A great deal of time and effort is given to defining what recreation and sport mean. Even the more inclusive term 'leisure' is often considered to be, in large part, recreation and sport. Most people seem to use these terms interchangeably, so rather than add to what can often be a confused theoretical discussion, let's accept that at the community level most sport is recreation and a significant number of recreational activities involve sport. As Stoddart (1986) points out, 'sport constitutes a large slice of leisure'.[1]

Rather than simply using definitions, it is more helpful to identify the main components of recreation and sport using all or some of the following terms:

• *Free Time.* Various dictionaries including Webster's (1990) tend to favour leisure (recreation) as involving the use of 'free time'.[2] When sport becomes professional, there is a constraint on free time and sport can in these circumstances become work. As Stoddart (1986) points out, 'top-level Australian sport will become more concerned with such issues (work-related complications)'.[3]

• *Activity.* Early definitions by Dumazedier (1974) and others tend to emphasise leisure (recreation) as, 'those activities that provided relaxation, diversion, or broadening of knowledge.'[4]

• *Competition.* Whereas recreation tends to be noncompetitive, sport has competitive activities associated with participation. As Coakley (1990) suggests, 'sport is an institutionalised competitive activity'.[5]

• *Social.* Recreation, sport and leisure all have strong social elements. Rowe and Lawrence (1990) emphasise that 'sport and leisure are profoundly social in character' [6] and the official publication of the Department of Sport, Recreation and Tourism (1985) points out 'that in particular, sport has a profound impact on the development of Australian society'.[7]

• *State of Being.* Attitude of mind or a state of being is used by Torkilsen (1987) and others who have adopted a psychosocial interpretation that links the more intangible reasons for involvement.[8]

• *Satisfaction.* The proposition of recreation as 'intrinsically satisfying pursuits'[9] is used by Howat and Earle (1986) and others.

• *Peak Experience.* Particularly when referring to some adventure activities and highly competitive sports events, Csikszentmihalyi (1991) uses the term 'optimal experiences' [10] and Hamilton-Smith (1990) talks about the 'peak experience'.[11]

• *Fun and Enjoyment.* Recreation and leisure are linked to 'pleasure, fun and enjoyment'[12] by Mobily (1989), while Parker and Paddick (1990) suggest that 'enjoyment' was the most common cited element when a sample of South Australians were asked the meaning of leisure.[13]

• *Play/Organised.* The element of play is a factor in recreation and sport activities. Most writers emphasise play components in each, but Coakley (1985) points out that 'sport is different from play . . . it is organised and structured'.[14]

REASONS FOR IDENTIFYING BENEFITS

There is intense competition for scarce financial and human resources at all levels of government and among organisations working in the private sector. Therefore, it is important to present decision makers with compelling evidence for providing adequate recreation and sport facilities and services.

USING THE BENEFITS ARGUMENTS

Planners and others using this manual will have a variety of reasons for wanting to identify the benefits of recreation and sport. There are those who will require short, concise statements, perhaps for speeches or press statements. Others may want key points with more detail for reports, strategic planning documents and planning approvals, while at various times more detailed arguments and supporting evidence are required to give statements more credibility.

BENEFITS IN DETAIL

These benefits are presented for easy reference under four categories:

1. Personal and individual benefits
2. Social and community benefits
3. Economic benefits
4. Planning and environmental benefits

The aim is to present powerful and convincing evidence to justify the allocation of resources (financial and physical) to recreation and sport.

Personal and Individual Benefits

Recreation and sport provides people of all ages with an opportunity to participate in activities that contribute to the growth of body, mind and spirit.

Prevention of Health Problems

Among the many benefits of physical activity (growth of the body) through participation in certain kinds of recreation and sport is the fact that it is one of the best ways to prevent health problems now and in the future.

The National Heart Foundation produced a policy statement in 1991 that categorically states, 'exercise can benefit everyone, including people with heart disease'. It also went on to detail the benefits of moderate activity.[15]

A report from the United States Surgeon General states, 'We have today strong evidence to indicate that regular physical activity will provide clear and substantial health gains. . . . Because physical activity is so directly related to preventing disease and premature death and to maintaining a high quality of life, we must accord it the same level of attention that we give other important public health practices that affect the entire nation'.[16]

High volumes of exercise for periods over years help produce the negative energy balance required for weight loss. In addition, physical activity leads to other important benefits for overweight individuals.[17]

Recent research suggests that Australian children are showing all the signs of adapting to a less active lifestyle in a way medical experts predict will have far reaching implications for their health.[18]

Stress Management

Recreation and sports can assist the mind and body relationship and in particular reduce the incidence of stress. Several studies have noted the role of outdoor pursuits in improving the mental health of participants. Ewert (1988) reported improvements in self-esteem and self-confidence.[19]

Of course healthy interpersonal relationships are important in stress reduction. Holahan (1988) reported that activity participation had an important role in psychological well-being.[20]

Physical activity can have a significant effect on mental health. Physically active adults have enhanced self-concepts and self-esteem, as indicated by increased confidence, assertiveness, emotional stability, independence and self-control.[21]

The Feldenkrais method is recognised throughout the world as a successful technique that people can learn to assist them with the use of the mind in relation to body movement. Rywerant Yochanan, an approved practitioner, says, 'this system is a way of teaching people to increase both their physical and mental awareness in order to maximise their inherent potential'.[22]

Studies have identified the psychophysical indicators of leisure benefits, such as the importance of leisure activities in stress-mediating functions to releasing tension.[23] Learning a new recreation or sport skill improves the sense of independence and autonomy and enhances personal and individual benefits. In a nationwide household survey, women rated a chance to learn new skills as the second most important skill. Men rated this benefit sixth in importance.[24]

Improved Quality of Life

Intangible benefits such as happiness, enjoyment, satisfaction or spiritual experiences add to the quality of life. There has been a tendency to steer clear of describing these benefits because they are considered too difficult to measure and things of the spirit are often linked in a narrow sense to religious experiences. Yet there are many people who are concerned with how to improve the quality of their lives both within a secular as well as a religious context. Recreation and sport participation can contribute significantly to providing the elements necessary to encourage deeper experiences that lead to personal growth and a sense of well-being.

To improve life one must improve the quality of experience. Mihaly Csikszentmihalyi has researched the positive aspects of human experience over a number of decades with a research team at the University of Chicago and in many countries throughout the world. He places emphasis on 'flow' as a means of achieving optimal experiences or intrinsically rewarding experiences. He suggests that activities such as sports, games, art and hobbies consistently produce flow which is (in part) the achieving of happiness through control over one's inner life.[25]

Research by Russell and others indicates that there is support for a higher level of leisure participation leading to a higher level of need-satisfaction, which in turn is positively related to life satisfaction.[26] Many high-performance sports people understand that the level of satisfaction is strongly linked to the level of performance.

In a review of outdoor recreation benefits, Driver and Brown indicated some of the more important intangible benefits such as improving self-image, self-actualisation (or the ability to freely reach high levels of 'being'), spiritual growth and development, enhanced creativity and aesthetic appreciation, stimulation and the opportunity for curiosity seeking.[27]

Outward Bound courses and similar adventure activities provide good examples of these intangible benefits that can often come close to spiritual experiences. Some research among university students indicates that one of the major benefits from experiencing the solitude and grandeur of the wilderness is the opportunity for spiritually uplifting experiences.[28]

Social and Community Benefits

Recreation and sport can be a positive influence on the development of social and community attitudes such as cooperation, understanding, character, team spirit, fair play, loyalty and the strengthening of the national spirit. These lead to satisfying recreation and sport opportunities that also enhance strong community values.

Social Cohesiveness

Recreation and sport can strengthen social cohesion at national and community levels.

The First World Forum on Physical Activity and Sport held in Quebec City suggested that by socialisation through sport, children develop discipline, respect for authority, and cooperative behaviour; recognise their roles in group activity; and learn self-expression and how to relate and interact with others. Sports are believed to be inspirational, satisfying and fun builders of emotional maturity and character.[29]

Improved Community Life

Recreation and sporting opportunities strengthen the quality of life within communities.

One of the best measures of community involvement is the number of volunteers who freely contribute their services without remuneration to recreation and sporting organisations. A 1991 study of volunteers undertaken by the South Australia Department of Recreation and Sport and the Australian Sports Commission estimated that over 170,000 volunteers were involved in community sport and recreation in South Australia. The study went on to state that if the volunteers were not available, their sport would be 'inoperable'.[30]

Strengthened Families

Satisfying relationships within families can be maintained and perhaps strengthened by involvement in recreation and sporting activities.

An Australian survey carried out in the 1960s indicated that there is a strong, positive and significant relationship between joint participation in leisure activities and marital well-being and happiness.[31]

High Community Priority

Leisure (recreation and sport) is generally rated a high priority by people when considered along with a range of community benefits that add to the quality of life. A South Australian study found that recreation is one of the best predictors of community satisfaction.[32] A review of national and local surveys and empirical studies by Marans and Mohai in 1990 indicated that there was a high correlation between leisure and life satisfaction.[33]

Involved Older Adults

Recreation and sport contribute significantly to the quality of life of older adults. A South Australian study looked at significant lifestyle considerations among older people. They ranked home-based recreation activities as one of their first preferences (25.8 per cent). Other popular first choices included walking and jogging (17.4 per cent).[34]

Recreation patterns among older Australians (55+ years) indicate that in the physical or sporting competitive category, the most sought after additional involvement was in walking (13.3 per cent males, 16.8 per cent females), golf (6 per cent males, 3.3 per cent females) and bowls (5.2 per cent males, 2.5 per cent females).[35]

Benefits to Women

Women receive many social and community benefits through recreation and sport. There are over one million women over 15 years of age (i.e. one in six) who are involved in organised sporting activities throughout Australia.[36] Their talents and the sporting skills of players, administrators, coaches and officials are valuable assets to strengthening community structures. Also, these skills are transferable to other community activities.

Canadian statistics show that young girls remain active and healthy by participating in organised physical education and sporting activities. They gain competitive drive that overlaps into school work and outside community interests. Also, when girls participate in physical education and sporting activities, they feel satisfied, cohesive, confident, active and skilful.[37]

Economic Benefits

Most personal, social and environmental benefits of recreation and sport have an economic dimension. Direct economic benefits are derived from the capital development of recreation and sport facilities and the production of goods and services in both the private and public sector.

Investment Opportunities

More than half of the Australian population participates in recreation and sport activities at various levels. This offers opportunities for significant investments in the provision of recreation and sport facilities and services.

During the 12 months ending March 1997, almost one-third of Australians aged 15 years and over (32.4 per cent or 4.7 million people) were involved in sport, either as players, nonplayers or both. This figure does not include those who participate in social sport or physical activity which is not organised.[38]

Reduced Health Costs

Significant health cost savings can result from increasing community involvement in regular physical activities. These health benefits range from better personal cardiovascular performance to reduced incidents of lower back pain, leading to greater capacity to cope with stressful lifestyle pressures. Fitness programs and exercise are often criticised for being repetitive and therefore boring. Recreation and sport activities can provide an ideal way of increasing interest in regular physical activities.

The outlays by the commonwealth on health services to individual states in 1996–97 was $19.3 billion (i.e. $1,000 per person). Health benefits through increased participation in recreation and sport reduce the outlays in this area and allow funds to be redirected into other areas of the health service.[39]

A New South Wales report suggests that the health and vitality of our community can be improved through greater commitment. The national economic benefit for encouraging an additional 10 per cent of the population to engage in regular physical activity has been estimated at $590.2 million annually, or over $1.62 million per day.[40]

Increased Wealth of Nation

Recreation and sport are a significant contributor to the wealth of the nation.

The recreation and sport sector of the economy provides a percentage of Gross Domestic Product (GDP) comparable with other major industry sectors such as iron and steel, motor vehicles, transport, insurance, water supply, defence, rail and community services.[41]

Employment Opportunities

Contrary to popular belief, the recreation and sport industry is a significant and growing generator of employment. The recreation and sport sector employs over 95,000 people. Around 44 per cent of this employment is on a full-time basis.[42]

In the 1996 census, 217,000 people indicated that they had a main occupation associated with sport and recreation activities.[43] (Note: This includes arts, culture, gambling and amusement.) The volunteer contribution to recreation and sport is conservatively valued at $1.6 billion.[44]

Economic Development

Tourism makes a substantial contribution to the nation's economic development. Sporting events and recreational activities are an important part of the tourist experience.

In 1995, 10 per cent of international visitors to Australia indicated that a spectator, participant or nature-based outdoor activity was an influence on their decision to visit Australia.[45] Based on 1995 tourism information on international visitor reasons for travel to Australia, a conservative amount of expenditure on tourism-related sports is in the order of between $234 million and $430 million per year.[46]

Growth

Government expenditure on recreation and sport at all levels has grown significantly over the past five years. This growth reflects the importance that people place on recreation and sport open space, facilities and services.

On the commonwealth level, the outlay on recreation (including sport) in 1991–92 was $173 million and in 1995–96 it had increased to $265 million.[47] On the state and territory level, the outlay on recreation (including sport) in 1991–92 was $770 million and in 1995–96 it had increased to $909 million.[48] (*Note:* The figures here are expressed in current prices, that is, measured at prices current at the times when the outlays occurred.)

Local Growth

Local governments spend as much on recreation and sport as state governments and the commonwealth government combined.

In 1995–96, the commonwealth government spent $265 million on recreation and sport. Over the same period, the state and territory governments of New South Wales, Victoria, Queensland, Western Australia, South Australia, Tasmania, Northern Territory and Australian Capital Territory spent $909 million. Local governments throughout Australia spent $1,030 million over the same period.[49]

Improved Worker Productivity

Productivity in the work place improves if employees participate regularly in sport or active recreation programs.

Corporate-sponsored physical activity programs decrease employee turnover, decrease absenteeism, decrease industrial injuries, decrease medical costs, and increase productivity.[50]

Environmental Protection

Parks and open spaces for outdoor recreation and sport pursuits are an investment in environmental protection.

Proximity to open spaces has also been shown to increase real estate values substantially. According to the 1994 Commonwealth Fund/Harris poll, 57 per cent of property owners living within two blocks of a city park in New York say that being located near the park enhances the value of their property. In Salem, Oregon, urban land next to a greenbelt was worth $1,200 more per acre than urban land 1,000 feet away.[51]

Economies can be found through linking recreation and sport with environmental protection. The River Torrens Linear Park in Adelaide has developed a flood mitigation project at a cost of $28.2 million. $16.1 million of that total was allocated to linear park works mainly in the form of cycle and walking tracks, open spaces for informal recreation and sport use and tree planting for the beautification of the river banks.[52]

Planning and Environmental Benefits

Through the provision of parks, open spaces and protected natural environments, recreation and sport contributes to the environmental health of the community.

Diversity

Open spaces encourage a variety of diversity of recreation and sport opportunities, increasing personal, community and health benefits.

In the extensive public consultation over four years that culminated in the preparation of the South Australian Recreation and Sport Strategy Plan, open space was high on the priorities people gave to their recreation and sport preferences. The strategy therefore emphasises a variety of recreation open spaces including parks (urban and national), sports grounds, children's play areas, linear parks for walking and cycling, botanic gardens, forests, conservation areas, drainage areas, urban buffer zones, lakes, rivers and other water areas for people to actively and passively participate in recreation and sport.[53]

Parks and recreation were a significant and important feature for every Canadian city or town chosen as the most enlightened 10 towns and cities in America and Canada. Features such as bicycle and walking paths, downtown forests, cultural diversity and great parks (both within the city core and in communities) were key factors.[54]

Beauty

There are visual and aesthetic values to be obtained from recreation and sport open spaces.

Most people can relate to the experience of looking out over pleasant parklands or open space views on their way to or from work or at other special times. As Williams suggests, 'there is a certain psychic relief in open space that can not be underestimated. It gives us visual relief from the tangled, jarring and often monotonous sight of urban development and a sense of orientation and community identity'.[55]

Development

Economic and social benefits are derived from the planning of recreation and sport open spaces and facilities before new housing, community and commercial facilities are put into place.

Seymour Gold suggests that 'no single element can better shape and complement urban form than well-placed open space. Its ability to differentiate, integrate or buffer different types of land use or activities is unsurpassed. Sensitively designed open space can give people a sense of identity and territoriality. It can define urban form and limit the physical size, shape or density of a city or neighbourhood'.[56]

The parklands surrounding Adelaide are an example of well-planned open space for recreation and other purposes that were put into place when Colonel Light founded Adelaide in 1836. They give the city definite shape and form. The benefits of recreation were appreciated over 150 years ago because the original Adelaide plan stated, 'one of the major purposes for setting aside the parklands has always been to provide for the, "recreation of the people"'.[57]

Stability

A high level of satisfaction with the environment in which people live is an important benefit to the stability of communities. Proximity to nature, the outdoors and the convenience of recreation and sport facilities are major preferences when people have a choice about where they live.

Among those people living in new communities, the use of leisure time ranked second among ten predictors of life satisfaction.[58]

Sensitivity

Outdoor education (recreation) is the best available method for fostering environmental sensitivity. David Foot suggests that in Canada over the next 10 years there will be a gradual focus away from facility-based recreational activities towards natural environmental-based recreational activities.[59] This may also occur in Australia.

Outdoor education teaches people how to enjoy nature and enlarge their lives, both cognitively and affectively. Environmental education programs show increases in knowledge of the environment, increased levels of social interaction, a decrease in socially inappropriate behaviours, and an increase in learning lifelong outdoor leisure skills.[60]

DISBENEFITS OF RECREATION AND SPORT

While emphasis has been placed on the benefits of recreation and sport, it is important to acknowledge there are some disadvantages that affect individuals and the community.

For example, excessive injuries result from participation in some physical activities and sports. The Better Health Report states that 'one in seventeen Australians will suffer from some form of sports injury every year'. Also, 'sports injuries cost Australia $1 billion in 1990—the worst sports for injuries are: Australian football, rugby league and union, soccer, basketball, netball, hockey and cricket in that order'.[61]

There are also disadvantages associated with attitudes that link excessive use of alcohol and illicit drugs with recreation and sporting activities. The use of recreational drugs to enhance experiences cannot be condoned. Also, the use of performance-enhancing drugs in competitive sport is banned.

Noisy sports in close proximity to residential areas provide environmental disadvantages to near neighbours.

With increased mass entertainment and the encouragement of major recreation and sport events involving large crowds, there are disadvantages in the form of massive dislocation of traffic and crowd control. In addition, this type of recreation and sport activity can be disruptive to neighbours with increased noise levels and other environmental disturbances that can raise tensions in the community.

Another disadvantage is the result of poor planning that exacerbates community conflicts because of an inequitable allocation of recreation open space and facilities.

REFERENCES

1. Stoddart, Brian [1986] *Saturday Afternoon Fever— Sport in the Australian Culture*. North Ryde, NSW: Angus and Robertson, p. 10.
2. *Webster's New Dictionary and Thesaurus* [1990] New York: Russell, Geddes and Grosset.
3. Stoddart, Brian [1986] *Saturday Afternoon Fever— Sport in the Australian Culture*.
4. Dumazedier, Joffre [1974] *Concepts of Leisure* [J.F. Murphy, ed.]. Englewood Cliffs, NJ: Prentice Hall, p. 133.
5. Coakley, Jay J. [1990] *Sport in Society—Issues and Controversies*. St Louis: Time Mirror/Mosby College, p. 15.
6. Rowe, David and Lawrence, Geoff [1990] *Sport and Leisure—Trends in Australian Popular Culture*. New South Wales: Harcourt Brace Jovanovich, p. 17.
7. Department of Sport, Recreation and Tourism and Australian Sport Commission [1985] *Australian Sport: A Profile*. Canberra: Australian Publishing Service, p. xi.
8. Torkilsen, G. [1987] *Leisure and Recreation Management*. London: Russell, Geddes and Grosset.
9. Howat, G. and Earle, L. [1986] *Leisure Lifestyle and Well-Being: The Holistic Viewpoint of Leisure and its Application to Contemporary Society*, in ACHPER National Journal, June, pp. 8–10.
10. Csikszentmihalyi, Mihaly [1991] *Flow—The Psychology of Optimal Experience*. New York: Harper Perennial, p. 71.
11. Hamilton-Smith, Elery [1990] *Directions for Recreation Benefit Measurement in Australia: Some Preliminary Thoughts*. Melbourne: Phillip Institute of Technology.
12. Mobily, K. [1989] *Meanings of Recreation and Leisure Among Adolescents,* in Leisure Studies 8, pp. 11–23.
13. Parker, S. and Paddick, R [1990] *Leisure in Australia: Themes and Issues*. Melbourne: Longman Cheshire.
14. Coakley, Jay J. [1990] *Sport in Society*, p. 14.
15. National Heart Foundation of Australia [1991] *Exercise and Heart Disease: Policy Statement 5*. Canberra: Author.
16. Surgeon General US Public Health Service [1996] *Physical Activity and Health*, in The Benefits Catalogue, Parks and Recreation Association, Canada, p. 26.
17. Bouchard, C., Shephard, R. and Stephens, T. [1994] *Physical Activity, Fitness and Health*, in The Benefits Catalogue, Parks and Recreation Association, Canada, p. 29.
18. O'Neill, H. [1996] *The Slide to Sloth*. Aussie Sport Action, winter edition, pp. 8–9.
19. Ewert, A. [1988] *The Identification and Modification of Situational Fears Associated With Outdoor Recreation*, in the Journal of Leisure Research, vol. 20, pp. 106–117.

20. Holahan, C.K. [1988] *Relation of Life Goals at Age 70 to Activity Participation and Health and Psychological Well Being Among Terman's Gifted Men and Women*, in the Psychology of the Ageing, vol. 3 (3) pp. 286–291.

21. Seefeldt, V. and Vogel, P. [1985] *The Value of Physical Activity*, in The Benefits Catalogue, Parks and Recreation Association, Canada, p. 23.

22. Rywerant, Yochanan [1983] *The Feldenkrais Method: Teaching by Handling*. San Francisco: Harper and Row, p. xviii.

23. Ulrich, R.S., Dimberg, U. and Driver, B.L. [1991] *Psychophysical Indicators of Leisure Benefits,* in Benefits of Leisure [B.L. Driver, P.J. Brown and G.L. Peterson, eds.]. State College, PA: Venture Publishing.

24. Hawes, D.K. [1978] *Satisfaction Derived from Leisure-Time Pursuits: An Exploratory Nationwide Survey*, in Journal of Leisure Research, vol. 10, pp. 247–264.

25. Csikszentmihalyi, Mihaly [1991] *Flow—The Psychology of Optimal Experience.* New York: Harper, p. 6.

26. Russell, R.V. [1989] *The Importance of Recreation Satisfaction and Activity Participation in Life Satisfaction of Age-Segregated Retirees*, in Mapping the Past, Charting the Future [Edgar L. Jackson and Thomas Burton, eds.] State College, PA: Venture Publishing.

27. Driver, B.L. and Brown, P.J. [1986] *Probable Personal Benefits of Outdoor Recreation*, in Literature Review. The President's Commission on Americans Outdoors. Washington, DC: Government Printing Office.

28. Rossman, B.B. and Ulehla, Z.J. [1991] *Psychological Reward Values Associated With Wilderness Use: A Functional Reinforcement Approach*, in Benefits of Leisure, p. 188.

29. Karch, R.C. [1995] *Promoting Values and Benefits of Physical Activity and Sport*, at the First World Forum on Physical Activity and Sport in The Benefits Catalogue, Parks and Recreation Association, Canada, p. 105.

30. SA Department of Recreation and Sport and Australian Sports Commission [1991] *Volunteers in South Australian Sport*. Canberra, ACT, p. 19.

31. Fallding, H. [1996] *The Family and the Idea of Cardinal Role*, in Human Relations, vol. 14, pp. 220–246.

32. Vreugdenhill, Anthea and Rigby, Ken [1987] *Assessing Generalised Community Satisfaction*, in Journal of Social Psychology, vol. 127, no. 4, pp. 381–390.

33. Marans, Robert and Mohai Paul [1990] *Leisure Resources, Recreation Activity, and the Quality of Life.* In The Benefits Catalogue, Parks and Recreation Association, Canada, pp. 354–355.

34. Earle, Leon [1992] *Social Network Needs Among Older People*, University of South Australia and Recreation for Older Adults SA, p. 22.

35. Earle, Leon [1989] *Recreation Patterns Among Older Australians*, in Ideas for Australian Recreation. Canberra: Australian Government Publishing Service, p. 39.

36. Australian Bureau of Statistics [1993] *Population Survey Monitor on Sport and Recreation Participation*. Adelaide.

37. Teaching Services Unit [1988] *When Girls Play—Activity and Self-Esteem.* Video cassette, Victoria College, Canada.

38. Australian Bureau of Statistics [1997] *Sport and Recreation: A Statistical Overview*, cat. no. 4145. O.P. 53.

39. Australian Bureau of Statistics [1996] *Government Finance Statistics*, cat. no. 5512.0.

40. Bauman, A., Bellow, B., Booth, M., Hahn, A., Stoker, L. and Thomas, M. [1996] *Towards Best Practice for the Promotion of Physical Activity in the Areas of NSW*. NSW Health Department, Centre for Disease Prevention and Health.

41. Confederation of Australian Sport [1997] *Economic Impact of Sport*. Tasman Asia Pacific and Ernst & Young, p. 24.

42. Confederation of Australian Sport [1998] *Economic Impact of Sport,* p. 26.

43. Australian Bureau of Statistics [1997] *Sport and Recreation: A Statistical Overview*, cat. no. 4156.0, p. 11.

44. Confederation of Australian Sport [1997] *Economic Impact of Sport,* p. 28.

45. Bureau of Tourism [1996] *International Visitors Survey 1995*. Department of Tourism, Canberra.

46. Centre for South Australia Economic Studies [1992] *The Australian Formula One Grand Prix—A Perspective*, in the Sports Economies Newsletter, February 1992, p. 5.

47. Australian Bureau of Statistics [1997] *Sport and Recreation: A Statistical Overview*, cat. no. 4156.0, p. 30.

48. Australian Bureau of Statistics [1997] *Sport and Recreation: A Statistical Overview*, p. 30.

49. Australian Bureau of Statistics [1997] *Sport and Recreation: A Statistical Overview*, p. 30.

50. Gibbons, L. [1989] *Corporate Fitness Programs and Health Enhancement*, in The Benefits Catalogue, Parks and Recreation Association, Canada, p. 126.

51. Trust for Public Land [1994] *Healing America's Cities: Why We Must Invest in Urban Parks*, in The Benefits Catalogue, Parks and Recreation Association, Canada, p. 146.

52. Chabrel, D.M. [1993] *Internal Report*, Department of Engineering and Water Supply, South Australia.

53. Daly, J.W. [1992] *Benefits of Recreation,* in Benefits of Recreation and Sport—Seminar Papers, Adelaide, p. 5.

54. Utne Reader [1997] *American's 10 Most Enlightened Towns,* in The Benefits Catalogue, Parks and Recreation Association, Canada, p. 77.

55. Williams, D.R. [1991] *A Development Model of Recreation Choice Behaviour,* in Australian Parks and Recreation, vol. 27, no. 4.

56. Gold, Seymour [1980] *Recreation Planning and Design.* San Francisco: McGraw-Hill, p. 32.

57. Daly, J.W. [1987] *Decisions and Disasters—Alienation of the Adelaide Parklands.* Adelaide: Bland House, p. 155.

58. Daly, J.W. [1992] *Benefits of Leisure,* p. 5.

59. Foot, David [1990] *The Age of Outdoor Recreation in Canada,* in The Benefits Catalogue, Parks and Recreation Association, Canada, p. 82.

60. Schleien, S., McAvoy, L., Lois, G. and Rynders, J. [1993] *Integrated Outdoor Education and Adventure Programs,* in The Benefits Catalogue, Parks and Recreation Association, Canada, p. 154.

61. Better Health Program [1990] *Sports Injuries in Australia: Causes, Costs and Prevention.* A Report of the Better Health Program, Canberra.

CHAPTER
2

Provision of Recreation and Sport Open Spaces

One of the fundamental planning and design requirements is the provision of adequate recreation and sport open spaces. In order to chart a path through the maze of conflicting opinions on the quantity of open space necessary for recreation and sport, an overview of the Australian legislation is provided, followed by a description of open space categories. A new approach is suggested using a number of templates identifying areas for local, district and regional outdoor recreation and sport activities. This approach could at least provide guidelines at the initial stage of planning to understand what is possible. Examples of open space standards used in Britain, Canada and the United States are then provided. Finally, an attempt is made to point out some future directions of recreation and sport open space planning.

There are no authoritative standards for the quantity of open space required because each application has its own characteristics. Certainly quality rather than quantity is always argued, but nevertheless the reality is that guidelines are needed if only to assure planners and policy makers that the long-term decisions that they are about to make have some rationality.

A review of recreation open space planning was carried out by Ken Marriott in 1980[1] in which he pointed out the dangers of using open space standards that have little relationship to community needs. Marriott admitted in the early 1980s that progress was being made by municipal councils in a number of

areas including, 'the process of introducing community-wide participatory planning processes'.[2] As we are entering a new millennium, planners need good arguments for considering recreation and sport open space provision. Knowledge of what is happening elsewhere can stimulate creative thinking at the regional and local levels and keep planners from slavishly following the standards approach of the past.

OVERVIEW OF THE AUSTRALIAN LEGISLATION

The best way to obtain an overview of the Australian scene is to identify the official government legislation and policy documents.

Commonwealth of Australia

Traditionally, land management issues are the responsibility of the states and territories. The only commonwealth legislation that is indirectly related to recreation and sport open space provision is the Australian Sports Commission Act, 1989.[3] In the objects of the Commission, there is reference to 'encouraging increased participation and improvement of performance by Australians'. Presumably this reference requires the provision of appropriate facilities, including open space for sport. Another object is contained in a specific reference to the 'provision of resources, services and facilities to enable Australians to pursue and achieve excellence in sport'.

Also, at the commonwealth level, nonstatutory policies and strategies impact on planning for recreation and sport. For example, the Australian Model Code for Residential Development[4] was developed by the Model Code Task Force of the Green Street Joint Venture and it provides a direction for planning residential areas around Australia. This model code is particularly relevant to recreation and sport in charting future directions for public open space planning.

New South Wales

Although there are no acts of legislation specifically for recreation or sport, direction for the allocation and management of open space is provided in the New South Wales Open Space Strategy in the Environment Planning and Assessment Act, 1979.[5]

An interpretation of Section 94 of the Act has been developed which assists local councils to prepare an open space plan. This plan is required in order to justify contributions for acquisition and embellishment of open space from developers.[6]

Victoria

Two pieces of legislation have an impact on recreation and sport planning in Victoria. The first is the Planning and Environment Act, 1987[7] which refers to the recreation environment. Of particular importance is the second piece of legislation which identifies facilities provision and defines sporting lands through the Sport and Recreation Act, 1972.[8]

In addition, there is the nonstatutory Metropolitan Open Space Plan, 1988[9] that provides policy directions and a classification of open space.

Queensland

Acts and legislation relating to recreation in Queensland include the Recreation Areas Management Act, 1988[10] and the Local Government Planning and Environment Act, 1990.[11] Both Acts provide guidelines for land management. Sport is not addressed at a statutory level.

Queensland has not developed classifications for open space and instead refers to the Standard Practices—Guidelines and Design Practices produced by the Australian Capital Territory.[12] Metropolitan directions for open space and recreation planning are also incorporated within the City of Brisbane Town Plan, 1986.[13]

Western Australia

Western Australia has no acts or legislation relating directly to recreation and sport. However, the Metropolitan Region Town Planning Scheme Act, 1959–1982[14] and the Town Planning and Development Act, 1928[15] provide guidelines for the provision and management of public open space and as such these will impact on the environment for recreation and sport.

The Policy Manual No. 1–Development Control Including Subdivision produced by the State Planning Commission also provides directions for the allocation and use of public open space.[16]

The Department of Planning and Urban Development has established a planning strategy for the Perth metropolitan area called METROPLAN, which indirectly impacts on recreation and sport.[17]

South Australia

In 1991, the Adelaide Planning Commission completed the 2020 Vision[18] which was a Metropolitan Adelaide Strategic Plan. It recommended a strategic planning system for the development of metropolitan Adelaide. An outcome of this strategic plan was an integrated planning and development assessment system encompassed in the Development Act, 1993.[19] Part of the Act specifies open space requirements.

A Local Government (Lands) Bill has been through an extensive public consultation process at the time of printing and awaits debate in parliament. It contains the concept of community land, which presumes that all local government land, except roads, will be classified community land after a two-year consultation period. Management plans for community land must be prepared which identify the use applied to the land, for example, for recreation and sport. Certain land, for example, the Adelaide Parklands, must be community land and its classification cannot be revoked.[20]

The Metropolitan Open Space System planning policy (MOSS) is an addition to the Development Plan. It defines and links open space in and around metropolitan Adelaide.

Nonstatutory strategic planning has been emphasised with the preparation of the State Recreation and Sport Strategy Plan in 1994.[21] This strategy further clarifies state government recreation and sport trends, issues and priorities.

Also, the government's social policy objectives with regard to urban development have been developed in the form of a Social Policy Aspects of Urban Development.[22] This policy paper provides a basis for the incorporation of social policies into the statutory planning process. There is a significant section of social policy and objectives relating to recreation open space and pedestrian paths and cycle routes.

Tasmania

Few legislative references directly impact on recreation and sport open space in Tasmania.

The Local Government Act, 1993[23] with amendments up until February 1997, identifies public land for health, recreation and sporting facilities and the Tourism and Recreational Development Act, 1977[24] highlights a commitment to funding recreation projects.

Northern Territory

Directions for open space planning for recreation and sport in the Northern Territory are provided within the Northern Territory of Australia Planning Act, 1987[25] and the Darwin Town Plan, 1990.[26]

Australian Capital Territory

The Australian Capital Territory has a Territory Plan with a section on urban open space, which provides objectives, purposes and controls.[27]

A number of ordinances determine the availability of existing facilities for recreation and sport. For example, the ACT Lakes Ordinance, 1992[28] and the Cotter River Act,

1994[29] prohibits and controls certain recreation activities.

Nonstatutory documents that provide a direction for open space and metropolitan planning include the Standard Practices—Guidelines on Planning and Design Practices, 1988[30] and the Metropolitan Plan, 1984.[31]

OPEN SPACE CLASSIFICATION

Various descriptions of recreation and sport open space are used throughout Australia and overseas. Below are examples of some more popular classifications being used.

Active and Passive

It is too simplistic to describe open space as either 'active' or 'passive'. This classification was popular in the 1970s and 1980s.

Functional

More functional classifications have been used since, such as

- indoor facilities (only where they occur on open space);
- civic spaces/malls;
- formal gardens;
- small parks or playgrounds;
- outdoor sports facilities;
- parklands;
- beach, foreshore, or river;
- bushland;
- ancillary (adjacent to road corridors); and
- underdeveloped (no present use)[32].

Recreation Opportunity Spectrum (ROS)

During the 1980s, another approach came to Australia from the United States Forest Service, called the Recreation Opportunity Spectrum (ROS). [33] This classification uses a 'settings approach' based on matching recreational needs to a range of experiences in different settings. A number of local councils used this approach but found it difficult to adapt to urban environments because it originated in broader, forestry-based recreational settings.

Hierarchy of Open Spaces

From the states and territories legislation and official planning documents, the hierarchy of open spaces (see figure 2.1) has been derived as a guide to what actually is in practice. This is not to say the hierarchy is acceptable for all situations, but various components of it are now being used throughout Australia.

OPEN SPACE DESCRIPTIONS IN DETAIL

The following descriptions explain in more detail the headings in figure 2.1. They bring together the collected wisdom of the Australian states' and territories' official planning documents and legislation.

Play Spaces

This term is not used in official publications, but it is a category that encompasses the

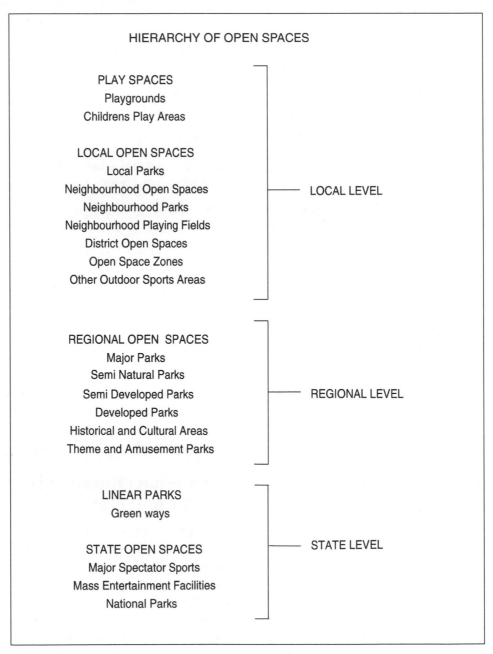

Figure 2.1   Hierarchy of open spaces.

types of children's play spaces that are different from the wider term of local open space.

Playgrounds

In Canberra, the National Capital Development Commission's policy is to provide playgrounds so that no residence is more than 400 metres from a playground. Consequently, each neighbourhood will contain several playgrounds. One of these is the central playground, which caters primarily for older children located within the central park adjacent to the local shops and the primary school. The others are local playgrounds, which cater for two- to six-year-old children, located in local parks throughout the neighbourhood.[34]

Children's Play Areas

In South Australia, careful consideration has been given to the design and location of children's play areas. The principles include the following:

- Playground facilities designed to allow for safety, flexibility, variety, imagination and creativity
- Location of play areas in public spaces adjacent to shops and community centres to promote social play and the watching opportunities which inform fantasy play
- Location of play areas on clearly defined pedestrian and cycle routes or next to shops, schools, sports grounds or parks
- Play areas which are visible from adjacent residential housing, streets and public areas to facilitate casual surveillance
- Play areas which offer opportunities for people with disabilities
- Play areas which include natural areas to allow for creative and interesting play opportunities[35]

Local Open Spaces

Under the heading local open space, New South Wales identifies land that is required to satisfy the general day-to-day needs of the local area population. An amount of 2.83 hectares per 1,000 population is the commonly accepted rate and the continued use of this standard is considered appropriate where no other basis has been established.

It is generally accepted that the provision of open space ranges from 10 square metres to 28 square metres per person.[36]

Local Parks

In Victoria, local parks are sites of local significance in urban areas, which provide space for informal, noncompetitive recreation and relaxation for residents within a local neighbourhood. Local parks are suitable for specific-purpose trips (e.g. children to use playgrounds) or as one destination in multipurpose trips to schools, shops and community facilities. Local parks commonly incorporate outdoor sporting facilities.

Local parks ideally should be distributed so that all urban households are located within a 300-metre safe walking distance. Where a 300-metre walking distance criterion is not feasible in these areas, first priority for open space acquisition should be directed towards obtaining some open space within 500 metres of all residents.

Ideally, local parks of at least one hectare should be provided within 500 metres of all urban households to allow flexibility in catering for a range of age groups, activities and population change over time.

A municipality may also wish to provide mini-parks of less than one hectare to cater for young families, especially in new subdivisions. These should be provided in addition to, not instead of, the larger local reserves and could feasibly be spaced so as to be within 200–300 metres of all households.[37]

Neighbourhood Open Spaces

This term is used in South Australia for areas of between five to ten hectares providing for both active and passive recreation needs.[38]

Neighbourhood Parks

In the Australian Capital Territory, neighbourhood parks contain children's playgrounds and are located so that no residence is more than 400 metres from a park.

The parks should be located to utilise and preserve areas of existing trees or other natural features. They should have an area in the range 2,500–5,000 square metres with the local parks having an area of 2,500–3,000 square metres and the central parks having an area of 4,000–5,000 square metres.

The recommended areas should only be exceeded where an increase is warranted by specific circumstances such as the inclusion of a stand of trees or other natural features. The minimum dimension should be 50 metres.

Parks should be located between the primary school and the local shops. Both central and local parks should be located to be readily accessible from the pedestrian and cycle network. Both central and local parks may be located within or partly within floodways provided they do not extend below the one in two year flood level.

The location of the playground within the park will depend on the detailed design of the park. However, the following general rules should apply:

- The edge of the playground should be a minimum of 20 metres from the boundary of a residential block.

- The edge of the playground should be a minimum of 20 metres from the curb line of a local or collector road.

- The edge of the playground should be a minimum of 30 metres from the curb line of a distributor road.[39]

The Australian Capital Territory also provides these criteria for nonorganised recreation, for passive relaxation and particularly for safe children's play. They may also contain and preserve features with a special landscape character such as a stand of trees, a natural rock outcrop or a fine 'view'. Generally neighbourhood parks will contain children's playgrounds, as one of the primary purposes of these parks is to provide for safe children's play. On this basis, neighbourhood parks can be subdivided into the same two groups: central and local.[40]

Neighbourhood Playing Fields

A distinction is made between neighbourhood parks and neighbourhood playing fields in the Australian Capital Territory. Neighbourhood playing fields are provided for sporting activi-

ties such as cricket, football, hockey and athletics. Residents may also use the fields for social sports. Fields may also be used for training and competition sport by primary school children. The neighbourhood playing fields should be used as the playing fields for the primary school and should be located immediately adjacent to the school.

There are two types of neighbourhood playing fields: Sports Combination Type 1 requiring 2.6–2.7 hectares and Sports Combination Type 2 requiring an area of 2.1 hectares.[41]

The playing fields should be located in natural terrain with a slope of 1:50 if possible. They should have frontage to a distributor road or collector road with good accessibility from a distributor road.

The playing fields should be located to the north of the primary school buildings. The distance between the edge of the field and the closest school building should be 25–30 metres. This provides adequate clearance between the building and the field and adequate space for casual play and observation of sports.

Provision should be made to enable sealed car parking to be provided for a minimum of 20 cars. The design of the playing fields and the school should be such that the school parking area is located to provide the parking space for community use of the playing fields out of school hours.

The playing fields may be located within or partly within floodways provided that the playing surface of the field does not extend below the one in two year flood level.[42]

District Open Spaces

Under the category of district open space there is a wide variation of terminology used.

In South Australia, district open spaces are areas of between 10 and 20 hectares providing a range of active and passive recreational opportunities.[43]

District Playing Fields

The Australian Capital Territory uses the following open space standards for district playing fields. District playing fields are provided for organised sport. They are used by high schools and by sporting associations for training and for competitive sport. District playing fields should be provided for a population of 16,000–20,000, that is, for a group of four or five suburbs.

District playing fields will have an area of 8 hectares or 12 hectares, depending on whether two or three basic sports units are provided, plus an area for tennis courts, basketball courts, pavilion, toilets and car parking.

The playing fields should be located in natural terrain with a slope of less than 1:50 if possible. They should have frontage to an arterial road so that they are easily accessible from the neighbourhoods which they serve.

Provision should be made to enable sealed car parking to be provided for a minimum of 200 cars. The parking area should be located to the west of the main oval to achieve optimum viewing of the oval from the car park.

The playing fields may be located within or partly within floodways provided that the playing surface of the field does not extend below the one in two year flood level.[44]

District Parks

This term is used in Victoria and the Australian Capital Territory.

In Victoria, district parks include sites of greater than local significance which attract and support longer duration (but less frequent) visits than local parks. Like local parks, they provide areas for informal noncompetitive recreation, appreciation of the natural or cultural heritage, relaxation, social interaction (including group outings) and solitude. Many district parks incorporate or adjoin outdoor sporting areas. District parks should serve as local parks for nearby residents, particularly at off-peak times.

District parks primarily service households within a two-kilometre radius, although many will also cater for visitors beyond this catchment area. These parks may also serve any employees from nearby industrial or commercial areas, particularly on weekdays.

The size of a district park is usually at least three hectares, although smaller areas (down to one hectare) may function as a district park if located and developed in an appropriate style.[45]

In the Australian Capital Territory, district parks are provided for nonorganised recreation and for passive relaxation. They cater for family or group outings and are equipped with barbecue and picnic facilities. They may contain children's play equipment, which is more sophisticated than that provided in neighbourhood parks, and other facilities such as fitness tracks. Car parking and toilets are provided. Landscaping is generally informal. The park may also incorporate natural or historic features.

A district park should be provided for a population of 16,000–20,000, that is, for a group of four or five neighbourhoods. The park should have an area in the range 2.5–4 hectares. The recommended area should only be exceeded where an increase is warranted by specific circumstances such as the inclusion of an extensive feature of significance in the park.

The district park should be located with the district playing fields to achieve efficient use of land and to provide a more attractive setting for the district playing fields. Access roads and parking areas should be located so that they serve the district park and the district playing fields.[46]

Open Space Zones

Both Brisbane and Darwin have established recreation or open space zones. In Brisbane, the zones aim to achieve three primary objectives:

1. To facilitate the satisfaction of the existing and future recreation needs of the community by the inclusion of adequate and appropriate land on which both active and passive recreation can occur

2. To conserve natural resources of particular significance for enjoyment by future generations

3. To facilitate the provision of recreation and tourist facilities in appropriate locations by private enterprise[47]

The Town Plan also identifies three recreation zones:

1. Open space zones intended primarily to be used for informal and casual recreational pursuits

2. Sport and recreation zones intended to accommodate organised sports with associated facilities, commercial recreational establishments as well as less formal recreational activities

3. Conservation zones comprising those parts of the city which, because of their significant environmental values, are considered worthy of preservation for the present and future residents of the city[48]

The Darwin Town Plan has adopted zones to describe the recreational and other uses for their open spaces.[49]

Other Outdoor Sports Areas

In Victoria a detailed description is given of other sports areas which include all types of outdoor facilities designed for competitive sport excluding those categorised as spectator sporting facilities. Some are restricted to use by club members at all times (or at specific times) while others are available for general community use. Most playing fields can also be used for informal activities outside the times set aside for organised competition. A hierarchy of facilities has been defined for many sports by the relevant sporting associations.

Sport facilities cater for teams or individuals beyond a local neighbourhood (i.e. beyond walking distance). Some may have catchment areas of the entire metropolitan or urban area, depending on the level of competition and the specialised nature of the sports.

Levels of provision are best determined at the local level according to community needs, availability of facilities in neighbouring municipalities and local funding priorities. However, as a (very broad) rule, developing urban areas generally need to allocate approximately 1.5 hectares per 1,000 people for various outdoor sports excluding golf courses and racecourses.[50]

Regional Open Spaces

In South Australia, regional open spaces are areas up to 200 hectares serving more than one council and providing a wide range of recreational and sport activities.[51]

Major Parks

Victoria identifies 'major parks' as areas that provide opportunities for informal recreation or appreciation of the natural or cultural heritage within, or close to, the metropolitan area. They generally allow scope for visits of several hours and attract visitors from all parts of the metropolitan area. These parks include features of regional, state or national significance and are often listed on tourist itineraries. Five categories of major parks are summarised below.

Semi-Natural Parks

Semi-natural parks primarily service a catchment area within 30 minutes' driving distance, but many areas may cater for visitors from beyond this distance, depending on the significance of the park's features. These parks should be large enough (e.g. 100 hectares) to allow extensive walking with visual and aural isolation from the urban environment. They should also be large enough to protect the natural environment while allowing informal, but carefully managed recreational use.

Semi-Developed Parks

As for semi-natural parks, these parks primarily service a catchment area within 30 minutes' driving distance, but many areas may cater for visitors from beyond this distance. Semi-developed parks should be large enough to allow extensive walking with visual and aural isolation from the city. A suggested minimum size is 30 hectares. They should also be large enough to cater for a wide range of informal recreation activities, while protecting significant natural features.

Developed Urban Parks

Developed parks primarily, service a catchment area within 30 minutes driving distance, but many areas may cater for visitors from beyond this distance. Developed parks of regional (or greater) significance should be large enough to allow extensive walking and a reasonable degree of isolation from other urban activities. They should also be large enough to cater for a wide range of recreational activities. Some major parks may be particularly significant due to their prime location, although size may be relatively small.

Historical and Cultural Areas

These sites would usually attract visitors from an entire urban area, and often visitors and tourists from farther afield. The size of the site will be highly variable and generally not critical, as a building or structure may provide the major attraction.

Theme and Amusement Parks

Theme or amusement parks are likely to attract visitors from an entire urban area, and usually from farther afield. The size of these parks will be highly variable, but need not be particularly large. They need only be large enough to allow scope for long-term financial success.[52]

LINEAR PARKS AND GREENWAYS

Victoria, South Australia and the Australian Capital Territory have specific aims, or objectives, for linear parks that also act as greenbelts or green corridors and have very important recreation and sport use.

Victoria has an excellent definition of a linear park. They generally provide links (and therefore access routes) between other parks, community facilities, shops and residential areas and areas of fauna habitat. The linear parks should provide opportunities for a wide range of informal, nonmotorised recreational activities.

The catchment area would depend on the importance of other parks and facilities, which are linked to the linear park, and the particular features, attractiveness and scale of the linear park itself. Catchment areas may range from a single municipality to an entire metropolitan area. They have the potential to enlarge the catchments of existing parks to which they feed people.

The size of a linear park is variable. Length is more important than width, although width should be sufficient to allow for a path or access route, tree planting and landscaping wherever possible.[53]

Also, the Victorian government is committed to creating a network of open space, which will meet the needs of Melbourne's population into the twenty-first century. Under the heading of 'Expanding and linking open space' the main aims are to

- increase the amount of open space to provide a range of recreational opportunities for future generations;
- link existing and proposed open spaces to provide a metropolitan-wide network for nonmotorised recreational use; and
- achieve a more equitable distribution and improve the accessibility of public open space, paying particular attention to areas relatively deprived of open space.[54]

In South Australia, the Metropolitan Open Space Strategy (MOSS) has been introduced into the Planning Act by means of a Supplementary Development Plan.[55] A network of private and public land of an open character is created around and through Metropolitan Adelaide. Among the objectives of MOSS are

- to accommodate a range of recreation and sporting facilities of regional or state significance, including facilities which may be used for national and international events;
- to accommodate a range of passive recreation and leisure areas;
- to provide for the integration of stormwater management in association with recreation, aquifer recharge and water quality management; and
- to develop open space recreation reserves through land purchases, contributions of open space and exchanges of land.[56]

In the Australian Capital Territory, an open space system will be planned to facilitate and improve visual and physical access. This open space system will also provide a balanced range of recreation opportunities and other uses in a manner that reinforces the National Capital Open Space System as a diverse ecological, cultural, scenic and recreational resource. It will also provide a land bank for future National Capital and recreational needs.[57]

Advocacy for greenways is a movement in the United States and it has spread to New Zealand. At least one state in Australia, South Australia, is considering its implications.

As the Salisbury City Council in South Australia points out, 'Greenways encourage the use of natural corridors such as rivers and creek floodplains, for linear park systems. These natural corridors can be supplemented as necessary by man-made corridors such as utility and transportation rights of way. The aim is to assemble a complete, interconnected system of linear open space ways within a community'.[58] There is a persuasive case for the adaptation of resources such as rivers, creeks, abandoned railroads and unused road reserves in South Australia to provide public routes for walkers, cyclists and in some instances horse riders. Cogent environmental reasons can also be mounted for advocating greenways, one of the most compelling being the movement of wildlife, particularly birds, along a natural corridor.

Some disadvantages are the significant financial costs of responsibly managing a public asset traversing other public land holdings already administered by local councils and various government agencies. Matters of potential public liability suits arising from claims by recreational users must also be addressed.

The greenways movement is a practical answer to the difficult task of providing open space in developed metropolitan areas and expanding outer urban and country regions where land preservation is becoming increasingly costly. 'To make a greenway is to make a community'.[59]

STATE OPEN SPACES

This term is used in South Australia and it has significance in the development of state recreation and sport strategies, including specialist facilities of state, national and international levels.[60]

Major Spectator Sport and Mass Entertainment Facilities

The Victorians use this category to describe major facilities of state, national and international significance. These facilities are usually designed for statewide, interstate or international competition, with extensive provision for spectators. They are likely to be fully enclosed and not available for general community use at other times. Many spectator sport facilities are also used for various forms of mass entertainment such as rock concerts, circuses and ice skating displays.

Major sport and entertainment facilities should serve an entire urban or metropolitan area and be located close to public transport, preferably a railway station.

The size of playing and spectator areas and adjoining car parks will depend on the requirements and popularity of particular sports.[61]

National Parks

Australia developed its first national park in New South Wales soon after the first national park was created in Yellowstone, USA. National parks are administered under appropriate acts of parliament in each state or territory. Their main objectives are to promote the use and enjoyment of a wide range of recreational opportunities, while at the same time preserving and protecting the natural environment.

PERCENTAGE OF OPEN SPACE

Most states and territories have legislation that allows for the acquisition of open space for a number of purposes including recreation and sport.

In New South Wales, one or a combination of three methods can levy open space:

- land contribution
- monetary contribution for land
- monetary contribution to improve existing or new open space[62]

In some cases the government will be in a position to acquire priority sites identified in regional plans, through the Sydney Region Development Fund. These priority sites include regional open space.[63]

The Outdoor Recreation and Open Space Guidelines point out that, 'Recreation demand standards enjoy wide spread usage in almost all NSW councils. The common standard of 2.83 hectares per 1,000 is derived from the British 7 acres per 1,000 standard of the early 1900s. . . .the planning and legal professions have to date shown a reluctance to question this standard, even though there is clearly no logic in the Australian context for its application'. [64]

In Victoria, each council has a planning scheme in which additional requirements for public open space are on the basis of 5 per cent of all the land in the subdivision intended to be used for residential, industrial or commercial purposes. Payment is made to the council of the site value of all the land in the subdivision intended to be used for residential, industrial or commercial purposes, or a combination of the above so that the total of the percentages required does not exceed 5 per cent.[65]

In Queensland, an area of land will be provided for use as a park. The means by which this is done is through a monetary contribution in substitution for the provision of that area of land or by works provided for the improvement of land for use as a park (including the development of recreational facilities) or any combination of the above.

If subdivision approval is sought, an area that is 10 per cent of the area of land to be subdivided is provided. Where the construction of a canal is involved within the meaning of the Canals Act 1958–1989, an area that is 7.5 per cent of the area of the land to be subdivided must be provided.[66]

In South Australia, the open space contributions apply for division of land into more than 20 allotments (except by strata plan), and one or more allotments is less than one hectare in area. Up to 12.5 per cent in area

must be vested in the council or the Crown (as the case requires) to be held as open space. Or the applicant makes the prescribed contribution given by a formula prescribed in the Act.[67]

In Tasmania, 1/20th of the whole of a subdivision can be acquired for public recreation or public gardens.[68]

In the Northern Territory, the acquisition of open space must take into account the physical, environmental, economic, cultural, social and human resources available in the locality.[69]

The Australian Model Code for Residential Development suggests the following percentages of open space: in the absence of an existing approved plan, where open space is required from a parcel of land to be subdivided, the amount of unencumbered open space required is not less than 6 per cent of the site area, and

- is of fair and reasonable quality relative to the total land in the subdivision;

- is located in such a way that each allotment in the subdivision is within 500 metres safe walking distance of any existing or proposed public open space in the vicinity;

- comprises reserves of at least one hectare in area, or where the resulting public open space is less than 0.5 hectare in area, the local authority may

  — require such public open space to be set aside for use as a linear connection between streets or to proposed or existing open space, community facilities or public services;

  — require such public open space to be combined with existing or proposed public open space on an adjoining property; or

  — require a cash-in-lieu payment to be used for acquiring land for additional, or improving, existing local public open space in the vicinity.[70]

OPEN SPACE TEMPLATES: A DIFFERENT APPROACH

A number of approaches have been used with varying degrees of success to determine the amount of recreation and sport open space required (for example, the standards approach and various classifications mentioned earlier in this chapter), while variations of the recreation opportunities spectrum (ROS) are still used. It is now time to consider a different approach.

In many situations where consultations on open space requirements are undertaken, it cannot be assumed that people are able to visualise the land required for recreation and sport activities. For example, not many people know the dimensions for a football oval, a soccer field or complex consisting of a number of tennis or netball courts. The five templates that follow are examples of local-, district- and regional-level open spaces. It is hoped that these templates, or similar ones, can assist in a realistic appreciation of open space requirements. They are therefore guidelines only to assist in the initial stages of the planning process.

Local Open Space Templates

The local open space templates are for open spaces primarily used by nearby residents. They can vary in size from as small as a house block up to approximately 0.5 hectares for informal use and 1.2–3.0 hectares for sporting use.

Local Open Space (Informal)			
Minimum area (ha)	Catchment	Typical recreation and sport facilities	Parking, ablutions, clubrooms, etc.
0.5	500 metres	Playground; informal play area; BBQ and picnic area; facilities for informal and ball sports	Kerb-side parking; shelter

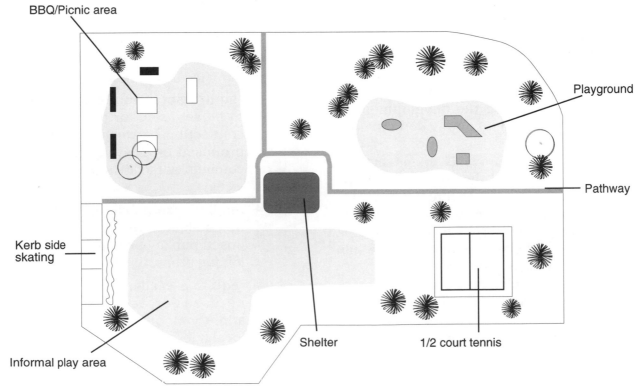

Playground	0.10	BBQ/picnic area	0.12
Kerb-side parking	0.10	Landscaping (25%)	0.12
Informal play area	0.20	1/2-court basketball	0.03
Shelter	0.01	**Total area**	**0.68 hectares**

Local Open Space (Sporting Park)

Minimum area (ha)	Catchment	Typical recreation and sport facilities	Parking, ablutions, clubrooms, etc.
1.2–3.0	500 metres	Playground; informal play area; BBQ and picnic area; facilities for formal and informal and ball sports; skating area	Parking for 20–30 cars; toilet block; shelter

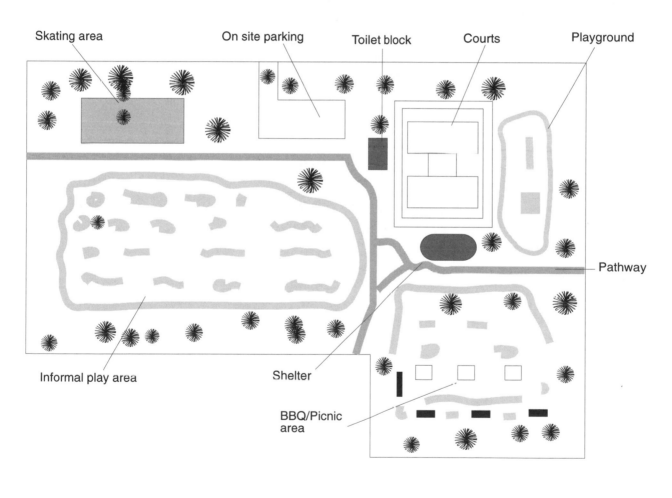

Playground	0.10	Toilet block	0.02
Hard area for skating	0.13	Courts (2 basketball, 2 tennis)	0.18
Informal play area	0.80	Shelter	0.04
On-site parking	0.11	Landscaping (25%)	0.40
BBQ/picnic area	0.20	**Total area**	**1.98 hectares**

District Open Space Templates

The district open space templates are for larger open spaces that provide activities for people who come from a wider catchment area and usually stay longer than those who use local open spaces. People living nearby also use district open spaces as a local park. The first of these templates is for predominantly informal use and is a minimum of 10 hectares catering for people within 1.5 kilometres or less than one-quarter of an hour's driving time. The district sporting open space or park is smaller, to demonstrate a minimum area that is possible for playing surfaces and ancillary facilities such as car parking, toilets and clubrooms. The catchment area is larger because the driving time to district sporting parks of up to half an hour is suggested because people playing competitive sports are prepared to travel longer distances.

District Open Space (Informal)			
Minimum area (ha)	Catchment	Typical recreation and sport facilities	Parking, ablutions, clubrooms, etc.
10.0	1.5 kilometres 1/4 hr. driving	Playground; informal play area; BBQ and picnic area; facilities for informal ball sports; skating area; special event area; walking and riding trails; water feature	Parking for 50 cars; toilet blocks; hall/ clubroom; shelter

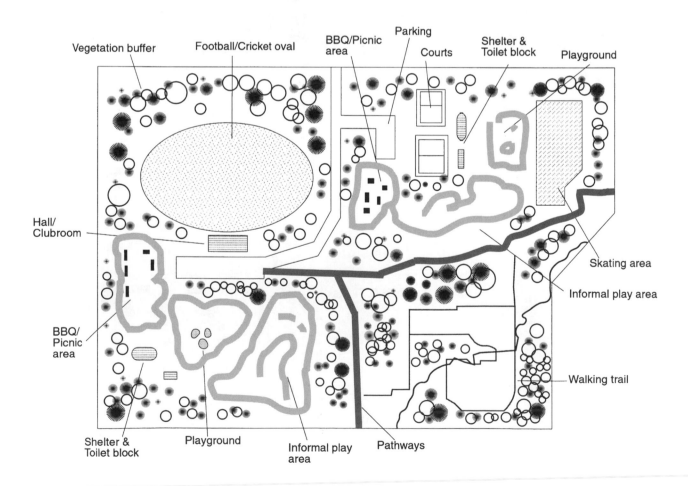

Playground × 2	0.28	Shelter × 2	0.18
On-site parking (100 cars)	0.37	Courts (2 netball, 2 basketball)	0.17
Informal play area × 2	1.60	Natural area for walking trail	2.25
Toilet block × 2	0.04	Skating ramps and circuit	0.45
BBQ/picnic area × 2	0.40	Landscaping (25%)	2.15
Hall/clubroom	0.25	Courts (2 tennis)	0.14
Oval (football/cricket)	2.47	**Total area**	**10.75 hectares**

District Open Space (Sporting Park)

Minimum area (ha)	Catchment	Typical recreation and sport facilities	Parking, ablutions, clubrooms, etc.
5.0	1.5 kilometres 1/2 hr. driving	Playground; informal play area; BBQ and picnic area; facilities for multiple formal ball sports; skating area	Parking for 50–200 cars; clubrooms; toilet blocks; shelter

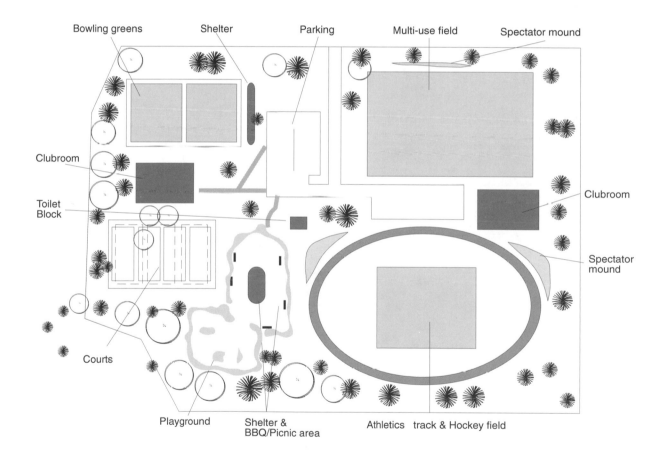

Playground	0.14	Toilet	0.02
On-site parking (160 cars)	0.59	Lawn bowls (2 greens)	0.32
BBQ/picnic area	0.20	Landscaping (25%)	1.28
Clubroom × 2	0.50	Rugby Union/League and	
Athletics track		Touch field	1.26
(with hockey field inside)	1.72	Courts (4 tennis, 3 netball)	0.27
Shelter × 2	0.11	**Total area**	**6.41 hectares**

Regional Open Space Template

The regional open space template is for open spaces that have a catchment area that attracts people who are prepared to drive significant distances to use the facilities, between 30 and 60 minutes. It has a minimum of 30 hectares and it depicts a range of facilities. These regional open spaces often have landscapes of cultural significance. For people nearby, regional open spaces also serve local and district purposes.

Regional Open Space			
Minimum area (ha)	**Catchment**	**Typical recreation and sport facilities**	**Parking, ablutions, clubrooms, etc.**
30.0	1/2 hr.–1 hr. driving	Playground; informal play area; BBQ and picnic areas; facilities for formal and informal ball sports; skating area; special event area; walking and riding trails; bridle trail; semi-natural area; water feature (boat ramp)	Parking for a minimum of 200 cars; toilet blocks; shelter; storage sheds; kiosk

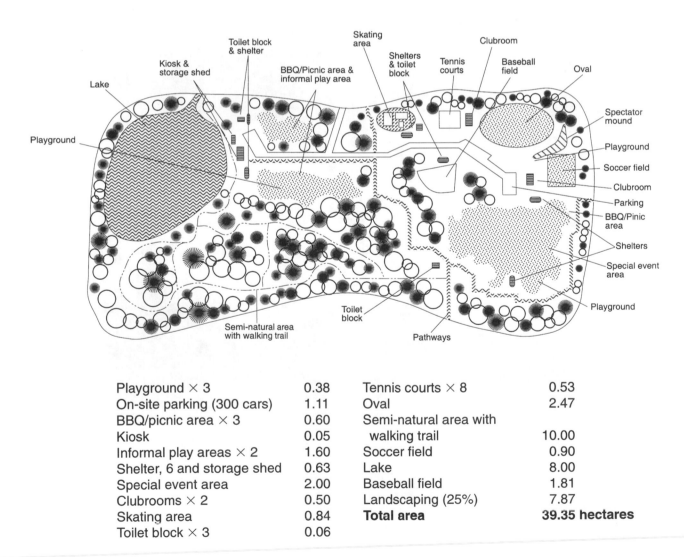

Playground × 3	0.38	Tennis courts × 8	0.53
On-site parking (300 cars)	1.11	Oval	2.47
BBQ/picnic area × 3	0.60	Semi-natural area with	
Kiosk	0.05	walking trail	10.00
Informal play areas × 2	1.60	Soccer field	0.90
Shelter, 6 and storage shed	0.63	Lake	8.00
Special event area	2.00	Baseball field	1.81
Clubrooms × 2	0.50	Landscaping (25%)	7.87
Skating area	0.84	**Total area**	**39.35 hectares**
Toilet block × 3	0.06		

Notes on the Open Space Templates

Buffer zones of 50 metres should be provided where car parking for more than 20 cars or major recreation and sporting facilities are located near residential housing. This may be reduced if mounding and densely planted trees are located within the buffer zone.

Clubrooms should be located so that several groups using various facilities within the one park can easily access them. *Shelters* should be provided wherever possible to allow persons protection from the sun and rain.

The retention of the natural landscape should be a priority for *playgrounds and informal play areas*. This should take preference over the installation of play equipment and should, wherever possible, be incorporated into the overall design.

Parking should, where possible, allow one space per 1.5 persons attending a recreation facility at a district to regional level. Turn-around areas for buses should be provided at district- and regional-level sporting parks and open spaces. Individual car park dimensions should be as follows:

- 2.5 metres wide
- 3.2 metres wide for disabled parks
- 5.4 metres long
- 5.8 metres apart (back to back in a blind aisle) (allow an extra 1.0 metre at the end of the car park for blind aisle parking)

Careful consideration should be given to the Disability Discrimination Act when planning *toilets,* either providing new toilets or upgrading existing ones. The following important issues regarding the provision of toilets have been raised through the Inner Southern Region Recreation and Open Space Strategy in South Australia:

- People with disabilities may have a carer who is of the opposite sex, therefore the provision of unisex toilets is more appropriate.
- Toilets should be located with concern for safety and crime-prevention measures.

The Unley City Council (South Australia) in their Strategy for Public Conveniences identified demand criteria for justifying the provision of public toilets in parks and open spaces. This was based on a minimum level of utilisation, being: 50 or more people at any one time; length of stay to exceed two hours; to be used at least on weekends.

Note: Provision for parking and toilets will ultimately be determined by local government policies.

The area required for dual-use *walking/riding trails* will naturally be determined by the length of the trail. The pathway itself should be 3 metres wide with 1.25 metres either side for safety as a minimum, although 2 metres either side is preferable. An easement of 20 metres should be allowed where a trail passes hazardous areas such as cliff faces. The area required for a trail can be determined using the following formula:

$$\text{Area (hectares)} = \frac{7 \times D}{1000}$$

where the length (metres) of the trail = D.

An equestrian (bridle) trail is usually one metre wide with a metre either side for safety. If placing an equestrian trail next to a walking/riding trail, it is beneficial to create a vegetation buffer between the two.

Parks that are designed with *wildlife corridors* to encourage biodiversity should be a minimum width of 120 metres to facilitate the movement of wildlife.

Allow adequate space for the following elements:

- *BBQ and picnic area.* 0.04 hectare per unit
- *Clubroom.* 0.09–0.25 hectare
- *Informal play area.* 0.2–0.8 hectare
- *Landscaping.* Approximately 25 per cent of the park area
- *Parking (on site).* 37.16 square metres per car
- *Playground.* 0.10–0.14 hectare
- *Shelter.* 0.01–0.09 hectare
- *Special event area.* 1.0–2.0 hectare
- *Toilet block.* 0.01–0.02 hectare

Table 2.1 lists the suggested area requirements for outdoor recreation and sport facilities.

COASTAL RECREATION: OPEN SPACES

Open space for recreation includes the vast expanses of coastal beaches and water. Chapter 7 provides details on how recreation planning and design criteria can be utilised for many coastal activities. It also develops criteria and guidelines for various recreation and sport activities and facilities along the coast.

Some Australian states and territories and the commonwealth have legislation relating to coast protection, marine parks, nature conservation, beach protection and coastal management, which refer to recreation.

The following references are the key pieces of legislation being used for coastal open space. There are references to recreation that provide guidelines for further policy development of recreation along Australia's extensive coast line.

- At the *commonwealth level,* a national coastal action plan was prepared with draft conclusions and recommendations

Table 2.1   Suggested Minimum Areas Required for Outdoor Recreation and Sport Facilities

Type of facility	Activity	Dimensions including safety buffer (metres)	Minimum area required (hectares)
Court	Basketball	32 × 19	0.06
	Netball	38 × 23	0.09
	Tennis	37 × 18	0.07
	Combined (2 basketball, 2 netball and 2 tennis)	40.0 × 45.3	0.18
	Combined (4 tennis and 3 netball)	38 × 72	0.27
Field	Baseball	125 × 145	1.81
	Hockey	99 × 61	0.60
	Lacrosse (based on women's field)	116 × 66	0.77
	Rugby League	134 × 80	1.07
	Rugby Union	156 × 81	1.26
	Soccer	118 × 76	0.90
	Softball	90 × 67	0.60
	Target archery (club level with safety mound) (state level without safety mound)	120 × 100 165 × 150	1.20 2.48
	Touch	70 × 50	0.35
Oval	Australian Rules Football	173 × 143	2.47
	Cricket	137.16 × 118.87	1.63
	Practice nets (2 nets) (3 nets)	7.8 × 34.82 11.4 × 34.82	0.03 0.04

Type of facility	Activity	Dimensions including safety buffer (metres)	Minimum area required (hectares)
Rink	Boules (bocce/petanque)	27.5 × 4.0	0.01
	Croquet	32.0 × 25.6	0.08
	Lawn bowls	40 × 40	0.16
Skatepark	Flat area (incorporating roller hockey)	50 × 25	0.13
	Street and fun circuit	50 × 50	0.25
	Ramp combination	20 × 40	0.08
	Combination (ramps and circuit)	50 × 90	0.45
	Combination (flat area, circuit and ramps with speed skating track around the outside)	140 × 60	0.84
Track	Athletics (8 lanes)	180 × 95	1.72
	Athletics (including space for field events)	183 × 110	2.01
	Cycling	200 × 150	3.00
Trail	Walking/riding (for every km in length)	N/A	0.70
Water	Motorised boating	various	60.00
	Paddleboat/rowboat/canoe hire	various	8.00

that could allow a sectorial approach to recognising recreation and sport open spaces as part of a coastal action plan. [71]

- In *New South Wales* three pieces of legislation relate to coast protection and marine parks. [72, 73 & 74]

- *Queensland* has legislation on coast protection and management, beach protection and marine parks. [75, 76 & 77]

- *South Australia* has legislation on coast protection within its planning legislation that allows local councils to establish recreation zones. [78 & 79]

- *Western Australia* has eight marine reserves under conservation and land management legislation. [80]

- *Northern Territory* has marine legislation on pleasure craft. [81]

- *Victoria* manages 50 per cent of its coastline under national park legislation. [82]

There is a need to further develop the concept of identifying recreation and sport open spaces as part of the coastal planning now being undertaken by various levels of government both in Australia and overseas.

EXAMPLES FROM OVERSEAS

To gain an understanding of how open space requirements vary, examples are given from Britain, the United States of America and Canada.

Britain: The National Playing Fields Association

For all new developments, the National Playing Fields Association recommends a minimum standard to be determined according to the local population profile and adopted as part of the statutory planning process locally. [83]

- Adult and youth outdoor playing spaces: within the range 1.6 to 1.8 hectares per 1,000 population.
- Children's play provision: within the range of 0.6 to 0.8 hectares per 1,000 population.
- Total outdoor recreation playing spaces per 1,000 population is therefore 2.2 to 2.6 hectares.

Within existing settlements, for reasons, say, of scarcity of land supply or density of population, the above minimum standard should serve as a target, with each local plan development setting a level of provision to be achieved within the plan period which represents an increase towards the minimum standard.

Youth and Adult

Looking at the provision of outdoor playing spaces for youth and adult use in existing urban settlements, it is unrealistic for many authorities to achieve the minimum standard at present. To take two extreme examples, if the London Boroughs of Kensington and Chelsea and Islington were to provide 1.8 hectares per 1,000 population, the land required as outdoor playing space would be marginally above one-fifth of all land available in each borough. However, the National Playing Fields Association believes that strong planning and provision policies are essential in all urban environments to ensure that playing spaces are not only protected but also increased. Otherwise, authorities will face a diminishing land bank drifting slowly but inexorably down towards the unacceptable levels illustrated by those two boroughs.

A minimum standard of between 1.6 and 1.8 hectares per 1,000 population is recommended in all new developments. The standard should also apply within existing settlements. Where there is a proven shortage of suitable land, the ratio should serve as a target and an intermediate local standard should be adopted as a first phase of moving towards the ratio.

Children

Children's needs for open spaces are significant in their own right. Of crucial importance is the provision of casual play spaces for the unrestricted use of children at play, situated at neighbourhood level—the type of spaces, for example, that can be used by a child and friends in the 10 minutes before tea.

A minimum standard of outdoor spaces for children's play should be within the range of 0.6 and 0.8 hectares per 1,000. The chosen level of provision should be determined according to the local population profile and adopted within the statutory planning process.

United States of America: Regional Parks

Space standards for regional parks suggest various units within the park. The minimum size for regional parks is 8.09 hectares.[84] Table 2.2 details regional park space standards in the United States. Table 2.2 is an ex-

Table 2.2   USA Regional Park Space Standards

Facility	Area in hectares
Play apparatus area—preschool	0.14
Play apparatus area—older children	0.14
Paved multipurpose courts	0.71
Tennis complex	0.40
Recreation centre building	0.40
Sport fields	4.05
Senior citizens' complex	0.77
Open or 'free play' area	0.81
Archery range	0.31
Swimming pool	0.40
Outdoor theatre	0.20
Ice rink (artificial)	0.40
Family picnic area	0.81
Outdoor classroom area	0.40
Golf practice hole	0.31
Off-street parking	1.21*
Sub Total	11.46
Landscaping (buffer and special areas)	2.43
Undesignated space (10%)	1.39
Total	15.28

*Based on 330 cars at 37.16 square metres per car

ample of typical areas allocated for a range or recreation and sports facilities.

Canada: Range of Canadian Urban Open Space Standards

It is recommended that the hierarchy of levels be followed in most communities. The smaller communities may not need to distinguish between 'district' and 'citywide' levels, of course. Table 2.3 summarises the urban open space standards in Canada. The range of Canadian urban open space standards are provided from a report prepared for the Canadian Parks and Recreation Association.[85]

TRENDS AND ISSUES FOR RECREATION AND SPORT OPEN SPACES

The following trends and issues may assist planners and policy makers to widen their understanding of the importance of providing adequate recreation and sport open spaces.

The values of recreation and sport open spaces as a significant influence on the *quality of life* within communities is changing the direction of recreation and sport from physical planning towards more emphasis on social planning.

There is a surprising depth of *commitment* by communities to the provision of open space for a wide range of purposes, particularly for recreation and sport.

While there is a commitment at the community level, governments at all levels are finding it increasingly difficult to fund the open spaces required from the public purse. Standards can assist in making the point that open space is necessary, but strategic planning must contain a thorough needs analysis that emphasises *quality* of open space above quantity.

Most councils and state or territory governments have recreation and sport *open space planning* as part of their overall planning. In many cases, separate recreation and sport open space plans are being developed at local and regional levels.

Management of open space is an important issue. Often the acquiring of the land is the easy part. The ongoing management of open spaces is another matter. Courage is sometimes required to either sell or exchange unsuitable land.

Community consultation is almost mandatory for any recreation and sport open space planning. If adequate consultation is neglected or superficially undertaken, it will be at the peril of a cherished project.

Environmental issues need to be addressed as part of any recreation and sport open space planning, especially along the coast or in

Table 2.3 Range of Canadian Urban Open Space Standards

Level	Acres/1,000	Service radius	Size of space
Subneighbourhood play spaces	*	100 yds to 1/4 mile	500 sq ft to 2 acres, typically 1/2 acre
Neighbourhood parks, play areas	1.0 to 2.5	1/4 to 1/2 mile, typically 1/2 mile	1/4 to 20 acres, typically 6 acres
District parks, playfields	1.0 to 2.5	1/2 to 3 miles, typically 1 mile	4 to 100 acres, typically 10 to 20
Citywide parks	5.0 usually	typically up to 3 miles or 30 minutes' driving time	25 to 200 acres, typically 100
Regional parks,	4.0 to 10.0	typically up to 1 hour driving time	typically over 100 acres

* No standard usual, but spaces are planned in conjunction with urban planners and developers, following recommended site planning practices, e.g. CMHC Site Planning Criteria.

areas that are environmentally sensitive. Recreation and sport must sustain the environment, not contribute towards its further deterioration.

Social justice and *equity issues* are now important in open space usage. People of all ages and those with disabilities have rights to access open spaces for recreation and sport purposes.

FINAL CAUTION

Again, it is worthwhile emphasising that the standards used throughout Australia and those quoted from other countries should be treated with caution. They are guidelines only and therefore must be placed in a context of preliminary information on which a thorough planning process is built.

REFERENCES

1. Marriott, Ken [1980] *Urban Recreation Open Space and Facility Planning*, in Recreation Planning and Social Change in Urban Australia [David Mercer and Elery Hamilton-Smith, eds.]. Melbourne: Sorrett.
2. Marriott, Ken [1980] *Urban Recreation Open Space and Facility Planning*, in Recreation Planning and Social Change in Urban Australia [David Mercer and Elery Hamilton-Smith, eds.]. Melbourne: Sorrett, p. 151.
3. Commonwealth of Australia [1989] *Australian Sports Commission Act, 1989*. Canberra: Author.
4. Green Street Joint Venture [1990] *Australian Model Code for Residential Development*. Canberra: Author.
5. Government of New South Wales [1979] *Environmental Planning and Assessment Act*. Sydney: Author.
6. Mandis Roberts Consultants [1992] *Outdoor Recreation and Open Space—Planning Guidelines for Local Government*. New South Wales: Department of Planning.
7. Government of Victoria [1987] *Planning and Environment Act, 1987*. Melbourne: Author.
8. Government of Victoria [1972] *Sport and Recreation Act, 1972*. Melbourne: Author.
9. Ministry of Planning and Environment [1988] *Metropolitan Open Space Plan*. Victoria: Author.
10. Government of Queensland [1988] *Recreation Areas Management Act 1988*. Brisbane: Author.
11. Government of Queensland [1990] *Local Government Planning and Environment Act 1990*. Brisbane: Author.
12. National Capital Development Commission [1988] *Standard Practices—Guidelines and Design Practices*. Canberra: National Capital Development Commission.
13. Brisbane City Council [1986] *City of Brisbane Town Plan*. Brisbane: Author.
14. Government of Western Australia [1959] *Metropolitan Region Town Planning Scheme Act, 1959–1982*. Perth: Author.
15. Government of Western Australia [1928] *Town Planning and Development Act, 1928*. Perth: Author.
16. State Planning Commission, *Policy Manual No. 1—Development Control Including Subdivision*. Western Australia: Author.
17. Department of Planning and Urban Development [1990] *METROPLAN—A Planning Strategy for the Perth Metropolitan Region*. Western Australia: Author.
18. Adelaide Planning Commission [1991] *2020 Vision—Ideas for Metropolitan Adelaide*. Adelaide: Premiers Department.
19. Government of South Australia [1993] *Development Act 1993*. Adelaide: Author.
20. Government of South Australia [1998] *Local Government (Lands) Bill*. Adelaide: Author.
21. Department of Housing and Urban Development [1994] *State Recreation and Sport Strategic Plan for Metropolitan Adelaide*. South Australia: Author.
22. Department of Housing and Urban Development [1993] *Social Policy Aspects of Urban Development*. South Australia: South Australian Urban Land Trust.
23. Government of Tasmania [1962] *Local Government Act*. Tasmania: Author.
24. Government of Tasmania [1977] *Tourism and Recreational Development Act, 1977*. Hobart: Author.
25. Government of Northern Territory [1987] *Northern Territory of Australia Planning Act 1987*. Darwin: Author.
26. Department of Lands and Housing [1990] *Darwin Town Plan*. Northern Territory: Author.
27. Australian Capital Territory [1993] *The Territory Plan*. Australian Government Publishing Service.
28. Australian Capital Territory [1992] *ACT Lakes Ordinance*. Australian Government Publishing Service.
29. Australian Capital Territory [1994] *Cotter River Act*. Australian Government Publishing Service.
30. National Capital Development Commission [1988] *Standard Practices—Guidelines on Planning and Design Practices*. National Capital Development Commission.
31. National Capital Development Commission [1984] *Metropolitan Canberra: Policy Plan Development Plan*. Australian Capital Territory: National Capital Development Commission.
32. Mandis Roberts Consultants [1992] *Outdoor Recreation and Open Space—Planning Guidelines for Local Government*. New South Wales: Department of Planning, p. 8.

33. Clark, R.N. and Stankey, G.H. [1979] *The Recreation Opportunity Spectrum—A Framework for Planning, Management and Research.* General Technical Report PNW-98. United States Forest Service.

34. Australian Capital Territory [1998] *Standard Practices Guidelines on Planning Designs.* National Capital Development Commission.

35. Department of Housing and Urban Development [1993] *Social Policy Aspects of Urban Development.* South Australia, pp. 39–40.

36. Department of Environment and Planning [1981] *Guidelines for the Administration of Section 94 of the Environmental Planning and Assessment Act.* New South Wales.

37. Government of Victoria [1987] *Planning and Environment Act.* Victoria: Author.

38. Department of Housing and Urban Development [1993] *Social Policy Aspects of Urban Development.* South Australia, p. 39.

39. National Capital Development Commission [1988] *Standard Practices.* National Capital Development Commission.

40. National Capital Development Commission [1988] *Standard Practices.* National Capital Development Commission.

41. National Capital Development Commission [1988] *Standard Practices.* National Capital Development Commission, p. 25, figures 1 and 2.

42. National Capital Development Commission [1988] *Standard Practices.* National Capital Development Commission.

43. Department of Housing and Urban Development [1993] *Social Policy Aspects of Urban Development.* South Australia: Author.

44. National Capital Development Commission [1988] *Standard Practices.* National Capital Development Commission.

45. Ministry of Planning and Environment [1989] *Planning Guide for Urban Open Space.* Victoria.

46. National Capital Development Commission [1988] *Standard Practices.* National Capital Development Commission.

47. City of Brisbane [1986] *Town Plan.* Brisbane.

48. City of Brisbane [1986] *Town Plan.* Brisbane.

49. City of Darwin [1990] *Town Plan.* Darwin.

50. Ministry of Planning and Environment [1989] *Planning Guide for Urban Open Space.* Victoria: Author.

51. Department of Housing and Urban Development [1993] *Social Policy Aspects of Urban Development.* South Australia: South Australian Urban Land Trust, p. 39.

52. Ministry of Planning and Environment [1989] *Planning Guide for Urban Open Space.* Victoria.

53. Ministry of Planning and Environment [1989] *Planning Guide for Urban Open Space.* Victoria.

54. Ministry of Planning and Environment [1989] *Planning Guide for Urban Open Space.* Victoria.

55. South Australian Metropolitan Open Space System [1993] *Supplementary Development Plan.* Adelaide: Ministry of Planning and Environment.

56. South Australian Metropolitan Open Space System [1993] *Supplementary Development Plan,* Objectives 36 and 39.

57. National Capital Development Commission [1984] *Metropolitan Canberra: Policy Plan Development Plan.* Australian Capital Territory: Author.

58. Salisbury City Council [1998] *Salisbury 2000 Open Space and Recreation—Policies.* South Australia, p. 1.

59. Little, Charles, E. [1995] *Greenways for America.* Baltimore: Johns Hopkins University Press, p. 38.

60. Department of Housing and Urban Development [1994] *Social Policy Aspects of Urban Development.* South Australia, p. 39.

61. Ministry of Planning and Urban Development [1987] *Planning Guide for Urban Open Space.* Victoria: Author.

62. Government of New South Wales [1979] *Environmental and Planning Assessment Act.* Sydney: Author.

63. Government of New South Wales [ND] *New South Wales Open Space Strategy.* Sydney: Author.

64. Mandis Roberts Consultants [1992] *Outdoor Recreation and Open Space—Planning Guidelines for Local Government.* New South Wales: Department of Planning, p. 17.

65. Government of Victoria [1988] *Subdivision Act, Section 18.* Victoria.

66. Government of Queensland [1990] *Local Government Planning and Environment Act 1990.* Brisbane: Author.

67. Government of South Australia [1993] *Development Act 1993.* Adelaide: Author.

68. Government of Tasmania [1962] *Local Government Act, 1962.* Hobart: Author.

69. Government of Northern Territory [1987] *Northern Territory of Australia Planning Act 1987.* Darwin.

70. Green Street Joint Venture [1990] *Australian Model Code—For Residential Development,* Canberra: Task Force.

71. Resource Assessment Commission [1993] *National Coastal Action Plan—Draft Conclusions and Recommendations.* Canberra: Coastal Zone Inquiry.

72. Government of New South Wales [1979] *Coastal Protection Act.* Sydney: Author.

73. Government of New South Wales [1998] *Coastal Protection Amendment Act.* Sydney: Author.

74. Government of New South Wales [1997] *Marine Parks Act.* Sydney: Author.

75. Government of Queensland [1995] *Coastal Protection and Management Act.* Brisbane: Author.

76. Government of Queensland [1968] *Beach Protection Act.* Brisbane: Author.

77. Government of Queensland [1982] *Marine Parks Act.* Brisbane: Author.

78. Government of South Australia [1972] *Coast Protection Act 1992.* Adelaide: Author.

79. Government of South Australia [1993] *Development Act 1993*. Adelaide: Author.

80. Government of Western Australia [1984] *Conservation and Land Management Act (CALM Act)*. Author.

81. Government of Northern Territory [1996] *Marine Act*. Author.

82. Government of Victoria [1975] *National Parks Act 1975*. Author.

83. National Playing Fields Association [1989] *Minimum Standards for Outdoor Recreational Playing Space*. London: Author.

84. National Park Recreation Association [1971] *National Park and Recreation Open Space Standards*. Washington, D.C.: Author.

85. Burton, Thomas L., Ellis, Jack B. and Homenuck, H. Peter M. [1977] *Guidelines for Urban Open Space Planning: A Report*. Parks and Recreation Association, Canada.

CHAPTER
3

Planning Methodology

It is now necessary to consider the methodology needed for developing local-, regional- and state-level recreation and sport strategy plans. Section 1 provides advice on how to manage the planning process including getting the basics right for success, then looks closely at the tendering process and the preparation of a planning brief. Section 2 suggests that there are no perfect planning strategies and identifies six different planning methods, the final being a simplified version that has been tried and tested. Section 3 focusses on how to develop a planning framework and use mapping tools. Because recreation and sport strategic planning is an ongoing process that needs to be flexible and able to evolve and change to meet new challenges, information systems need to be reviewed constantly if the planning methodology is to be kept up to date.

DEFINITIONS

Because the terms 'planning' and 'design' are used in the title of the manual, the following clarification of their use is necessary within the context of recreation and sport planning.

Planning is a people-oriented process that brings together information about the rational allocation of recreation and sport resources to meet the present and future requirements of people at the state, regional and local level.

Design is the practical application of recreation and sport resources identified in the planning process. The designer's task is to create specific open spaces and built facilities for recreation and sport that are compatible with the environment and add to the quality of life of the present and future user.

Throughout the manual, planning and design terms are often used together because it is not possible to plan without taking into account the design of the recreation and sport facility or open spaces. Similarly, the design of a facility including open spaces for recreation and sport must take into account the rational allocation of resources in a wider planning context.

Planners use a plethora of terminology such as vision, mission, aims, goals, policy, objectives, principles, strategies and action plans. *Objectives*, as used in this manual, represent an end-point of planning. They are where visions, missions, aims or goals are focussed prior to formulating principles.

An endeavour has been made to use the term *principles* in this manual to explain in greater detail the beliefs or philosophies underlying the objectives. They are the basis on which priorities and action plans will be determined.

SECTION 1: MANAGING THE PLANNING STRATEGY

Outcomes in the form of tangible planning strategies that can be implemented and evaluated depend on getting the planning strategy right.

It is difficult to conceive of poor management and methodologies leading to satisfactory projects. Sometimes it is instructive to learn from our past mistakes so that they are not repeated.

Why Projects Fail

Getting the fundamentals wrong usually guarantees failure in managing the planning process. The following failure guarantees should be avoided:

1. Rushing into the project without identifying clear terms of reference that detail the scope and task with expected outcomes.

2. Setting unrealistic time frames for completion of the project.

3. Establishing a project management committee; after all, the members should have more important things to do with their time.

4. Fragmenting the tasks to be undertaken and insufficiently briefing the people selected.

5. Allowing the project to be coordinated by someone who has no experience with the project.

6. Burying the project strategy document among a myriad of other tasks and conveniently forgetting to report on progress until the originators of the project give up in frustration or proceed on a unilateral basis without a strategy.

Success: Getting the Basics Right

Rather than concentrating on failure, get the basics right with thorough preplanning and then choose the most suitable planning method.

The following are some important matters to consider in developing the strategy methodology.

Appointment of a Project Management Committee

It is essential to appoint a project management or advisory committee to manage and oversee the planning process. Usually some of the members of the committee represent the agencies that are funding the project.

Large committees can be cumbersome. Therefore, the selection of a right mix of people who are able to 'own' the project and give it credibility is important when government agencies and the community consider the recommendations.

Key factors in the appointment are:

- *Availability.* Make sure that the person has the time and a strong commitment to the project, which could mean involvement in some additional tasks to assist the project.

- *Skills and authority to act.* It is not necessary for project management committee members to be experts in recreation and sport planning. Rather they should have an ability to think conceptually and represent broad points of view. Ideally, some skills in working with committees involved in strategic planning with an understanding of recreation and sport issues are desirable.

- *Commitment.* Committee members should have a sense that the project is exciting and worthwhile; they must work as a team in order to produce practical outcomes that can be implemented through their support.

Options for Making the Planning Process Work

Coordinating and managing the process requires a focus. While a number of tasks require expertise with special skills, it is important to consider who has responsibility for bringing the project together. Four options are:

- *Using existing staff.* If there are staff available with the necessary expertise, consideration should be given to adjusting existing work responsibilities to allow for the preparation of a recreation and sport plan. Experience suggests that no matter how good the intentions, there is a danger that ongoing work commitments will impinge on the development of a recreation and sport plan by existing staff.

- *Using consultants.* External consultants are generally able to 'step back' and provide objectivity by raising and examining new issues. As they are independent, their views may also be more readily accepted. Fortunately, there are a number of consultants who have either developed experience in recreation and sport planning as part of their other work in the planning field, or have formal training in recreation and sport. Therefore, consideration should be given to tendering out the preparation of a recreation and sport plan.

- *Existing staff supported by consultants.* By combining existing staff with consultants, the expertise of both can be used. This method also ensures that the consultants' time, which is expensive, is not employed preparing reports on information that is already known. Using existing staff to work with consultants can be a cost-effective method of employing consultants to the best advantage of the project.

- *Short-term contract staff.* Increasing opportunities are available for the appointment of temporary or short-term staff to work on specific projects. While it is possible for the project officer to focus on this assignment without getting caught up in other extraneous tasks, when the project is finished there could be a problem of ownership when that officer leaves.

Tendering Process

More than likely, consultants will be involved in some aspects of planning strategy development. The following summary from a Western Australian Planning Guide[1] is useful in making sure there is a level playing field when engaging consultants.

Expressions of Interest

Expressions of interest provide opportunities for clients to prepare an indicative study brief and establish a budget limit. They can then negotiate with a selected number of consultants, seeking their advice as to the best way to undertake the study within this context. This usually requires less 'up front' time in preparing the brief and provides better opportunities for communication between the client and prospective consultant. The final project brief can then be determined and the consultants invited to submit their final proposals, including fees.

Expressions of interest usually involve a two-phased approach for selecting consultants. From an initial publicly advertised notice, or by direct invitation, consultants submit a proposal outlining their initial understanding of the study brief, individual or team skills, capability, previous experience and availability.

Usually three consultants are selected from the initial submissions and invited to prepare a detailed proposal addressing the study brief, including costs for undertaking the work. The final selection process should involve an interview so that the client can assess potential working relationships with the consultant.

Open Tendering

Open tendering, generally advertised in newspapers, is the usual process adopted by governments and public tender boards responsible for overseeing the process of engaging publicly funded projects. Tender submissions are required to follow a specified format, addressing the study brief and the selection criteria and including a fixed price for service provision.

Selective Tendering

If there is no legal requirement for public tendering, a selective tendering process may be adopted. This involves inviting a selection of suitably qualified and experienced consultants to prepare a submission, which will form the basis for selection of the preferred tenderer. This approach has the benefit of saving time in comparison to the open tendering approach. The disadvantage, however, is that consultants with particular skills may not be readily known to those that are responsible for deciding on the invitation list, and therefore may be missed in the process.

Invitations to Quote

Invitations to quote are normally used when consultants with particular expertise are required or when the client has worked with consultants before and wishes to assess current fees for service based on a comparison with similar consultants.

The time and effort required to prepare a submission can vary depending on the previous approaches. It is therefore important for the client to identify the type of service required and the most appropriate way of engaging consultants.

For example, tendering requires the client to prepare a detailed and accurate study brief so that the consultant can establish a fixed price. There is little opportunity for dialogue prior to tendering and to a great extent the quality of the outcome will be directly related to the clarity of the brief and the consultant's understanding. Both the client and the consultant will therefore need to invest a considerable amount of time in the process.

Preparation of the Brief

The quality of the recreation and sport plan is directly related to the contents of the brief. Therefore, careful attention should be given to drawing up a document that clearly outlines the tasks to be undertaken.

It is important to specifically detail the tasks to be achieved because if the brief is not clear, the results are likely to be unsatisfactory.

Consultants should be allowed to prepare an accurate estimate of the probable costs of preparing the recreation and sport plan. It is not necessary to spend large amounts of money gathering information and conducting investigations if the information is already available. Using existing material is more cost efficient than wasting time (which costs money) collecting information already available. For example, most surveys that identify the most popular recreation and sport activities in which people participate draw similar conclusions. Therefore, the brief should specify exactly what additional information is needed.

The following information should be included in the brief:

- Clearly identify the *client* or *clients* who are responsible for the plan.
- Give a brief *background* of how the proposal has developed to this point, any factors that brought about the proposal and the reasons the recreation and sport plan should proceed.
- Provide clear *objectives* for the strategy plan. It is helpful if these are placed in priority order.

- Detail any particular *procedures* the consultant will need to relate to other officers or planning projects that may be proceeding at the same time. If this is part of a larger planning study, for instance, the procedure by which this plan integrates with others should be laid down clearly. Any additional assistance by means of access to computer information or office space for the consultant should be indicated.
- Give potential consultants a *suggested methodology,* information on how the project should be developed leaving scope for them to introduce their own ideas. Stress that an innovative approach would be welcome.
- The consultant should be given a clear understanding of the *consultative process,* including the level of consultation required. Because consultation is expensive, the client needs to be clear about the depth of consultation necessary.
- Detail the *major planning areas* that should be covered in developing the plan. For example, recreation and sport open spaces may need to be identified and the type of outdoor and indoor facilities specified, including suggested management arrangements.
- Specify the form that the final *documentation* should take (for example, there are likely to be maps, plans and tables) and the number of copies required (usually six to ten).
- Be clear on the *timetable*—when the project starts and ends. Plenty of lead time should be given so that the successful consultant has an opportunity to clear up other tasks to concentrate on this project.
- A *project management* committee should be established to supervise the development of the plan. This was discussed earlier in the chapter. A designated leader of the consultancy should be identified, if a team approach using specialists in different areas is proposed by the tenderer.

- The brief should ask for curriculum vitae containing the professional *qualifications* and practical experience of each member of the consultancy team.

- Finally, the brief should request a breakdown of the *budget details* and costs. This is important because negotiation may be possible if the fee is above budget. Also, additional work may be required in some special aspects of the project. If there are itemised costs, then adjustments can be made if necessary.

Whatever consultant is finally agreed upon, it should be made clear that an 'issues paper' is required during the early part of the investigation process so that the project is kept on track and any differences of opinion with the project management committee can then be discussed. The extent to which the key issues paper is circulated to others such as council members, officers of agencies and other interested individuals and organisations needs to be clarified.

If the planning involves controversial issues such as the location of facilities and environmental factors, then consultants should be required to state their experience in conflict resolution techniques.

Consultants should be encouraged to adopt the most productive methods of obtaining feedback by using workshops, focus groups and different survey techniques, for example, in shopping centres. An example of a good consultation process can be found at the end of section 2 (page 43) in this chapter.

The question of whether the consultants should be given an indication of the funds available needs to be considered. Tenders based on price usually encourage keen competition, but significant differences may occur in the quality of the final product. Another alternative is to set the cost for the work to be undertaken based on previous strategy plans that have been prepared. This eliminates the possibility of unfair advantages occurring through leaks about the amount of funding available. Also, it is easier to make comparative assessments of the proposals if all tenderers have the same information about the amount of money available. See an example of a typical planning brief in appendix A.

SECTION 2: SIX DIFFERENT PLANNING METHODS

The following planning procedures have been used with varying degrees of success in preparing recreation and sport plans. They should be considered carefully, then adapted for the local situation.

Three Key Questions Method

This method has been successfully used in both local and regional recreation and sport planning in South Australia. It poses three key questions that need to be addressed:

1. *Where are we now?* To answer this question, a *situational analysis* is developed that reviews the current situation by providing population statistics, an inventory of recreation and sport facilities and their usage patterns.

2. *Where do we want to be?* An *opportunity analysis* can be undertaken to answer this question. It should look at future favourable circumstances for meeting the needs of the community through better recreational and sport services and facilities.

3. *How do we get there?* This question seeks to provide objectives, goals and actions for addressing the answers obtained from the first two steps. It is critical to then develop an implementation process for monitoring and reviewing the progress of the plan. This involves an ongoing assessment of the current situation and future opportunities.

Figure 3.1 places these questions within a five-step planning process.

Four-Phase Method

This planning process described in the *Sport and Recreation Victoria* manual[2] highlights 'key outputs' at the conclusion of each phase (see figure 3.2). Tangible products or outcomes are required.

Six Strategy Stages Method

The British Sports Council suggests a six-stage process for developing sport and recreation strategies.[3] They are:

1. *Review of local authority current policies.* An inventory of facilities and open spaces as well as major recreation and sport services is required. Questions such as why are the services provided and who uses them should be posed.

2. *External influences on the local authority.* This stage deals with population, economic and environmental changes, policies and practices of other key organisations and should, in the case of South Australia, take into consideration legislative changes through the development plans.

3. *Identification of local authority roles and aims.* Broad aims of the strategy and the future roles the local council will want to play are now drawn out of the work of the first two stages.

4. *Identification of key issues.* An examination of the key recreation and sport issues are now identified covering the quality of the services and facilities provided.

5. *Key issues: examination, policy and courses of action and review.* Having identified the key issues, this stage gathers relevant information so that informed policies can be made and courses of action taken.

6. *Strategy review.* This last stage seeks to establish a timetable for reviewing the plan annually on the basis of the recreation and sport services; establish policies every three

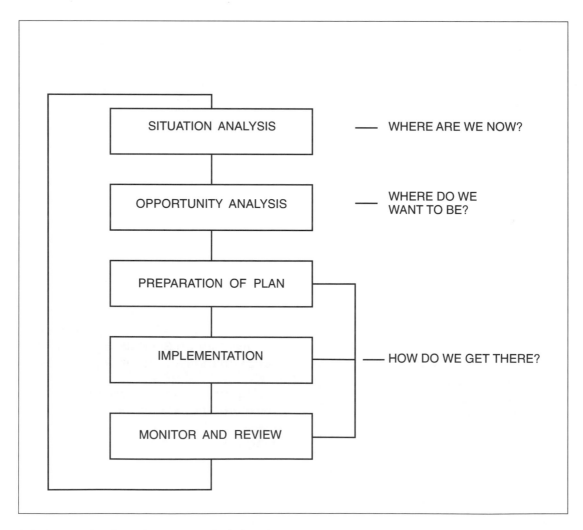

Figure 3.1   Three Key Questions method of planning

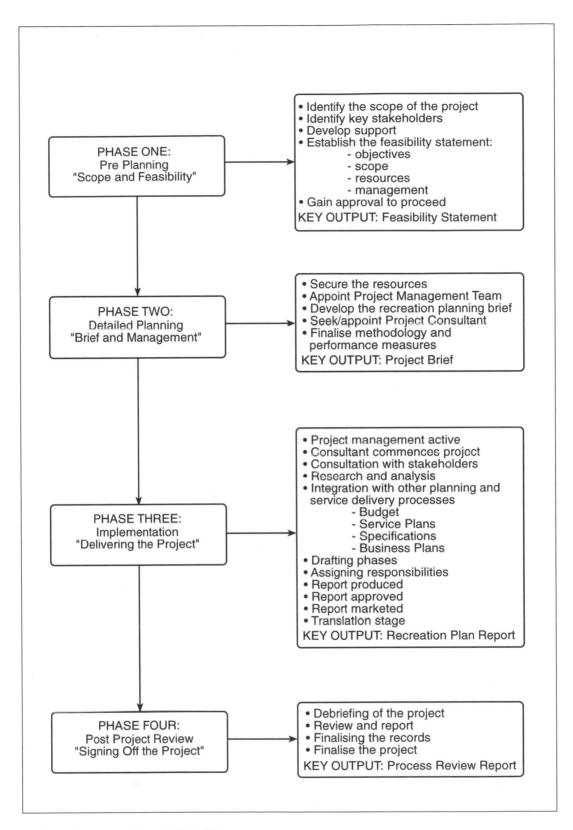

Figure 3.2 Four-Phase method of planning.

years; and undertake a major review of the role, aims and objectives of the strategy every six years.

An Eight-Step Method

A recreation planning manual for local government prepared by Ken Marriott for South Australia[4] describes an eight-step planning process.

1. *Preplanning.* Covers the need for a comprehensive plan clarifying the purposes of planning and considering who should do the planning.

2. *Policy formulation.* Includes preparation of draft goals, objectives and principles. Also, policy formulation identifies specific actions and guidelines.

3. *Social-economic analysis.* Involves the collection and analysis of population—for example, housing and tourism data.

4. *Previous reports review.* Consists of a review of previous reports, studies and working papers dealing with recreation.

5. *Existing provision review.* This step reviews the existing council structures, recreation facilities, programs and services.

6. *Community consultations.* Community consultations are considered to be an important part of any recreation planning review. Since the needs of the community should be of paramount importance, consultation should be seen as a means of developing awareness of wider community needs rather than those of organised minorities. Emphasis is placed on the dangers of overconsultation. Methods of consultation are then detailed.

7. *Policies and recommendations for action.* Ken Marriott suggests that this is one of the most demanding steps in the process because it brings together the key elements, identifies priorities and makes final recommendations.[5]

8. *Implementation and evaluation.* This step entails action to make sure the strategy plan is a reality by promoting the findings and introducing evaluation process.

SWOT Analysis Method

As part of the methodology, particularly after the information has been collected on recreation and sport services and facilities, the SWOT analysis has been effectively used in a workshop environment to synthesise policies. Some project management committees have found this analysis particularly helpful to assist in clarifying strategies and prioritising policy areas.

SWOT identifies:

• **(S)trengths:** The major strengths of recreation and sport provision such as good management techniques and facility maintenance should be highlighted.

• **(W)eaknesses:** These are sensitive areas that need to be faced in a nonthreatening environment. Such matters as lack of funding for programs and services and poor location of recreation and sport facilities could be raised.

• **(O)pportunities:** In every local and regional strategy plan there exist opportunities for the development of recreation and sport services and facilities. For example, addressing social justice and equity issues related to the use of facilities and services can be important to challenge existing thinking. Opportunities for multiple use of facilities and better management practices must certainly be considered in any strategy planning process.

• **(T)hreats:** Major threats have to be faced. These could include changes in the demographics of a local council area, competitive tendering changes and government decisions outside the control of the local council and recreation and sport associations.

A Simple Planning Method

Most council members and representatives of community groups including various recreation and sporting clubs and associations are not experts in recreation and sport strategy planning. Therefore, this easily understood planning method was introduced to assist in preparing a number of local and regional recreation and sport plans.

First, analyse the existing situation using

- past reports;
- population trends at state, regional and local levels as applicable;
- inventories of recreation and sport open spaces and facilities, including an assessment of their effectiveness and efficiency;
- current and future demands for recreation and sport in the light of changing social and economic patterns; and
- results of consultations with key groups, i.e. recreation and sport clubs and associations, council members and staff, relevant state government officers.

Second, assess the following major areas:

- Key issues: through the recommended key issues paper prepared for discussion by the consultants with the project management group and others who may be able to input constructive comments.
- Open spaces allocated to recreation and sport.
- Outdoor and indoor recreation and sport facilities.
- Capital costs of any proposed development.
- Maintenance and management costs of recreation and sport open spaces and facilities.

Third, implement planning by doing the following:

- Formulating policies.
- Preparing action plans for
  — short-term development, i.e. one to two years;
  — medium-term development, i.e. up to five years; and
  — long-term development, i.e. up to ten years [Note: the long-term case can be almost meaningless because of the rate of change, and the emphasis is on the need to be flexible with all aspects of planning—although in some circumstances a long-term plan is required].

- Identifying priorities, following the establishment of clear objectives, goals, priorities and actions.
- Establishing management structures for recreation and sport facilities and programs.
- Preparing evaluation and review procedures that will provide information which will be valuable in determining the future development of recreation and sport in the planning area.

  Appendix A provides a consultancy brief detailing how this planning approach can be is used.

Figure 3.3 will assist in making this methodology clear.

Examples of Successful Planning Processes

Two examples of successful planning processes follow.

The Adelaide City Council flow diagram in figure 3.4 sets out a comprehensive consultation process for a major city parkland project over an 18-month period.[6] A second example is the executive summary of a local recreation and sport planning strategy for Victor Harbor (figure 3.5).[7]

SECTION 3: DEVELOPING A FRAMEWORK

Having identified a number of planning methods, it is now important to consider a planning framework for recreation and sport. Figure 3.6 identifies the planning responsibilities.

Local

At the local level, recreation and sport planning is primarily the responsibility of the local government authority with input from the state government authority with responsibility for recreation and sport. Some council areas will have recreation and sport facilities and open spaces that have regional and state significance, therefore state and local-level planning responsibilities need to be coordinated.

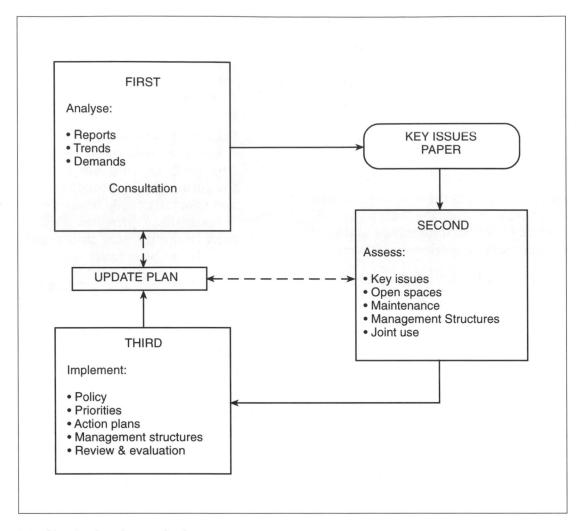

Figure 3.3   Simple planning method.

Local planning can be further segmented into district and neighbourhood areas. These areas include parks, playing fields, children's play areas, passive open spaces, built facilities such as indoor recreation facilities and sport facilities such as basketball and netball courts, swimming pools (indoor and outdoor), squash courts, fitness and health studios and clubrooms.

Regional

At the regional level, recreation and sport planning is primarily the responsibility of the state government agency in which the functions of recreation and sport reside. The planning task is to coordinate the overall planning with input from other government departments and agencies such as education, health, tourism, national parks and the environment. Often there is an overlap between what is

designated a regional facility and what is designated a local facility. A regional facility involves significant usage from outside a particular council area.

Cooperation of local councils and regional organisations of councils is important if a commitment is to be made to a regional recreation and sport strategy.

State

Planning of state recreation and sport facilities and open spaces is the responsibility of the state government, not necessarily one particular department. There are facilities of international, national and state significance such as major spectator sport facilities, mass entertainment facilities, coastal recreation and sport facilities and major parks, which have planning and management linkages across various state government agencies.

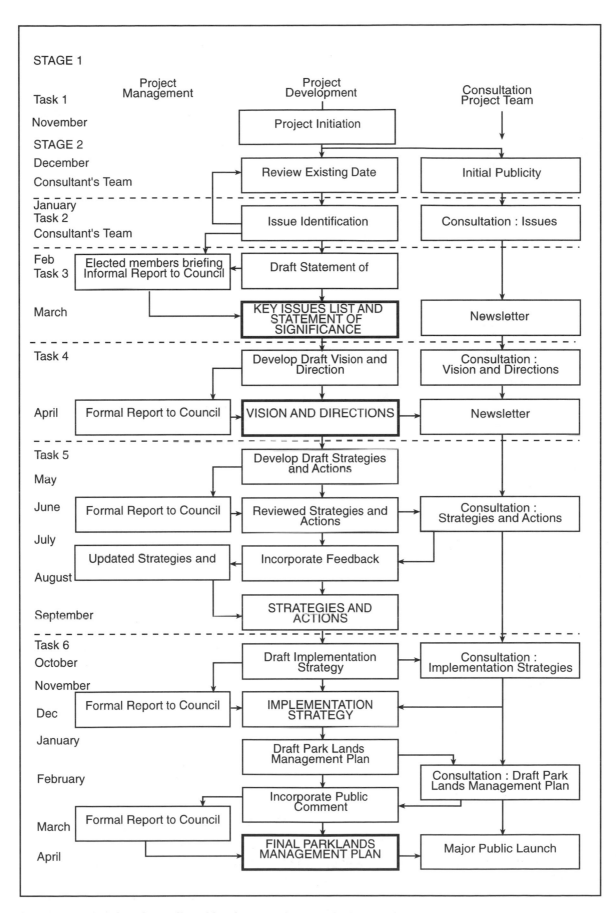

STAGE 1

Project Management	Project Development	Consultation Project Team

Task 1
November

STAGE 2
December
Consultant's Team

January
Task 2
Consultant's Team

Feb
Task 3

March

Task 4

April

Task 5
May
June
July
August
September

Task 6
October
November
Dec
January
February
March
April

- Project Initiation
- Review Existing Date — Initial Publicity
- Issue Identification — Consultation : Issues
- Elected members briefing Informal Report to Council ← Draft Statement of
- KEY ISSUES LIST AND STATEMENT OF SIGNIFICANCE — Newsletter
- Develop Draft Vision and Direction — Consultation : Vision and Directions
- Formal Report to Council — VISION AND DIRECTIONS — Newsletter
- Develop Draft Strategies and Actions
- Formal Report to Council → Reviewed Strategies and Actions → Consultation : Strategies and Actions
- Updated Strategies and ← Incorporate Feedback
- STRATEGIES AND ACTIONS
- Draft Implementation Strategy → Consultation : Implementation Strategies
- Formal Report to Council → IMPLEMENTATION STRATEGY
- Draft Park Lands Management Plan
- Incorporate Public Comment ← Consultation : Draft Park Lands Management Plan
- Formal Report to Council
- FINAL PARKLANDS MANAGEMENT PLAN → Major Public Launch

Figure 3.4   Adelaide City Council parklands management strategy program.

45

Local Recreation and Sports Planning Strategy
Victor Harbor - South Australia
Table of Contents

Figure 3.5   Recreation and sport planning strategy for Victor Harbor.

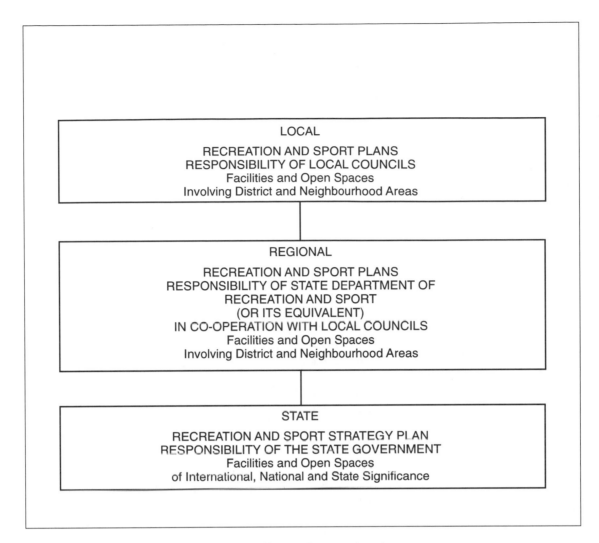

Figure 3.6   Hierarchy of responsibility for recreation and sport planning.

Also, some of the major sporting associations, such as football, basketball, netball, hockey and athletics have responsibility for large facilities. It is necessary to identify these planning responsibilities in order to prepare an overall strategy.

An Integrated Approach

The integrated approach involves developing partnerships among the three spheres of government, local communities and the private sector to work towards establishing and achieving shared objectives for enhancing local well-being.[8]

Before irreversible decisions are taken on the location and construction of recreation and sport facilities, an integrated strategic approach to planning and design can provide an opportunity for making sure other factors such as access to public transport, linkages with other community facilities and demographic trends are taken into account.

Past practices that allowed sports clubs, government departments or local councils to develop major facilities in isolation are fortunately now disappearing. There are increasing pressures for multiuse of recreation and sport facilities, particularly the community use of schools. Strategic recreation and sport planning assumes that an integrated approach is linked with other planning being undertaken at national, state and local levels.

In most states and territories, emphasis is being placed on integrated social, economic and environmental (including heritage) planning before proceeding with all major projects. Unless recreation and sport planning has an overall strategy with clear objectives, it will continue to be treated as an afterthought as other planning areas receive higher priorities.

At the heart of the following suggested planning framework is an integrated recreation and sport strategy plan that provides the outcomes that follow.

Outcomes from the planning framework must be tangible, relying on inputs through the collection of sound data that is then accurately interpreted. If the information system is effective, the following outcomes should result.

Inventories

Most local councils and state governments have inventories of various facilities for which they have responsibility. There is a need to develop a comprehensive facilities and land use database or audit of recreation and sport facilities covering those owned by local councils, community sports and recreation organisations, educational institutions and the private sector.

One major problem with the collection of such data is its cost, because the task of developing a system to cover local-, state-, national- and international-level recreation and sport facilities would be prohibitive. Another problem just as challenging would be updating such a system.

A recommendation to a commonwealth inquiry into funding of community and recreation facilities suggests that not only is such a system necessary, but also that it should be linked to a Geographic Information System (GIS) mapping capability to provide 'a consistent system of grading facilities for all sports'.[9] The feasibility of such an ambitious inventory, which includes a grading of facilities at the national level, is being considered along the lines of the international and national facilites inventories introduced by South Australia.[10 & 11] Similarly, Queensland has a questionnaire for a sporting facilities needs analysis.[12]

Local councils and state and territory governments are already developing databases and GIS mapping capabilities. These can be utilised for recreation and sport facilities.

Mapping Capabilities for Recreation and Sport Planning

An important tool for strategic planning is a flexible mapping database that provides a visual method of presenting information. The quality of the data and its relevance to recreation and sport planning must be constantly questioned to avoid the collection of meaningless information which is costly and can be counterproductive by overloading planners with information.

In recreation and sport strategic planning it is important to go further than producing maps that merely present an historical snapshot of the situation as it exists; this information will be out of date within a short period of time.

It is now possible to use mapping to identify the gaps in the existing range of recreation and sport facilities and open spaces at state, regional and local levels and introduce various options in a visual form with accompanying relevant data. This allows priorities to be established to take account of the more efficient use of existing facilities or justification for additional facilities in the right locations. Good examples of this mapping capability are found in appendix D which provides two examples of questionnaires for international and national sporting facilities and regional recreation and sporting facilities.[13 & 14]

Outcomes From the Planning Framework

The previous outcomes can then be applied to local-, regional- and state-level recreation and sport strategy plans or specific projects. Figure 3.7 identifies the links between the information systems; local, regional and state strategy plans; and specific projects.

Requirements of a Computer Mapping Program

When using computer mapping programs, it is important to address clearly the following questions:

- Is the mapping system user-friendly?
- Are there sufficient personnel with the

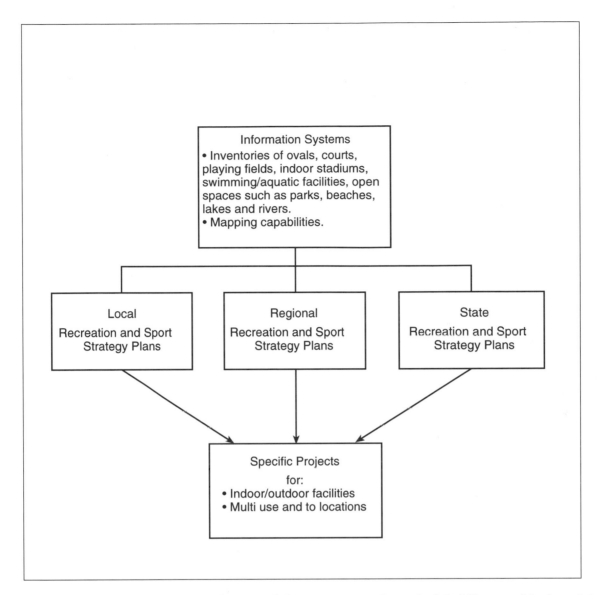

Figure 3.7   Outcomes from the planning framework. Inputs are more important, but they must be translated into these outcomes.

knowledge necessary to operate the system?

- What is the cost?

- Who updates the information on a regular basis?

- Is the data from the program compatible with other mapping programs?

- How many other government authorities—state, local and national—use the system?

- Does the system 'talk' to other databases?

- Has the system capacity for expansion?

- What sort of service backup is available from the provider?

- What type of hardware is required to operate the system, including printer for maps?

- Can confidentiality of information at various levels be assured?

Components of a Recreation and Sport Mapping Program

Having asked the right questions about the requirements of a mapping program, it is now necessary to make sure that the components of a database are in place. A program should at least assist in identifying trends, strategies, facilities and open space, and cost and benefits.

Figure 3.8 provides more details of each component.

Range of GIS Systems

There are a range of systems, but the Geographic Information System (GIS) has been found to be most effective and readily available at state and local government levels. Two of the most popular programs are Map Info and ARC Info. There is no clear market leader and the present recreation and sport users of computer mapping throughout Australia are fairly evenly divided. Arrangements can be made for either state departments or local governments to contract out their GIS services rather than duplicate expensive personnel and hardware.

Future Possibilities

The value of making computer mapping an integral part of the strategic planning process should not be underestimated. At least there should be efforts made to develop a compatible state or territory system including the recording of international, national, state and regional recreation and sport facilities and open spaces. If possible, encouragement should be given to local councils in developing their own mapping databases in such a way that they are compatible to the regional and state system. The question of a national computerised inventory should remain on the agenda for future consideration.

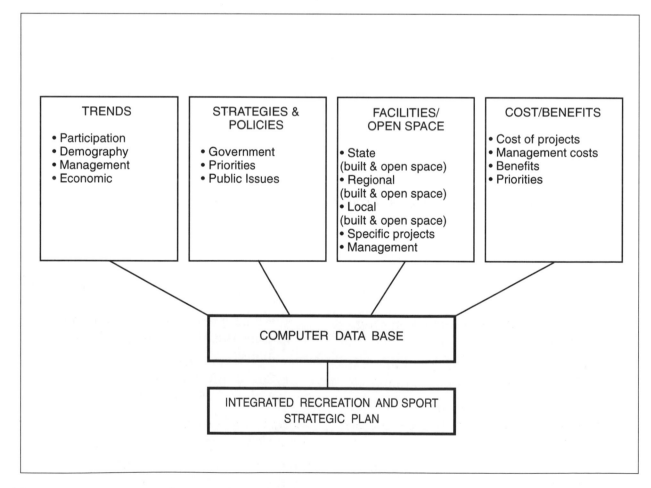

Figure 3.8   Components of a recreation and sport mapping program.

National Initiatives

The government sector is not the only sector that has been hindered in its efforts at effective planning and development as a result of the lack of reliable, comprehensive and accessible statistics on recreation and sport. The lack of data has also limited the ability of nongovernment organisations to form sound strategic policies.

Statistical Information

In cooperation with the Australian Bureau of Statistics (ABS), a Recreation and Sport Industry Statistical Group (RSISG) has been established with representation from each state and territory and the commonwealth to provide relevant statistics for the recreation and sport industry.

Various publications are available on a range of subjects that are useful in developing recreation and sport strategic plans. Information on demographics, participation, economic indicators and employment are available.

National Sport and Recreation Industry Data Base and Directory (NSRIDD)

Each state and territory has a computer database provided by the Australian Bureau of Statistics (ABS), which enables the user to retrieve and analyse a range of statistical information on recreation and sport. Over 60 ABS tables and extensive data on organisations and occupations within the recreation and sport industry are available. The data is updated and added to each year.

NSRIDD also has sections on sport, recreation, amusements, gambling, services, construction, retail, wholesale manufacturing, industry, finance, agriculture and culture. Over time it will become the repository for all nationally reliable and comparable statistics on recreation and sport.

Any person or organisation requiring statistics on recreation and sport can access this information. The computer program is hands-on and 'user-friendly' and the data is available through the agency responsible for recreation and sport in each state or territory.

As more data is added each year, there will be opportunities for extensive trend analysis and eventually it may be possible to link the statistics with a computer mapping capability.

IMPLEMENTING THE PLANNING FRAMEWORK

No single method of implementing recreation and sport strategies works in every situation. The methodologies described in this chapter highlight the need for a flexible planning system to improve the quality and range of opportunities for people at all levels to participate in recreation and sport activities. Above all, the methodology must be open to revision as priorities change.

REFERENCES

1. Ministry of Sport and Recreation [1997] *Recreation Planning Guide*. Government of Western Australia, p. 10–11.
2. Sport and Recreation Victoria [1996] *Recreation Planning in the 90's—An Integrated Approach*. Melbourne: Department of Arts, Sport and Tourism, p. 14.
3. Sports Council [1991] *District Sport and Recreation Strategies—A Guide*. England: Belmont Press.
4. Marriott, Ken [1990] *Recreation Planning—A Manual for Local Government*, second edition. Adelaide: South Australian Recreation Institute.
5. Marriott, Ken [1990] *Recreation Planning—A Manual for Local Government*, p. 81.
6. Hassell Pty Ltd [1998] *City of Adelaide Parklands Management Strategy Programme*. Adelaide.
7. Phillip Gray and Associates [1996] *Victor Harbor Recreation and Sport Plan*. District Council of Victor Harbor and Office for Recreation and Sport.
8. Sport and Recreation Victoria [1996] *Recreation Planning in the 90's—An Integrated Approach*.
9. House of Representatives Standing Committee on Environment, Recreation and the Arts [1997] *Rethinking the Funding of Community Sporting and Recreational Facilities: A Sporting Chance*. Canberra: Australian Government Publishing Service, p. 55.
10. Office for Recreation and Sport [1999] *Questionnaire GIS Sporting Facilities Inventory (International, National and State)*. Department of Industry and Trade. Adelaide.
11. Office for Recreation and Sport [1999] *Recreation, Sport Facilities and Open Space GIS Inventory*. Department of Industry and Trade. Adelaide.
12. Office of Sport and Recreation [1998] *Queensland*

Sporting Facilities—A Needs Analysis, Queensland Government, Department of Emergency Services. Brisbane.

13. Office for Recreation and Sport [1999] *Questionnaire GIS Sporting Facilities Inventory (International,*

National and State). Department of Industry and Trade. Adelaide.

14. Office for Recreation and Sport [1999] *Recreation, Sport Facilities and Open Space GIS Inventory.* Adelaide.

CHAPTER 4

Local Recreation and Sport Strategy Plans

This chapter focuses on the all-important issue of developing a policy framework. It includes a step-by-step process on how to prepare and implement recreation and sport during planning of facilities, services and programs at the local level. Clear objectives and principles for local facilities and open spaces are then proposed, followed by an extensive discussion on methods by which particularly facilities can be funded at the local level. Some key issues that have arisen in the preparation of recreation and sport strategies at the local level are discussed and finally an example of best planning practice is provided.

This chapter should be the one most referred to because the majority of recreation and sport happens at the local level where thousands of people of all ages engage in a wide range of daily recreation and sport activities. If the provision of local open spaces for recreation and sport and adequate facilities is not right, then it is that much more difficult for effective regional and state recreation and sport strategies to be put in place.

DIFFERENCES AT THE LOCAL LEVEL

Because local councils are responsible for the care, control and management of most public land at the local level, they are the important providers of recreation and sport facilities and services for the community.

Not all councils are the same. Therefore it is important to recognise that the characteristics of councils will significantly influence the planning process. The four categories of councils below identify certain characteristics that impact on policy formulation.[1]

Inner Metropolitan Councils tend to be characterised by

- an ageing or declining population;

- an ageing recreation and sport infrastructure, in particular facilities;

- decreasing membership of recreation and sporting clubs and groups and hence declining financial viability resulting in the amalgamation of clubs; and

- location of most international and national standard facilities.

Outer Metropolitan Councils tend to be characterised by

- an increasing population with a high proportion of young families;

- the development of new, or expansion of existing facilities;

- difficulties in meeting the demand for recreation and sport facilities and services;

- an emphasis on development of local-level facilities and activities; and

- dormitory suburbs from which residents commute to very different communities to work.

Provincial Cities tend to be characterised by

- an ageing population with a significant proportion of retirees who have moved from the surrounding rural areas;
- service centres for surrounding rural areas; and
- a population which is not large enough to support major facilities, but a community which expects a comprehensive range of facilities to be available.

Rural Communities tend to be characterised by

- a declining population;
- problems in sustaining junior sports teams as a result of declining junior numbers;
- the necessity to travel long distances for recreation and sport activities;
- an amalgamation of clubs and rationalisation of facilities in recent years;
- relatively homogeneous communities; and
- significant natural outdoor recreation resources of national and international significance.

LOCAL POLICY SETTING

Because policies set future directions, policy setting is an important function of strategy planning at the local level. Therefore, it is important to ensure that recreation and sport priorities are considered and pressures are resisted. Sometimes unreasonable demands are made by pressure groups within the community for their priorities in developing recreation and sport facilities and services.

Ten Steps to Policy Formulation

A 10-step process (figure 4.1) is recommended for the development of policies. Depending upon the nature of the policy to be developed, a number of these steps may be combined, resulting in a simpler process that is also provided.

These steps are adapted from a publication produced by the Office for Recreation and Sport in South Australia for the use of local governments,[2] but they can apply equally to policy setting by a range of other clubs, associations and government agencies with a recreation and sport focus.

1. *Identify policy issue.* Formally acknowledge that a policy is required to address a particular issue.

2. *Appoint a facilitator.* A facilitator, coordinator or policy manager is required to drive the policy development process. A facilitator can be an individual, usually an officer, or a group, which may be termed an advisory committee, a reference group or a working party.

3. *Establish a methodology.* Generally speaking a major policy issue will require a comprehensive and exhaustive process, whereas a relatively minor policy will involve a simpler process in which many of the ten steps are combined. The process must allow for flexibility to accommodate unforeseen circumstances and hitches. Draft time lines and a schedule should be established, and tasks and responsibilities allocated to officers, consultants and the community.

4. *Collect data.* Primary or secondary data may have to be collected depending on the nature of the policy. Primary data could include attitudes and opinions of stakeholders, as well as raw data relating to frequency and time of use of facilities, and can be collected through surveys, interviews, observation and group sessions including focus groups and workshops. Secondary data involves reviewing existing material, including council policies, reports, documents, legislation and regulations, as well as operational data such as budgets, attendances, maintenance standards and usage patterns.

5. *Present a position paper.* A position paper will summarise a policy issue and the data collected and present a series of policy options.

6. *Consult.* Consultation involves discussing the position paper with all affected stakeholders, both internally and externally with

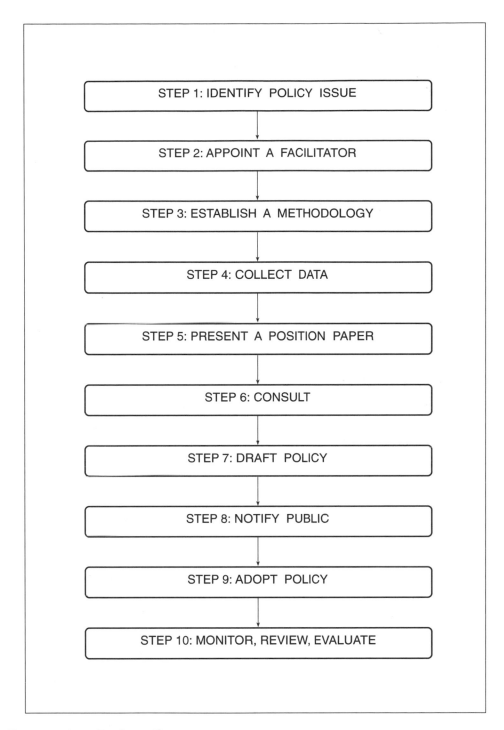

Figure 4.1   Ten steps to policy formation.

the community. A range of techniques can be used including personal interviews, workshops and focus groups, press releases, newsletters and public displays.

7. *Draft policy.* As a result of feedback received during the consultation, a draft policy will be prepared.

8. *Notify public.* Having established a draft policy, place it in the public arena using consultation techniques similar to those in step six. The public notification period should be for a set period in which formal submissions and comments will be received. These submissions may be verbal or written. It is

important that the community is fully aware of the time lines during which comment will be received, and the acceptable method for making comments.

9. *Adopt policy.* Based on comments received from the community, the policy may be modified and presented for adoption. A formal policy statement should also include an implementation program, administrative procedures and evaluation program.

10. *Monitor, review and evaluate.* This final step is often ignored, but it is an extremely important part of the policy development process. Major policies should be evaluated periodically, possibly annually, but probably every two or three years, whereas minor policies are reviewed as required, possibly as circumstances change and the policy becomes outdated.

Simple Four-Step Process

In many instances it is possible to use a shorter policy development process, particularly when issues are relatively simple. Rather than using the 10 steps just outlined, some steps can be combined.

1. *Planning.* Having decided that a policy needs to be drafted, appoint a facilitator with responsibility for coordinating the policy formulation process.

2. *Data collection and consultation.* Collect relevant information and consult stakeholders prior to preparing a draft policy.

3. *Draft policy and public comment.* Prepare a draft policy and circulate it to stakeholders and special interest groups for information. Based on comments received, the draft policy may be modified.

4. *Policy adoption.* A formal policy statement including an implementation program, administrative procedures and evaluation program is presented for adoption.

POLICY CONTENTS

There is no one best outline for developing a policy document. Sometimes the policy document can be simply a number of points within a broader community development policy.

Preferably, recreation and sport policies should be presented in a self-contained, comprehensive document.

The following suggested outline is a guide to the contents of a policy document:

- *Opening statement.* The opening statement should contain the aim, vision or mission of recreation and sport at the local level.

- *Principles.* The principles statement should contain the main points that underpin and justify the aims, vision or mission.

- *Objectives.* The objectives are the 'working tools' of the policy document. They should provide a broad outline of the areas in which the organisation will be dealing.

- *Strategies.* The strategies are the practical way in which each objective is to be achieved.

- *Actions.* Actions should be achievable outcomes of the strategies.

- *Outcomes.* Outcomes are the results of each of the actions and they usually are in the form of performance indicators that can be measured easily.

- *Management plans.* Management plans are in effect a separate document and are the day-to-day operational tools governing all aspects of service delivery. In chapter 6 the contents of management plans are covered in more detail.

- *Review process.* Policy reviews should be carried out every two to three years. The management plans above are yearly reporting mechanisms to check on progress towards the achievement of the policy.

DEFINITION OF LOCAL FACILITIES AND OPEN SPACES

Local recreation and sport facilities and open spaces are those within a designated local council's boundary and consist of district and neighbourhood areas. Examples of local recreation facilities and open spaces include the following:

- Playing fields
- Sports ovals and pitches
- Courts
- Golf courses
- Recreation centres
- School recreation and sports facilities
- Swimming pools—indoor and outdoor
- Parks
- Walking, cycling and horse riding trails
- Informal recreation areas for picnicking and unstructured activities including quiet areas
- Kick-about areas for unstructured games
- Children's play spaces
- Playgrounds

CONTENTS OF LOCAL RECREATION AND SPORT STRATEGY PLANS

There is no one format that satisfies the underlying reasons for local communities developing their own recreation and sport strategy plan. All communities are different; however, some general guidelines can be helpful if for no other reason than to act as a checklist.

The following suggested contents for a local recreation and sport strategy plan have been derived from many local recreation and sport plans prepared in South Australia by local councils. You will need to vary them to meet your own purposes. The following guide will assist in clarifying the contents in a particular circumstance.

Preliminaries

Have you prepared a consultant's brief? The key to developing an effective plan is to work from a clear brief that has been prepared and agreed to by all parties before work on the plan commences. There are usually some major issues underlying the reasons for developing the plan in the first place and these will inevitably influence the end result.

Executive Summary

Usually an executive summary including the main recommendations is placed at the beginning of the plan. This allows readers to obtain an overview and summary of the main recommendations or action plans. The assumption is that at least most people who commence reading the plan will have the key information up front without the details. It may even stimulate them to read further.

Introduction

All the planning documents have an introduction that usually includes the background to the plan, objectives or purposes and a clarification of any methodology used such as community consultation techniques employed. Also, any definitions such as what is meant by recreation, sport and leisure are described early in this section.

Analysis

An analysis of the current situation usually follows. The demographics are usually analysed to obtain population projections in age groups within the local area. This section also analyses existing recreation and sport policies at the council level and, if necessary, the policies of key sporting clubs and recreation bodies within the council area.

An audit or inventory of where the recreation and sport facilities and open space are located is essential. Sophisticated computer mapping techniques are now available. See chapter 3 for further discussion on the possibilities of computer mapping capabilities. Appendixes D and E provide two examples of recreation and sport facilities inventories.

An analysis of financial information on recreation and sport income and expenditure can be helpful in determining the efficiency of present recreation and sport services.

Most consultants also identify local recreation and sport trends at this stage and compare them with regional, state and national trends.

Identification of Key Issues

At this stage, a key issues paper is prepared from the information gathered. It is then circulated to those who have the major responsibilities for recreation and sport in the local area. Valuable feedback will ensure that all issues have been covered.

Policy and Strategy Development

This section can be presented in a number of different ways:

- Aims, goals or purposes are sometimes used to clearly define the parameters of recreation and sport.
- Vision or mission statements are increasingly being developed.
- Objectives and principles should be introduced into the local recreation and sport strategy plan because they provide the basis for the next step.

Prepare Action Plans

The preparation of action plans, goals or recommendations provides a focus on particular outcomes that should be achieved within a specific time. Inevitably, the question of funding sources is raised. There should be opportunity to develop these, but experience has found that if too much emphasis is placed on trying to commit local councils or state governments to funding of specific projects, the overall strategy may be jeopardised.

Implementation of the Planning Strategy

Some ongoing evaluation and monitoring structure should be considered. Increasingly specific structures such as sport and recreation councils or community recreation and sport forums are being recommended to make sure that the strategy becomes a reality. A review process with specific time frames should also be considered.

Appendices

The relevant collected material should be included in the appendices for closer analysis and reference, for example,

- questionnaires or surveys used in the consultation phase;
- inventories of facilities;
- reports of workshops;
- expenditure details;
- maps of facility and open spaces locations; and
- schedules or timetables of recreation and sport services.

For more details on the contents of recreation and sport plans, see chapter 3.

OBJECTIVES AND PRINCIPLES FOR LOCAL FACILITIES AND OPEN SPACES

Each local council or community will have different reasons for preparing recreation and sport plans. These can range from objectives dealing with efficiency of provision of sports and recreation facilities through to qualitative objectives related to social justice and the equitable distribution of community recreation and sport services.

The Victorian Department of Sport and Recreation's Community Recreation Planning Guide points out that 'individual communities will have their own set of beliefs about goals or desired state of affairs in their local area . . . it is the responsibility of councils to ascertain and document their own set of principles within their communities'.[3]

Given that each local plan is prepared for different reasons, it is possible to provide some generally acceptable objectives and principles as a guide for planners. The following eight categories are guides only; they are the result of an extensive review of various planning documents and recreation and sport literature in Australia and overseas.

1. Outdoor recreation and sport facilities
2. Indoor recreation and sport centres
3. Swimming pools and aquatic centres
4. Local open spaces and facilities
5. Neighbourhood parks
6. Children's play facilities

7. Cycle tracks, walking trails and horse riding trails
8. Recreation and sport use of rivers and lakes

Outdoor Recreation and Sport Facilities

Recreation and outdoor sport facilities need to be designed to accommodate as many different activities as possible with only minor adjustments, for example, change of goalposts to soccer nets, redrawing of line markings in a different colour, etc. See appendix C for outdoor sports grounds dimensions for the most popular sports.

Passive and informal active recreation opportunities, such as picnic and barbecue areas, children's play spaces and walking and cycle paths need to be developed in association with formal outdoor sports areas. Seating, toilets, shade, shelter and other amenities are required to meet user needs.

Objectives

- Local-level planning for expansion or relocation of recreation and sport facilities that takes into account the overall requirements of council residents.
- The provision of future recreation and sport facilities that do not alienate land that could be suitable as open space for unstructured recreation.
- Multiple use of existing recreation and sport facilities wherever practicable.
- New facilities that meet multiple-use criteria and are both cost-effective and efficient through sharing of club facilities and car parking.
- Recreation and sport facilities to cater for the needs of people from all cultural backgrounds and that provide equitable access for people regardless of age, sex or ethnic background.

Principles

- Ensure that all residents are able to gain access to recreation and sport facilities giving priority to locations close to shopping centres, schools and residential areas.
- Encourage lease arrangements between clubs and organisations and councils to assist clubs and organisations that have an efficient management structure to provide an effective service to participants.
- Encourage multiuse of recreation and sport facilities by developing land adjacent to schools wherever possible.
- Develop a regional strategy for the substantial development or redevelopment of existing facilities, particularly when approached by state sporting associations or clubs seeking to establish a major presence in a council area.

Indoor Recreation and Sport Centres

There is an increasing demand for multipurpose indoor sport and recreation facilities that cater for a wide range of both 'wet' and 'dry' activities. These include the traditional basketball, netball and volleyball facilities as well as the specialised gymnastics, fitness and health facilities. Increasingly, aquatic facilities are being linked into larger regional sport and recreation centres. See chapter 6 for local and regional indoor centre designs.

Objective

- The creation of recreation and sport centres to accommodate a wide range of uses that are linked with other community facilities.

Principles

- Whenever possible, locate regional recreation and sport centres in or adjacent to regional shopping centres.
- Ensure that facilities are served by efficient public transport so that people (especially children and teenagers) can access them.
- Provide safe pedestrian and bicycle access especially for children and teenagers.
- Ensure that the design of facilities takes into account the needs of physically disabled users and parents with children in pushers. Attention should be given to safe pedestrian access, wide doorways, shallow ramps and appropriately designed toilets and changing facilities.

- Enable women and those with primary responsibility for the care of preschool children to use the facilities by providing creche facilities.

- Resolve the management style for the centre before the construction stage to enable a link between building design and the proposed activities.

Swimming Pools and Aquatic Centres

Indoor swimming and other aquatic activities are growing in popularity and there is a need for local councils to consider the refurbishing of older outdoor pools that are reaching the end of their economic life into more acceptable facilities. A number of myths have grown over the years about the provision of aquatic facilities. A recent study in South Australia clarifies what councils need to take into account when developing swimming facilities. See chapter 6 for suitable designs of aquatic facilities.

Objectives

- The provision of a range of adequate swimming and aquatic facilities at local and regional levels.

- The upgrading of existing facilities at the local level to improve swimming and aquatic activities to ratepayers at a reasonable cost.

- A distribution of new aquatic facilities that does not unduly overlap existing catchments to the extent that they impact on viability. This can be in the form of a regional hierarchy of aquatic and other indoor facilities.

- The provision of effective management of any facility developed to maximise usage and financial return.

- The linking of other recreation and sport facilities whenever possible with the aquatic centre.

Principles

- Provide at local, district and regional aquatic facilities for competitive swimming, recreational aquatic activities and fitness swimming.

- Consider the long-term viability of outdoor pools and opportunities for extending their use by developing other aquatic facilities or enclosing the existing outdoor facilities.

- Develop intercouncil cooperation to avoid replicating expensive aquatic facilities by introducing a hierarchy of local and regional aquatic facilities.

- Consider linking aquatic facilities with other indoor recreation facilities at local and regional levels to obtain greater use and economies of scale.

Local Open Spaces and Facilities

Local open spaces and facilities include recreation areas for picnicking, unstructured areas including areas for quiet activity, sports grounds (such as ovals, grounds and pitches), games areas, children's play areas and areas for passive recreation for the aged. The size of these facilities will vary according to the function they perform and the location of other similar facilities. See appendix C for outdoor sports grounds dimensions for the most popular sports.

Objectives

- The provision of adequate open spaces in the form of parks, reserves and linear linkages in convenient locations of a quality to meet the recreational and sporting needs of the community.

- The development of small reserves, local parks and playgrounds for general recreational use (active 'kick-about' areas as well as passive places).

- A network of cycle and pedestrian linkages between local and regional parks and reserves.

- A councilwide greening approach that promotes the planting of trees in all reserves, along streets and on vacant or underutilised land.

- Access to council and regional parks and reserves for people with disabilities.

Principles

- Review the opportunities for more efficient use of major open space in each council area and then assess any proposed developments to ensure they provide multipurpose recreation opportunities to meet the needs of different age groups.

- Encourage the development of landscaping and public access to land made available to sporting clubs so that additional community use such as unstructured activities including walking, picnics and children's play can be considered.
- Seek opportunities to include publicly accessible recreational elements into major residential and commercial developments.
- Introduce, wherever possible and with safety, recreational use along rivers, creeks and stormwater channels.
- Ensure that current, proposed and future cycle paths provide direct and safe links between major parks and open space areas. See chapter 6 for guidelines for walking, cycling and horse riding trails.
- Initiate appropriate planting including shade areas for picnic and play areas. Use recycled water wherever possible to contain open space maintenance costs.
- Provide public open space in accordance with an approved local recreation and sport strategy plan that has taken into consideration
  - the needs of the community to be served reflected in population density and demographic structure;
  - the classifications of user groups and perceived user requirements;
  - projected demand based on participation rates;
  - the use of and access to existing facilities;
  - environment, location, safety and weather factors, including shade areas;
  - opportunities to link open space net-

works, community facilities and public services;
  - opportunities for dual use of open space for recreation and drainage functions;
  - ongoing open space maintenance costs;
  - opportunities for dual use and multifunctional use; and
  - the provision of adequate lighting.

Neighbourhood Parks

Each park should have its own particular character to reflect the neighbourhood in which it is located. Neighbourhood parks should offer the opportunity for both getting together and socialising, or watching the world go by. See chapter 6 for a play space development model and other planning guidelines on playground design. Appendix C provides dimensions for outdoor sports grounds.

Objectives

- The provision of smaller, user-friendly parks catering for a wide cross section of users from a neighbourhood area.

Principles

- Provide for passive and active informal use by local residents containing play areas for children of different ages.
- Provide a range of play environments to meet the needs of
  - preschoolers (0–5 years);
  - primary school children (5–12 years);
  - teenagers (12+ years); and
  - physically disabled users.
- Cater for predictable activities and minimise undesirable activities (such as crime, inappropriate behaviour and vandalism).
- Include large grassed areas for active play and informal sports. Also, neighbourhood parks can include tennis courts for social use and hard paved areas for basketball, netball, volleyball, etc.

- Introduce topographical variations through mounding and depressions, especially in children's play areas, and to provide play opportunities and shelter from harsh weather conditions.

- Locate neighbourhood parks centrally or close to linear parks or pedestrian and cycle routes to schools, shops and bus stops.

- Consider other hard-surfaced areas off the main pedestrian route and away from passive sitting areas for activities such as roller sports, in-line skating, skateboarding, basketball and volleyball.

- Provide seating areas to enable overview of play areas. These need to be sheltered from the sun and wind by trees and constructed shelters such as gazebos, shelter sheds, etc.

- Ensure that toilets are provided including facilities for the disabled and a unisex toilet for parents of young children (these could be combined and include a table for changing babies and young children).

- Include drinking fountains and strategically placed and viable rubbish bins as part of the park furniture.

- Install appropriate signs to direct residents to the park by the shortest, safest routes.

- Provide sports fields, ovals or parks for active play. These active play areas should be clear of obstruction and buffered from adjoining housing and other uses.

- Use changes in the level and planting to help define boundaries.

- Provide areas especially designed for children's play including
  - shrubs, trees and bushes mounds;
  - paved surfaces;
  - opportunities for water play;
  - sand play playground;
  - equipment including climbing structures, swings, slides;

  - some small-scale equipment for preschoolers;
  - places to sit and watch (the seating should be circular or semicircular); and
  - landscaping.

- Encourage opportunities for children to be inventive by ensuring that some elements of the play environment are not fixed, but able to be picked up and moved by children.

- Provide challenging play equipment with gradually increasing levels of risk to enable children to test their limits.

- Offer play opportunities for children with disabilities.

- Involve children in the design of play areas and the selection of play equipment.

- Separate active and passive play areas.

- Place play equipment close together to allow children to establish a circuit.

- Provide shock-absorbing surfaces under play equipment and regularly replace them before they show signs of wear.

Children's Play Facilities

Play is the recreational activity of children. It is a voluntary activity essential for children's growth and development. It is the way they learn about their environment. Play is largely spontaneous and so tends to happen reasonably close to home. The play space development model and playgrounds facility guidelines that can be found in chapter 6 provide practical, logical and easily adaptable planning tools. These are derived from the South Australian *Playground Manual* [4].

Objectives

- Safe, accessible and interesting play areas for children.

- Play areas for children of different ages, that is, preschool (two to five years), middle childhood (five to twelve years), and teenagers.

- Play opportunities for children with disabilities.

Principles

- Provide children's play areas within easy walking distance from home and free of major barriers, on a clearly defined pedestrian and cycle route or next to shops, schools, sports grounds or parks.

- Incorporate traffic management features in areas around children's play areas that discourage through traffic and reduce the speeds of cars using the surrounding local streets.

- Make pathways wide enough to be comfortable for walking and to allow easy movement of prams, wheeled toys and wheelchairs. Paths should have a hard surface.

- Preserve natural areas where possible and make these accessible to children as an integral part of their creative and interesting play environment.

- Provide sports fields, ovals or parks for active play. These active play areas should be clear of obstructions and buffered from adjoining housing and other uses.

- Use changes in the level and planting to help define boundaries.

- Provide areas especially designed for children's play including
  — shrubs, trees and bushes mounds;
  — paved surfaces;
  — opportunities for water play;
  — sand play playground;
  — equipment including climbing structures, swings, slides;
  — some small-scale equipment for preschoolers;
  — places to sit and watch (the seating should be circular or semicircular); and
  — landscaping.

- Encourage opportunities for children to be inventive by ensuring that some elements of the play environment are not fixed, but able to be picked up and moved by children.

- Provide challenging play equipment with gradually increasing levels of risk to enable children to test their limits.

- Offer plays opportunities for children with disabilities.

- Involve children in the design of play areas and the selection of play equipment.

- Separate active and passive play areas.

- Place play equipment close together to allow children to establish a circuit.

- Provide shock-absorbing surfaces under play equipment and regularly replace them before they show signs of wear.

- Establish a regular maintenance schedule for checking such items as ropes, chains and fastenings.

- Place seating for adults within the view of play equipment.

- Provide drinking water and toilets that are easily accessible to users of all ages and by persons with disabilities.

Cycle Tracks, Walking Trails and Horse Riding Trails

Recreation tracks and trails are usually designed for people to enjoy a leisurely ride. They can also be used as pedestrian paths with simple traffic management techniques such as explicit signage.

If commuter cyclists use these tracks, they can be dangerous for pedestrian use because of the faster pace of cyclists. Similarly, if cyclists or joggers use walking trails or paths designed for fitness, there can be a safety problem that, if not recognised at the planning and design stages, can cause serious future conflicts.

Urban councils are under increasing pressure to limit the stabling and use of horses, but with creative planning there can be opportunities for local councils to provide recreational horse riding facilities. Cooperation of adjacent councils by developing a regional approach is recommended. See chapter 6 for guidelines for walking, cycling and horse riding trails.

Objectives

- The provision of a hierarchy of local, regional and state linear walking and cycling trails that link local communities to trails of state or national significance. Similarly, the provision of local horse riding trails that link to a regional and state network.
- Safe pedestrian and cycle access to and between local and regional recreation and sport facilities.

Principles

- Encourage cooperation between councils in seeking funding for a hierarchy of cycle and walking trails that link local trails to a regional and state network. Give priority to those pedestrian and cycle routes that will provide greatest accessibility between facilities and high-quality recreation experiences for users.
- Consider a range of alternative designs for cycling routes including on-road and off-road alternatives: for example, the use of linear parks, waterways and reserves along train and tramlines and median strips on main roads.
- Establish a liaison among the council, the appropriate bicycle planning authority and recognised cycling organisations in the design and development of recreational cycling routes.
- Develop separate horse riding trails because they are considered incompatible with walking trails and cycling tracks.

Recreation and Sport Use of Rivers and Lakes

Aquatic areas on rivers and lakes have major recreation and sport possibilities.

Objectives

- The provision of opportunities for the development of water sports within the council and region.
- The maintenance and enhancement of the coast as a recreation facility for public enjoyment including a wide range of recreation and sport activities.

- Increased access to lakes, rivers and water reserves for the provision of recreation and sporting opportunities.

Principles

- Increase the council commitment to a range of facilities and activities along the coast, rivers and on lakes for water sports and other recreational activities, concentrating activities wherever possible in designated focal areas.
- Support the development of water sports, particularly at the junior level.
- Seek new and alternative ways of funding recreation and sport facilities and areas, which cater for a metropolitan-wide catchment.
- Provide opportunities for the physically disabled and older people with limited mobility to experience direct contact with the beach.
- Ensure that people of non-English-speaking backgrounds are able to access the beach safely with improved signage in other languages.
- Encourage water catchment areas and reservoirs to be considered for use for recreation and sporting purposes.

KEY LOCAL RECREATION AND SPORT PLANNING ISSUES

Each recreation and sport plan must at some stage come to grips with a number of issues that need to be addressed before strategies are determined. Although these issues vary with each local situation, it is useful for planners and others involved in recreation and sport to know some of the key issues that may arise. Often information shared can lead to finding solutions. Identifying the following issues does not imply that they are the only ones. Also, they are not listed in any particular priority order.

Analysing recreation and sport plans and other documents in South Australia identified over 100 issues. The following are the key local ones that should be considered prior to developing strategies or action plans.

Trends in Local Recreation and Sport

Councils are under increasing pressure to be more businesslike in their operations, which includes not being able to offer 'in kind' support to the extent that was once possible. [5] Concerns are being expressed about the long-term viability of local sporting clubs because of

- the impact of drunk driving laws on the ability of clubs to raise funds through the operations of licensed bar facilities;
- the impact of poker machines on the ability of clubs to raise funds;
- the increasing amount of club funds allocated to paying for professional coaches and players or to the governing bodies to meet the growing expenses of state, national and international elite sport commitments;
- the increasing cost to participants for uniforms and equipment; and
- the difficulty in attracting volunteers to officiate in club operations and the regular changeover of personnel on management committees.

There has been a reduction in available financial resources for leisure and recreation, both in terms of funding from the public sector and personal disposable income. Continuing high levels of unemployment have resulted in a higher proportion of people not being able to afford costly recreation pursuits.

Resource sharing is becoming recognised as being in the best long-term interests of the community. Joint school and community facilities, multipurpose sport clubs, public and private joint ventures and cross-council projects are examples of this.

Councils are exploring alternative funding opportunities to finance community infrastructure. See chapter 6 for funding options.

The leisure industry, including tourism, is now a significant part of the Australian economy, employing large numbers of people and generating significant dollars. A consistent and high level of service is required to attract and retain customers.

Pricing Policies for Recreation and Sport Facilities

The spiralling cost of maintaining facilities has forced local councils to increase user fees. The issue is exacerbated by the lack of consistency between local councils in their respective pricing policies and pricing structures. Underlying this issue is the question of continued viability of many facilities.

A perennial planning issue faced by local councils is the setting of fees and charges for

- sports grounds;
- buildings such as change rooms and social club rooms;
- tennis courts, bowls and croquet greens;
- parks and reserves;
- playgrounds;
- indoor recreation and sport centres; and
- swimming pools (outdoor and indoor) and aquatic centres.

As Ken Marriott suggests, there is no one best solution to establishing a pricing policy. [6] Therefore, the following questions should be asked in determining the pricing policies:

1. Are the pricing policies fair and equitable without favouring any particular group unless there are good, clearly stated social justice reasons?

2. Are the users of the recreation and sport facilities predominantly ratepayers?

3. What cost recovery techniques are to be used?

4. Are the charges easily understood and consistent for all recreation and sport users?

5. Are the pricing policies in line with other nearby councils' fees and charges?

6. Can the proposed charges be seen as a way to strengthen weak clubs and organisations by assisting them to evaluate their viability?

Some suggested strategies for setting the pricing policy are:

1. Establish an independent body on which both the council and users are represented with the proceedings open to the public.

2. Provide an appeal procedure that allows clubs and organisations to recover from extenuating circumstances.

3. Encourage constant reviews of pricing policies.

4. Introduce a flexible pricing policy that is open to public scrutiny.

5. Consider the separation of management functions from users of facilities such as recreation centres, sport stadiums and aquatic centres.

6. Introduce any radical changes over a reasonable period of time.

Whatever strategies are used, all clubs and groups should be encouraged to consider sharing facilities and management procedures, which increases efficiency and reduces costs that will benefit players, participants and ratepayers and therefore everyone wins.

Management of Recreation and Sport

The range of recreation and sport management issues include the following:

• The operational management of recreation and sport facilities both indoors and outdoors. For example, councils are under increasing pressure to contract-out recreation and sport services and the maintenance of both indoor and outdoor facilities.

• Corporate management structures within local councils for the delivery of recreation and sport services. The tendency has been to consider recreation and sport as a part of either the parks and gardens department, the community services department, or even sometimes the engineers' department. As recreation, sport and leisure become increasingly important, there are strong arguments for departmental status.

• Risk management in a recreation and sport context is concerned with minimising the potential losses resulting from accidents. For example, playground accidents resulting in public liability claims have sometimes led to a reaction by councils to take out all or most of the children's play equipment.

• Asset management of recreation and sport facilities and open spaces are linked to the overall asset management of councils to meet the requirements of the Australian Accounting Standard (AAS 27), which lays down the financial reporting standing for local governments.

For recreation and sport, this means accounting for assets such as recreation and sport buildings and plants, sports grounds, parks and other open spaces including natural environments such as rivers, beaches, waterways and forests. Asset management also includes the difficult task of determining economic value of social infrastructure, with reference to recreation activities such as school holiday and after school programs and other recreation and sport activities linked to health and education. Some methods of valuation are discussed in a paper given by John Hatch at a National Seminar on Asset Management in 1994.[7]

Local councils are affected by these issues as well. As a starting point, the inventories of recreation and sport facilities and open spaces prepared as part of the local recreation and sport strategy plan should form the basis of the overall council corporate approach to asset management. Councils can use the objectives and principles for various recreation and sport facilities and open spaces identified in this chapter, for example, by

• establishing policies for the *acquisition* of future assets;

• setting criteria for the *disposal* of existing assets; and

• introducing *performance measures* to maintain the assets to the standard necessary to deliver a high-quality recreation and sport service.

There is no doubt that the various recreation and sport services strategies and action plans identified in the local recreation and sport strategy plan will need to be quantified by developing credible economic costing techniques.

Community Consultation

While the principle of community consultation in planning for recreation and sport is well accepted, the practice still falls short of establishing an unbiased understanding of community recreation and sport preferences.

A variety of techniques are used for improving the community consultation process; these are discussed at some length in *Recreation Planning—A Manual for Local Government*.[8] Above all other considerations, effective consultation depends to a large extent on the ability to communicate effectively.

The following is an example of good community consulting. The Port Adelaide Recreation and Sport Plan received a national award from the Royal Australian Planning Institute in 1994 partly because the consultation undertaken deliberately surveyed people from non-English-speaking backgrounds as well as Aboriginal populations who are often missed in general community consultation processes. Six researchers with the necessary language skills and sensitivity were employed. Also, discussions were held with a number of ethnic groups.[9]

The Adelaide City Council Parklands Management Strategy Plan[10] consultation process provides details on how this process can work in practice. Some suggested strategies are:

- Appoint consultants who have a proven record of good communication skills and techniques.
- Identify who is to be consulted. There is no general public but rather specific public: for example, residents, representatives of sport and recreation organisations, elected council members, council officers and various age groups from children, youth, young-marrieds, employed and aged.

- Avoid consultation for consultation's sake. Identify the purpose of consultation before embarking on what can be an expensive process.

Multiuse of Recreation and Sport Facilities

There are good examples of multiuse of recreation and sport facilities. These facilities range from shared grounds by sports in alternate seasons (e.g. football and cricket), to combined sports clubs (e.g. tennis and netball). Another multiuse combination could be groups with similar interests (e.g. croquet and bowls). There are also multipurpose indoor recreation centres for a wide range of indoor sports and recreational and aquatic activities.

Renewal of Existing Leases

There are a number of implications for councils when considering renewal of existing leases or the granting of new ones to recreation and sport organisations.

Avoid Duplication

It is not sensible to duplicate existing local facilities

Assess Recreation and Sport Usage

Before any new facilities are approved, there should be an analysis of the usage of existing recreation and sport facilities to assess whether the present facilities can be more efficiently utilised for the benefit of the community.

Change Attitudes

Most sports clubs or recreation organisations seem to want to own their facilities. They fail to realise that managing properties often diverts energies away from their main purpose, which is to play the sport or enjoy the recreational activities. Owning facilities does not mean that the sport and recreation activities can be provided more cheaply. Often, the expertise in facility management is not available at the club level and the consequence is that owning and managing a facility can become a liability rather than an asset to a club or organisation.

A number of professional facility management organisations now provide this expertise on a contract basis.

It is in the interests of the council to assure sporting clubs and recreation organisations that their future is secure without exclusive leases to their own grounds or facilities.

Consider Using School Facilities

School sports grounds and indoor facilities can be made available for recreation and sport purposes.

Australian and overseas experience indicates that it is often cheaper to inject new capital into upgrading school facilities for community recreation and sport use than to build new facilities on another (perhaps less central) site. For local-level recreation and sport activities, there are advantages in encouraging the use of schools for both outdoor playing areas and indoor facilities usually associated with physical education, but extended into other school facilities as the confidence in management grows.

Following are some advantages of using school facilities:

- Schools are usually one of the central points of a local community and significant numbers of people can reach them in many instances by walking.

- The facilities are usually occupied only during the day, leaving expensive publicly owned facilities with spare capacity for use during periods of peak community demand, in the evenings and on weekends and during holidays.

- Valuable links are formed between school staff and students when recreation and sports organisations use the facilities. This could encourage ongoing participation in activities after students have left school.

- By increasing community use, overhead costs can be shared.

- Because of population shifts, some schools became underutilised; community use could be a way of retaining the

education facility by making it a viable community asset.

- If the Education Department finds that the school is surplus to requirements, then every possible way should be explored to make sure that this community asset is retained for public use. Particularly the sports grounds, play areas and recreation open space should be retained if there are shortages in open spaces. Once lost, the open space rarely becomes available again.

Social Justice: Equity and Access

Geographical and historical factors sometimes lead to an imbalance in the distribution of local recreation and sport open spaces and facilities. Often, social justice issues particularly related to equity and access are neglected if there is not a conscious effort to highlight the need for these issues to be given priority.

Local councils should be aware of the following implications:

- Councils should consider the equitable distribution of resources as part of their social justice policies.

- Proximity of both recreation and sport facilities and open spaces to public and private transport should be given major consideration.

- Both recreation open spaces and facilities should be available to people with disabilities as far as practicable. This does not mean that people with disabilities are only spectators; they should be encouraged to participate by providing any special equipment needed for active involvement in recreation and sport activities.

- Often, parents, particularly women, cannot participate in recreation and sport activities because they have no one to mind the children. Facilities for childcare should be provided in recreation and sport facilities.

- Consideration should be given to providing access to

  — sports grounds;

— indoor recreation and sport facilities;

— swimming pools (indoor and outdoor);

— recreation trails;

— bars, restaurants and social amenities associated with recreation and sport centres; and

— viewing areas.

- With pressures on councils to adopt the 'user pays' principle for those using recreation and sport services, there is a need to consider the obligation to provide all residents living in the council area with equal access to facilities that is not based on financial ability to pay.

A range of pricing policies can be introduced to allow children and families access. Also, special arrangement for people with disabilities should be given consideration outside the 'user pays' principle.

Cost and Supply of Water for Outdoor Sport and Recreation Facilities

One of the major issues is the cost and supply of adequate water for playing surfaces. Councils and sports clubs should consider the following:

- More extensive research on ways of minimising the use of mains water, for example, cost-effective irrigation, the use of drought-resistant turf and the use of synthetic surfaces.

- Education of residents to accept that natural areas in some parks can brown off at some times of the year, and that heavily watered green areas are not always suitable to the Australian situation.

- The use of stormwater retention as a means of supplementing water requirements for recreation and sport facilities. This can mean the extension and development of lakes, wetlands and ponding basins as a water resource.

- In some outback areas where water is very scarce, councils should consider

adapting the playing conditions to suit the area. This particularly applies to the provision of football and cricket surfaces and golf courses (which don't need grassed fairways or greens). The need for multipurpose artificial surfaces for a range of sports such as tennis, basketball, netball and hockey should be considered.

Synthetic Playing Surfaces

In recent years, the range and quality of synthetic surfaces has increased enormously. Artificial surfaces can increase usage and decrease the number of grassed playing surfaces. The economic and playing advantages should be given consideration. Following is a list of advantages and disadvantages of artificial sport surfaces.

Advantages

- Useable in almost any weather conditions.

- Will withstand almost constant use and if well lit, can be used 24 hours a day, 52 weeks of the year (subject to the wishes of local residents).

- Usually require much less routine maintenance and remarking.

- Usually give a truer and faster playing surface with consistent bounce.

- Where existing ancillary facilities exist (e.g. stadium with catering facilities and bar of a high standard), the additional use that can be made of these surfaces can be cost effective.

Disadvantages

- Very expensive to install and, when necessary, to repair. It may consequently take a very long time—if ever—for a surface to break even financially.

- The high rebound resistance and high speed of a ball off many surfaces may be undesirable in some sports.

- Some governing bodies may not accept artificial surfaces as appropriate for some competitions.

- The nature of the surface may cause a high incidence of friction, burns or stress-related injuries.

- It may be necessary to purchase special footwear to protect either the surface or the participants from damage or injury.

A useful publication on the subject of artificial playing surfaces is *Recreation and Leisure—City Guilds Course*. [11]

Funding for Recreation and Sport

Although the local recreation and sport strategy plans should not be constrained by funding limitations, it is inevitable that funding issues will arise.

The single most important issue related to funding is the need for local councils to develop a regional strategy that shares the funding of major costly facilities such as indoor recreation and sport centres and swimming pools rather than have each council try to provide a complete range of facilities. Regional recreation and sport strategies are dealt with in the chapter 5.

Councils should use their local recreation and sport strategy plan to determine priorities and then consider the availability of funding from internal council budgets as well as other sources such as the various commonwealth and state and territory programs.

The private sector is beginning to appreciate the potential for investment in sport and recreation enterprises. There are possibilities for joint ventures between the private sector and councils as well as direct sponsorship of both recreation and sport programs and even the development of facilities.

There are pressures on councils to use more efficiently existing funds allocated to the operation of existing recreation and sport facilities and services. The issues of council pricing policies, which include leases and rentals for sports grounds and other facility hiring arrangements, have been discussed earlier in the chapter.

Other funding issues including sources for fund-raising are discussed in chapter 6.

CONCLUSION

A great deal of emphasis has been given to the preparation of a local recreation and sport strategy plan. As councils become involved in contribution to regional and state strategies, there is a need to have in place local recreation and sport strategies. In addition, there is increasing emphasis on state sports associations and recreation organisations developing their strategies. Therefore, it is important that local clubs and organisations are encouraged to consider their future development with the preparation of appropriate strategies.

The objectives and principles in this chapter can be used as guidelines to prepare local-level recreation and sport strategy plans. Maybe the accompanying issues raised will assist in identifying priorities and outcomes, which can be in the form of action plans. It is up to the planners and policy makers to develop local strategies using the objectives, principles and issues and then adapt them to the community in which they will operate.

There is an inevitable overlap between local and regional recreation and sport open spaces and facilities. Local government authorities within a region should cooperate in the development of local recreation and sport plans that fit into a regional structure. This will allow for economies of scale in the provision of facilities and a variety of recreation and sport activities to meet the needs of local people in the immediate areas where they live.

REFERENCES

1. Gray, Phillip [1998] *Recreation and Sport Policy Development—A Guide*. Adelaide: Office for Recreation and Sport.
2. Gray, Phillip [1998] *Recreation and Sport Policy Development—A Guide*.
3. Department of Sport and Recreation [1990] *Community Recreation—Municipal Recreation Planning Guide*. Victoria, p. 43.
4. Office for Recreation and Sport [1997] *Playground Manual*, revised edition. South Australia.
5. Hassell Pty Ltd and SA Centre for Economic Studies [1997] *The Economic Impact of Recreation and Sport at the Local Level*. Office of Recreation and Sport, South Australia, p. 9.
6. Marriott, K.L. [1993] *Pricing Policy for User Pays*. In Australian Parks and Recreation Journal, spring, 1993.
7. Hatch, John [1994] *The Economics of Recreation and Open Space Areas: The Market and Beyond*, In

the conference proceedings for the National Seminar Asset Management in Parks and Recreation, Glenelg, South Australia.

8. Marriott, K.L. [1990] *Recreation Planning—A Manual for Local Government*, second edition. Adelaide: South Australian Recreation Institute.

9. Hassell Planning Consultants [1993] *City of Port Adelaide Recreation and Sport Plan*. Prepared on behalf of the City of Port Adelaide, the Department of Recreation and Sport and MFP Australia.

10. Hassell Pty Ltd [1999] *City of Adelaide Parklands Management Plan*. Adelaide.

11. Wright, Jonathan [1989] *Recreation and Leisure - City Guilds Course 481, parts 1 and 2*. London: Croner.

Regional and State Recreation and Sport Strategy Plans

This chapter defines regional and state planning and proposes an approach for developing regional recreation and sport strategy plans. Objectives and principles are clearly identified followed by discussion on practical regional planning elements. Key state planning issues are raised and some examples of plans for indoor recreation and sport facilities are provided. Because of the growth in demand for indoor aquatic facilities, significant emphasis is placed on planning and design elements for swimming facilities. Finally, the responsibility for regional and state recreation and sport strategy planning is discussed.

Australian states and territories have different regional structures based on a local government structure, which is in turn based on councils or corporations, district councils, or shires. In some states, small isolated communities in outback areas have no local government structure. For example, in South Australia, community progress associations administered by the Outback Areas Community Development Trust serve these areas. All these local administrations value their autonomy and, despite the organisational differences, there are some common themes that could be useful for consideration when developing regional and state strategy plans. Rather than continuing to reinvent the wheel,

there are increasing opportunities for us to learn from each other.

DEFINITIONS OF REGIONAL AND STATE PLANNING

As with local- and regional-level planning there are overlaps between regional and state planning responsibilities. Following are definitions of regional and state planning.

Regional Planning

Regional planning integrates local recreation and sport plans within a specified geographical district or territory that has some agreed characteristics based on communities of interest.

In Australia, regions differ from states. The Australian Constitution clearly identifies state rights and therefore they have legality under federal legislation. Although regions and states often overlap when agencies such as education, health, industry groups and local government have different purposes for establish regions, regions have no constitutional legality.

Of particular interest to regional recreation and sport planning is the need to establish a rationale for developing expensive facilities in suitable locations to meet regional needs distinct from local needs.

State Planning

State planning is the provision of coordinated recreation and sport facilities and services for people governed by a constitutionally established entity.

The state planning has an additional role of not only taking into consideration regional recreation and sport priorities, but also identifying and providing facilities and services that have national and international significance with the support of the commonwealth government.

PLANNING VISION FOR RECREATION AND SPORT

If there is no vision at the state level, there can be no effective strategy planning at regional or local levels. It is important that a clear vision or mission statement provides a sound philosophical basis on which to build the state planning strategy.

The following example of a vision or mission statement used in South Australia's State Recreation and Sport Strategy Plan[1] emphasises the need for equity and social justice in the allocation of both land and facilities for all people regardless of age, sex and culture.

> *To encourage participation in a wide range of recreation and sports opportunities for South Australians of all ages and levels of abilities through providing well-designed and located state, regional and local level facilities, open spaces and services.*

Careful planning is required at the state, regional and local level to increase opportunities for recreation and sport participation across all ages and ensure that equity is a reality for the disadvantaged in the community. This does not just happen by chance. In order to meet the anticipated growth in recreation and sport, strategy planning should provide well-designed recreation and sport facilities in the right locations at an affordable cost.

SUGGESTED PLANNING APPROACH

Consider the following two planning approaches and adapt the suggested one to your own situation.

A *top-down approach* is attractive because planners have more control over the plan, but the results are often not owned by the key participants who are local councils, sports associations and clubs, recreation organisations and community groups at regional and local levels.

By far the most effective way to develop a state strategy is by using the *bottom-up approach* (figure 5.1) beginning where most recreation and sports activities occur—at the local level, with the preparation of recreation and sport strategy plans. Regional strategies are then formulated based on local planning strategies that have already been identified and from these, state strategies can be formulated. This bottom-up approach is time consuming but it has a greater chance of being owned by those who have participated in the planning process.

PREPARING REGIONAL RECREATION AND SPORT STRATEGY PLANS

Ideally, all councils in the region should prepare local recreation and sport plans, which should be taken into account when developing regional strategies. After the regional strategies are completed, it is relatively easy to bring together the state strategy.

The preparation of each regional strategy will vary because it must primarily meet the recreation and sport needs of the particular region. Usually, there are some common elements among regional strategy plans that are helpful to planners and those responsible for preparing overall regional plans.

In some country regions where financial limitations prevent local councils participating in the preparation of the regional strategy, a questionnaire could be sent to the local

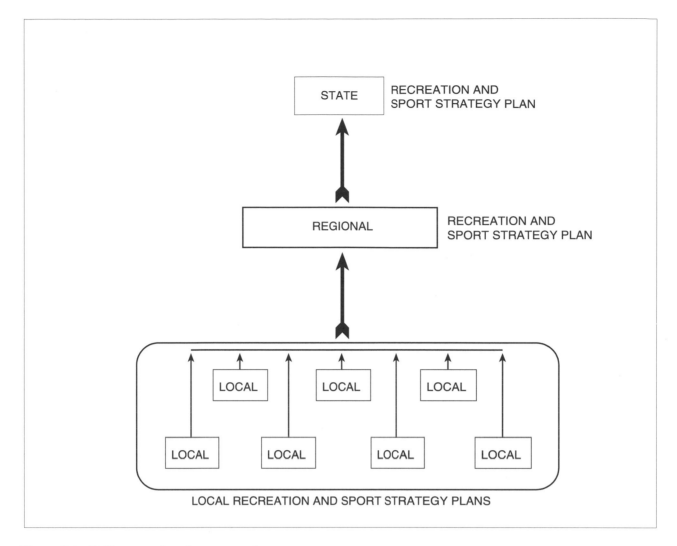

Figure 5.1   Bottom-up planning approach.

councils in the region seeking their participation. The letter could suggest that they involve interested people in their area through arranging a meeting which a consultant from the state recreation and sport agency or department could attend.

PLANNING PROCESS

It is important to get the planning process right. Each regional plan will be different, but essentially there are three key steps to building a successful planning process (figure 5.2).

For more details on preparing a thorough regional plan, see chapter 3 where there is discussion on eight alternative planning methodologies. Also, it could be useful to refresh your understanding of the overall framework in which the recreation and sport planning operates, which is also detailed in chapter 3.

EXAMPLES OF REGIONAL FACILITIES AND OPEN SPACES

Regional recreation and sport strategy planning is a coordinated approach to the provision and management of recreation and sport facilities and open spaces that serve more than one local government area and provide a focus for major sporting events or recreational activities in both urban and rural settings. Often regional facilities and open spaces

STEP 1 Analyse

> Bring together data from past reports, surveys, inventories and results
> of consultations with key groups and individuals.

STEP 2 Assess

> Identify key issues by assessing all information brought together
> in Step 1.
>
> Don't forget to take into account the feedback from the various major recreational
> and sport clubs and organisations, council members and strong supporters of
> recreation and sport development. A realistic assessment of what can be acheived
> rather than a wish list of vague possibilities is important.

STEP 3 Implement

> Formulate goals, objectives, strategies and action plans, with priorities and
> measure of performance with a realistic time frame for the implementation to
> occur.

Figure 5.2   Planning process.

are determined by their catchment areas and size, which can vary markedly from urban to country areas.

The following examples of state, regional and open spaces are provided as a 'thought starter' for considering the wider implications of regional planning.

- Major spectator sports stadiums
- Mass entertainment venues
- Indoor multipurpose recreation centres
- Major outdoor sports venues such as tracks, courses and playing areas
- Championship golf courses
- Swimming pools (usually heated 50 metre and multipurpose)
- Specialist single-purpose facilities for sports such as equestrian, shooting or hang gliding
- Major developed parks
- National parks
- Regional parks
- Semi-developed parks
- Semi-natural parks
- Theme and amusement parks
- Natural parks
- Linear parks
- Lakes with regional or state features
- Rivers of state or regional significance

REGIONAL INVENTORIES

With the assistance of powerful computer-generated mapping programs, it is now possible to introduce a sophisticated recreation and sport facilities and open spaces database using information already gathered at the local level.

By overlaying other database information collated for other purposes such as transport routes, location of schools, shopping centres, public facilities, population distribution and open spaces, it is possible to demonstrate clearly the type of regional facilities required and where they should be located.

Further information on computer mapping can be found in chapter 3. Appendix D provides two questionnaires: one for international-, national- and state-level facilities and another suitable for regional and local recreation and sport facilities.

OBJECTIVES AND PRINCIPLES FOR REGIONAL AND STATE FACILITIES AND OPEN SPACES

There are useful objectives and principles that can be identified to assist planners in providing effective regional and state-level recreation and sport planning strategies. Every effort should be made to integrate all levels of planning to encourage rational and economic use of scarce physical and human resources.

The following six objectives are the basis of the South Australian State Recreation and Sport Strategy Plan, now being revised as part of an ongoing process.[2]

1. Equity and social justice
2. Rational distribution
3. Integration
4. Access
5. Future provision
6. Conservation and environmental sustainability

The following three steps were taken to establish the objectives.

1. Three planning teams with specific expertise in recreation and sport planning were invited to prepare papers on the development of recreation and sport planning guidelines, then these were presented at a workshop for discussion by selected state and local government planners.

2. Over 100 local government authorities and 80 state recreation and sports associations were circulated with initial draft objectives and principles. After the comments were taken into consideration by an independent planning consultant, a follow-up opportunity was provided to comment further on the second draft.

3. State government agencies with an interest in recreation and sport were given opportunities to comment on both the first and second drafts.

Six objectives were then incorporated into the South Australian State Recreation and Sport Strategy Plan as the basis for metropolitan and country regional strategic plans.

An opportunity to place these objectives into a social planning context became available through the preparation of the Social Policy Aspects of Urban Development, which provides a guide to local and state government planning authorities, developers, planners and social service agencies.[3]

Objective 1: Equity and Social Justice

When developing recreation and sport facilities and open spaces, consideration should be given to the needs of all sections of the community they intend to serve regardless of age, gender, ethnicity or ability.

Principles
- Identify and set aside land for recreation facilities and open spaces to meet the needs of the existing and future population.
- Provide facilities and open spaces capable of being adapted to suit the changing

needs over time of the community they serve.

- Maintain an appropriate balance in the provision of areas and facilities available for active and passive uses.
- Provide open space areas incorporating sites of high amenity value including
  - linear parks incorporating, where appropriate, rivers or creeks and notable strands of vegetation;
  - parks of various sizes and types for both active and passive recreation (see a description of the hierarchy of parks in chapter 2);
  - formal and informal parks and gardens;
  - urban plazas, squares, courtyards and malls; and
  - conservation parks to conserve or establish areas of environmental or landscape significance.

Objective 2: Rational Distribution

There should be a rational distribution of recreation and sport facilities based on a hierarchical structure which ensures that state and metropolitan facilities, regional facilities and local facilities complement each other with minimal duplication, thereby providing better services to the community.

Principles

- Locate *local* facilities and open space areas that provide a range of district, neighbourhood and children's recreation and sport services within the designated boundaries of one council or operating authority.
- Locate *regional* facilities and open space areas serving more than one council area and providing a wide range of recreation and specialist sport facilities.
- Locate *state* facilities and open space areas that have significance for the development of recreation and sport in the state, including specialist facilities at the state, national or international level.

Objective 3: Integration

Whenever possible, recreation and sport facilities and open spaces should be integrated with other community facilities (e.g. town centre or shopping centre locations). Preference should also be given to multiple use of recreation and sport facilities for compatible activities.

No longer can recreation and sport planning be undertaken in isolation from other regional planning. Initially, this was possible because regional planning was rather a new planning process. Now, however, other agencies such as tourism, environment and natural resources, coastal management and regional economic development all have impacts on recreation and sport regional planning.

While it is important to integrate regional planning, experience has shown that unless recreation and sport has its own planning document, inevitably other regional planning priorities overshadow recreation and sport objectives, principles and issues making them minor sections of a much larger plan and potentially losing them altogether.

Principles

- Encourage the co-location of facilities and services in centres to promote ease of access as well as the integration, multiple use and sharing of facilities between compatible uses, for example, near education, shopping, office and community facilities.
- Design facilities that accommodate as many different activities as possible with only minor adjustment.
- Provide facilities and open space areas for a range and combination of uses including
  - children's playgrounds and adventure play activities (see chapter 6 for a play space development model and a checklist for playground design);
  - informal and passive recreation for the aged;
  - formal sporting activities and associated activities (see appendix C for

dimensions for outdoor and indoor sport facilities);

— community activities and events;

— pedestrian and cycle movements from shopping centres and schools to recreation and sport facilities (make sure local area bike plans are integrated with regional linkages across council boundaries);

— linear recreation and sports areas along creeks and drainage reserves wherever possible including walking and cycling routes; and

— appropriate management structures for multiple use of facilities early at the concept and design stage, a major factor in the success of these type of facilities.

Objective 4: Access

Access to recreation and sport facilities by public and private transport should be maximised.

Principles

- Develop facilities and open spaces that are served by public, private and community transport and linked to residential areas by pedestrian paths and cycle routes.

- Provide facilities and open spaces that are accessible for children and their caregivers, older people and people with disabilities, incorporating wide doorways, shallow ramps and hard surfaces to facilitate easy movement of prams and wheelchairs; creche facilities; and appropriately designed toilets and changing facilities.

- Where practicable locate open space areas within 500 metres of all households (see chapter 2 for further discussion on recreation and sport open space provision).

Objective 5: Future Provision

Adequate land in appropriate locations for recreation and sport facilities should be provided.

Principles

- Identify and set aside land for recreation facilities and open spaces to meet the needs of the existing and future population.

- Provide facilities capable of being adapted to suit the changing needs over time of the community they serve.

- Create an appropriate balance in the provision of areas and facilities available for active and passive recreation and sport.

- Provide open space areas incorporating sites of high amenity value including

  — linear parks, incorporating where appropriate, rivers or creeks and notable stands of vegetation;

  — parks of various sizes and types for active and passive recreation (see chapter 2 for a hierarchy of open spaces including parks);

  — formal and informal parks and gardens;

  — urban plazas, squares, courtyards and malls; and

  — conservation parks to preserve or establish areas of environmental or landscape significance.

Objective 6: Conservation and Environmental Sustainability

Designing and locating recreation and sport facilities should take into account conservation of the environment and also ensure user safety.

Principles

- Enhance the conservation of the area in which recreation and sport facilities are developed by using environmentally suitable designs. Attention should be paid to landscaping for visual impact. Both the participants and the surrounding neighbours should be consulted at the appropriate time.

- Locate recreation and sport facilities in areas in such a way that maximises use with as little as possible obtrusive effects on the living environment.

- Orient abutting facilities and open space areas towards those spaces and facilities and appropriate landscaping, particularly of pathways, to enhance casual surveillance.

- Provide adequate lighting of facilities and open spaces, particularly at entrance and exit points.

- Use signs and open space design features to define the edges of public spaces and to assist in direction finding. Multilanguage signage should be considered.

TOURISM, RECREATION AND SPORT OBJECTIVES AND PRINCIPLES

Most people who travel for pleasure can be assumed to be engaging in recreation and sometimes sport. The growth of international, national and regional sports events and festivals are economic generators at the local, regional, state and national levels. Therefore, it is appropriate to at least identify two recreation and sport strategic objectives and principles in the tourism sector for consideration when preparing state and regional recreation and sport strategy plans.

Objective 1: Tourists' Preferences

Recreation and sport activities for tourists should clearly identify and take into account tourists' preferences.

Principles

- Consider the possibility of extending the use of recreation and sport facilities to international, interstate, intrastate and local tourists by taking into account their preferences.

- Provide effective marketing and management of state and regional recreation and sport to guarantee a high-quality experience for tourists who may have special interests in particular recreation and sport activities.

- Develop a clear understanding of the overall tourism strategy of the particular region and how recreation and sport facilities can be developed to cater for tourists.

- Ensure that facilities are readily accessible by public and private transport.

Objective 2: Environmental Impacts

Tourism impacts on environmental fragility raise a number of issues. Specifically, when tourists become involved in recreation and sport, it is important to assess this impact carefully and develop policies for protecting the environment and still allow for the enjoyment of recreation and sport activities.

Principles

- Give a high priority to the provision of well-designed recreation and sport facilities and open spaces that are compatible with the environment.

- Consider appropriate methods of preserving fragile environments used by tourists and others for recreation and sport activities by awareness, education and, if necessary, prioritising recreation and sport access to these environmentally fragile areas.

- Allocate special areas for sport and recreational activities that have a high noise level.

PRACTICAL ELEMENTS OF REGIONAL PLANNING

Keep in mind the following regional planning elements that arise whenever regional plans are being developed. They could cost you considerable time and energy if they are forgotten or ignored.

Consider the Differences Between Urban and Country Areas

The major differences between country and urban settings should be considered carefully when planning a regional strategy. Rural areas may have large areas with small and scattered population densities. For example, the Outback Areas Region in South Australia's far north covers 85 per cent of the state but contains only 6.3 per cent of the population, whereas the Adelaide Metropolitan Region has 73 per cent of the population.

Defining regional and local facilities tends to be more difficult in country areas where local recreation and sporting facilities become regional facilities when visiting teams participate in regional competitions.

Sometimes there is a bias towards focusing on metropolitan planning because this is where the pressure for facilities and services is the greatest to meet population growth. Preparation of both urban and country regional strategies should have the same priorities.

Gather Only Relevant Information

There is a tendency to collect information without having a clear reason or use in mind. A great deal of time and effort can be avoided by spending time on analysing and assessing only relevant information in the region such as

- demographic data;
- recreation and sport activity trends;
- inventories of regional sport and recreation facilities and open spaces including the identification of specialist sport facilities that require international standards as laid down by the particular sports;
- existing policies and proposals of local councils and major sports and recreation associations;
- management structures for recreation and sport facilities and open spaces; and
- financial analysis of council and if necessary major recreation and sports associations' budgets, costs and expenditures.

Don't Overconsult

Target key people to consult. This is a regional not a local strategy. Most likely in the prepa-

ration of local recreation and sport plans, the community has already been consulted and in some cases overconsulted on a range of community, social and other issues. It is expensive to consult widely. Therefore, consult with state government departments, local councils, relevant regional local government organisations, and state, regional and district recreation and sports associations.

Identify Key Issues or Guiding Themes

The identification of key issues or guiding themes is critical. Once identified, they should be tested by wide circulation to key people for feedback before being accepted by the project management group.

Provide Sound Reasons for Strategy Formulation

After agreement has been reached on the key issues, it is then up to the consultants or planning group to address these issues by providing sound reasons for the preferred strategies. Action plans and priorities should be prepared at this stage.

Implement the Strategy

Strategies are only worthwhile if they can be translated into practice. Therefore, at the preparation stage, a great deal of thought needs to be given to how the strategies are to be implemented.

Chapter 3 suggests a number of ways to develop ongoing mechanisms that will assist the implementation of regional and state strategies. The aim is to facilitate regular review procedures and update strategies to meet changing recreation and sport needs and preferences. It is recommended that major reviews occur every three to five years.

Protect With Disclaimer

Governments at various levels sometimes have difficulty committing themselves to strategies that may have financial and other implications. It has been found that the following statement allows both levels of government to agree in principle with the overall strategy.

The preparation of this recreation and sport strategy plan is in no way a commitment from the state government to provide funds or make any other contribution now or in the future.

KEY REGIONAL ISSUES

Having outlined some practical elements in the preparation of regional strategies, it is now possible to consider some key issues in detail. These issues are those most frequently identified by project management committees when preparing regional recreation and sport strategy plans.

Because overlap often occurs between regional and local recreation and sport issues, regional issues should be considered alongside local ones. There is value in knowing what others consider to be key issues and sharing knowledge can assist in avoiding expensive mistakes and save planners and policy makers time and effort.

Indoor Regional Recreation and Sport Facilities

These are usually the most expensive facilities. Therefore, the indoor regional facility planning is an important component of the state strategy because the costs of 'getting it right'[4] can be high if the facilities are in the wrong places and do not serve the wider community. Also, the location of regional facilities determines state strategies for facility development and influences local councils in the provision of local recreation and sport facilities.

Co-Location of Indoor Recreation and Sport Complexes

Major recreation and sport facilities and services should be co-located in or close to regional centres to promote ease of access as well as the integration, multiple use and sharing of facilities between compatible uses, for example, near education, shopping, office and community facilities.

Funding of Regional Facilities Across Council Boundaries

Because regional facilities serve more than one council area, regional funding strategies across council boundaries should be considered. Agreement to fund regional recreation and sport facilities by councils over the region is an important part of developing a realistic regional strategy for recreation and sport. Such an agreement assists in setting state and commonwealth government funding of projects that attract regional support. In South Australia, regional funding of facilities is more likely if they are identified in the state strategy through the preparation of regional recreation and sport strategy plans.

Funding methods for major recreation and sport facilities are discussed in chapter 6.

Rationalisation of Aquatic Facilities

Many councils have significant investments in outdoor 'Olympic pools' (50-metre pools with the accompanying diving pool and usually a smaller toddlers pool). Because these pools are used by many other people besides their own council ratepayers, they are therefore regional.

Falling attendances at outdoor swimming pools have forced many councils to try to extend their use by introducing heating, water slides and leisure features, particularly shade protection from the sun. At the same time, rising operation and maintenance costs have led to significant deficits.

There is a move towards integrating indoor aquatic facilities with other recreation and sport facilities.

Location Characteristics

An extensive report on the 'Provision of Public Aquatic Facilities'[5] identified that recreation facilities that are easily accessible, highly visible, central to the population they intend to serve and close to other attractions are more likely to be successful. Therefore, the location of an aquatic facility is crucial to its viability.

As a general rule, new aquatic facilities should be located in or near centres and, more important, be part of larger recreation facilities. This is considered necessary as centres offer multipurpose single-trip functionality. Different transport modes are often available at a centre. There must be adequate car parking in the vicinity of the facility, either on site or shared parking on an adjoining site. A Victorian study indicates that an average of 88 per cent of users arrived by car.[6]

With regard to access, the facility should be on a major road and close to public transport. Being on a major road should also assist with visibility.

While hiding a facility behind a mass of landscaping has been a popular design response in the last couple of decades, this does reduce the visibility of the facility. The design of the facility must provide simple clues as to where its entry point is and where the various components are located. Locating part of the facility close to where the public will continually see it will enhance its visibility.

Proximity to other facilities should take the following factors into account:

- Type of facility proposed and that of adjoining facilities
- Distance (travel time)
- Sociodemographic characteristics of the catchment population
- Population density within primary and secondary catchments

Aquatic facilities that aim at different target markets can be located close together (i.e. less than five kilometres apart). Over 70 per cent of users travel less than 15 minutes to use a facility. The higher the population density, the closer facilities can be located to each other. The higher the household income and qualification levels, the higher the visitation rates.[7]

A careful and detailed assessment of each of these criteria will need to be made if an existing facility is to be retained or upgraded or if a new facility is proposed.

Implications for Councils

Although the continued provision of outdoor swimming pools should not be dismissed, careful assessment of the potential usage patterns and operating costs should be undertaken before the construction of new outdoor pools at regional level are contemplated.

Indoor aquatic centres are expensive to develop, but they can be economically viable if they are located in easily accessible positions, for example, adjacent to regional shopping centres, and have competent management.

Councils urgently need to develop a regional strategy for meeting regional aquatic needs. A rationalisation of existing swimming facilities should produce regional strategies that allow some councils to close inefficient and worn-out pools and provide a hierarchy of aquatic facilities at the local, district and regional level.

Country Aquatic Facilities

The value of a regional strategy for aquatic facilities becomes just as important in country regions as in the metropolitan regions. Further discussion on the detailed design of aquatic facilities can be found in chapter 6.

Lack of Recreation and Sport Opportunities in Country Areas

There is a perceived imbalance between metropolitan and country areas when allocating government resources. This imbalance is manifest in both the development of recreation and sport facilities and the provision of services such as sport coaching and trained recreation personnel, which are available in the metropolitan area.

Regional implications may include the following issues:

- In the majority of country regions, there is decreasing population and increasing costs of maintaining existing competitive team sports and providing for popular noncompetitive recreation and sports activities.

- Not all country towns can sustain the range of expensive facilities such as artificial surfaces for sports such as hockey and athletics, indoor aquatic facilities, large indoor stadiums and specialist sport training facilities. Therefore, a rational distribution of facilities within the region is required.

- Schools provide a major resource for community sport and recreation in country areas. With a drop in the numbers of young people in country areas, there is an increasing concern that schools may close. Apart from the educational issues, such closures would have a major impact on the recreational and social life of rural communities.

- Increasing recreation and sport resources for the older age range are required in country towns. They often become the centres for retirees who should have the opportunity to participate in recreation and sport activities.

Golf Facilities

Most councils are under pressure to provide additional golf facilities or upgrade the existing ones. These facilities vary from a championship standard 18-hole golf course to a par three course to a golf driving range. These facilities should be considered on a regional basis because of their development costs and the large areas of land involved.

Councils, particularly in country regions, are finding that there are expectations to upgrade courses by grassing both fairways and greens all the year around. The problem of water is often a major issue.

Although the capital costs of developing golf courses are expensive, the ongoing operating costs including maintenance of the large area of land involved can be profitable if the right mix of facilities are provided and the course has an attractive layout and other features. Therefore, golf courses should be considered with the following planning and design principles in mind:

• Careful consideration should be given to the need for a course in the region and whether sufficient land is available without seriously depleting the total land available for public use at the regional level.

• Bearing the preceding factors in mind, an average 18-hole golf course takes up between 48.56 hectares and 72.84 hectares.

• Another way of meeting the growing demand for golf would be to consider a nine-hole 'executive' golf course. This is less costly to develop and with a modification of the tee placements for the second round, these courses can provide even expert golfers with some of the challenges of a regulation 18-hole golf course. Approximately 20.23 hectares to 44.52 hectares of land would be needed.

• For beginners and older players, par three or 'pitch and putt' courses are popular. A nine-hole par three course can be constructed on approximately 2.02 hectares to 10.12 hectares of land.

• If a regional golf facility is justified, then the possibility of developing an 18-hole course with a par three course and maybe a golf driving range should be considered. Such a facility would attract a greater range of users and both operating and maintenance costs could be shared. The land needed for such a package of uses would be between 51.79 hectares to 85.38 hectares.

• The possibility of involving the commercial sector in the development or management of golf courses should be considered. If public regional open space is to be used for this purpose, careful consideration should be given to playing rights for nonmembers, public access to the course and a policy of no fences.

• A landscape architect should be employed, preferably a golf course architect, to ensure that the course is both attractive and challenging.

Regional Recreation and Sport Open Spaces

Recreation and sport must compete with many other demands for open spaces. How priorities are determined is an important issue. Regional open spaces for recreation and sport purposes are needed for the following purposes:

• Organised sports and associated activities at regional, state, national and, in some circumstances, international levels

• Regional and community festivals, activities and events

• Networks of walking and cycling trails

• Linear parks containing facilities for walking, cycling, active and passive recreation

• Natural parks for informal and passive recreation for all ages

• Children's play areas for playgrounds and adventurous play activities

Retention of Open Spaces

There is a fine balance between the demands to develop open spaces and the retention of community open spaces for future needs including recreation and sport. The question of how much open space is enough cannot be determined by sets of standards or formulas. (See chapter 2 for a detailed discussion on standards.) The selling of open space is a heavy responsibility because once gone it usually is gone forever. There is justification in selling open spaces to provide funds for other community purposes including the better management of the regional open space system and also to provide for recreation and sport facilities.

Conflicts Between Residents and Sports Groups

Regional open space for recreation and sport is highly valued by people when determining where they wish to live[8] (see also references in chapter 1 on the social and community benefits of recreation and sport). There is a need to address the potential conflicts between residents and sports groups that require a large amount of land in central areas on which to place regional or national standard facilities that could alienate open space.

Use of Creeks and Drainage Reserves

Creeks and drainage reserves are now being used wherever possible as linear recreation and sport areas and walking and cycling routes. The issue is who pays for their additional costs of maintenance and management of these regional open spaces now used for recreational and sport activities.

Recreational Use of Reservoirs and Water Reserves

The recreational use of watershed reserves and particularly the use of reservoirs has long been an important issue. As pressures are placed on the use of existing open spaces for many purposes, the issue of recreational use of water reserves and reservoirs will need to be resolved.

Walking, Cycling and Horse Riding Trails

Long distance walking, cycling and horse riding trails of state significance are increasing in popularity. Enthusiasm for their origi-

nal development needs to be tempered with thought given to the issues of public liability and ongoing maintenance. See chapter 6 for guidelines for walking, cycling and horse riding trails.

Environmental Recreation and Sport Conflicts

The growing popularity of outdoor recreation activities such as camping, walking, cycling, fishing, boating and four-wheel driving generates potential conflict between visitors and locals particularly in country regions.

Potential Conflicts

The increasing use of specialised vehicles such as four-wheel-drive units, trail bikes and dune buggies may become a major threat to nature conservation because they are not restricted to travelling on roads or tracks.

Where recreation facilities are to be provided on public open spaces, careful consideration should be given to the probable impact these facilities will have on the character of the surrounding areas. Their size and function should be related to the type of reserves or open spaces in which they are located.

Indiscriminate movement of visitors seeking recreational opportunities can cause damage to areas of environmental or heritage significance. There are potential conflicts with the traditional rights to movement of the Aboriginal people and the interference with pastoral and mining activities. However, the economic, recreational, social and educational value of travel in outback areas should be recognised.

The impact of off-road vehicles such as trail bikes and dune buggies on environmentally sensitive areas raises not only conflicts of land use, but questions of who bears the cost.

Because most motor sports are noisy, their location away from environmentally fragile and residential areas can minimise potential conflicts.

Regional Implications

By careful regional strategy planning involving all councils and appropriate state government departments and relevant recreation and sports organisations in the region, it is possible to rationalise the allocation of suitable land for recreation and sport purposes well in advance of need.

RESPONSIBILITY FOR STATE AND REGIONAL PROVISION

A recent Commonwealth Parliamentary Inquiry recommended that a basis of commonwealth funding to states and territories for regional sporting and recreational facilities include regional plans.[9] Therefore, it is apparent that responsibility for facilities at this level is primarily a state and commonwealth responsibility with the involvement of local councils and the relevant sports and recreation organisations.

The one overriding principle that should be considered at the regional level is:

The recognition of recreation and sport facilities as public assets that add value to the quality of life in the region and not just an additional extra to be built on the cheap.

Regional facilities must be considered as part of the overall state planning process and not as an expensive extra.

REFERENCES

1. Office for Recreation, Sport and Racing [1994] *State Recreation and Sport Strategy Plan—A Planning Strategy for South Australia.* Recreation and Sport Planning Unit, Adelaide.
2. Office for Recreation, Sport and Racing [1994] *State Recreation and Sport Strategy Plan.* Adelaide: Office for Recreation, Sport and Racing.
3. Department of Housing and Urban Development [1993] *Social Policy Aspects of Urban Development.* South Australian Urban Land Trust.
4. Department of Tourism, Sport and Racing and Hillary Commission [1994] *Getting it Right— A Guide to Planning and Developing Sport and Recreation Facilities.* Queensland and New Zealand.
5. Hassell Pty Ltd and Nicholas, J.A. [1997] *Provision of Public Aquatic Facilities—Strategic Directions.* Local Councils in South Australia and the Department of Recreation and Sport, p. 23.
6. Department of Sport and Recreation [1995] *Unpublished Study.* Victoria.
7. Department of Sport and Recreation [1995] *Unpublished Study.*
8. Vreugdenhill, Anthea and Rigby, Ken [1987] *Assessing Generalized Community Satisfaction*, in Journal of Social Psychology, vol. 127, no. 4, pp. 381–390.
9. House of Representatives Standing Committee on Environment, Recreation and the Arts [1997] *Rethinking the Funding of Community Sporting and Recreational Facilities: A Sporting Chance.* Canberra: Australian Government Publishing Service, p. 141.

6

Facilities Planning, Design and Management

It is important to address the specific issues of facility planning, design and management. The first section outlines a suggested planning approach for the provision of facilities. Section 2 provides practical designs for a variety of indoor facilities. Section 3 has some creative designs for a range of aquatic facilities and section 4 details planning and design criteria for children's play facilities. Section 5 brings together walking, cycling and horse riding designs and a new section 6 on skateboard planning and design offers advice on local-, district-, regional- and state-level facilities. Sections 7 and 8 assist in implementing the designs of facilities by discussing the finding of funds for construction and then addressing the efficient management of facilities.

It is assumed that by the time the needs for specific recreation and sport facilities have been identified, thorough consultation has taken place with sporting and recreation organisations, the community and government agencies.

PLANNING APPROACH

The methodologies suggested in chapter 3 are helpful in clarifying the most suitable planning approach. Three tasks should have been undertaken before the design and construction of facilities are commenced: an audit of existing facilities; a future needs or opportunity analysis; and classification of the facility types required at local, regional, state and international levels.

While existing facilities are being audited, location of existing facilities should be plotted accurately on a map and coded in a way that makes it easy to link to a computer mapping package such as a Geographical Information System (GIS) (see chapter 3 for a discussion on GIS). Then, the current situation should be determined by gathering demographic and participation data from sources such as the Australian Bureau of Statistics (ABS) and membership records from local recreation and sporting organisations. It is important to identify actual registered numbers and participants clearly.

It is important to identify needs that may arise in the future, say, in the next three to five years. The future needs analysis should include costs and anticipated sources of funds. Also, any feasibility studies or preliminary works undertaken should be itemised at this stage. A more detailed discussion can be found in chapter 3. See appendix D for an example of a questionnaire suitable for auditing existing facilities at the state level. This questionnaire can be adapted for other levels of facilities.

Steps 2 and 3—an audit of existing facilities and a needs analysis—can be determined together. Most consultants and planners have their own methods of information collection, but the key is thorough consultation with relevant sports and recreation associations, local councils, other government agencies and private sector sports and recreation deliverers (where necessary).

A suggested framework of responsibilities for state-, regional- and local-level facilities is provided in chapter 3. To this framework is now added facilities that meet international standards. The following definitions down to district level are suggested in the Queensland Sporting Facilities Plan:[1]

- *International level.* Facility standards meet the requirements of nominated sports or recreation peak bodies to conduct training or an event at international level or under international rules.

- *National level.* Facility standards meet the requirements of nominated sports or recreation peak bodies to conduct training or an event at a national level or under national rules.

- *State level.* Facility standards meet the requirements of nominated sports or recreation peak bodies to conduct training at a state level or hold a state open event.

- *Regional level.* Facilities of regional significance attract users from a substantial part of the region, as defined by the regional boundaries (determined by the state or territories departments) or the regional boundaries of the relevant organisation.

- *District level.* A district facility will meet the needs of people in more than one town or suburb.

- *Local level.* A local-level facility will cater for local sports and recreation groups and other community groups.

Specific Recreation and Sport Project Planning

Recreation and sport facilities require project planning methodology. For example, if the proposed facility is an outcome of the overall strategy plan developed after extensive consultation, the specific project planning can proceed.

Important Management Factors

Often, projects result from an enthusiastic person or group in a sport club, association or community recreation organisation who has a vision of what is required and comes forward with an idea or concept and an architect is appointed to draw up a plan. Sometimes no specific brief has been prepared and the planners have not considered how the facility will be managed. This can result in a poorly conceived and hastily constructed project. This leads to expensive changes if, for example, there is not enough storage, or the roof in the main gym is too low for volleyball and badminton, or the run-off areas are not adequate for netball and basketball, or the lighting is not adequate, or the front entrance cannot be supervised because of lack of staff.

It is important that the planning and design takes into account operating and management structures at the same time as the planning of the facility is undertaken.

A Suggested Project Planning Approach

Figure 6.1 represents an approach that incorporates the feasibility stage with an important second stage linking concept design and construction with management before the final operation stage is reached. The contents are the result of project planning to develop the Elizabeth Recreation and Sports Hub,[2] as outlined by the consultant, John Thompson.[3]

Stage 1: Project Feasibility

This stage begins with the identification of the need for the project and plans for fitting the project into the local or regional recreation and sport strategy plan. This includes consultation on present and future needs and priorities. It is then possible to develop a project brief along the lines suggested in appendix B.

Often a proposal to develop a new facility comes forward without much research into the community use of existing facilities. One method of assessing needs is the SWOT method that identifies **S**trengths, **W**eaknesses, **O**pportunities and **T**hreats. See further discussion of this method and other methods in chapter 3.

Consultation with potential users about their requirements for facilities should be a

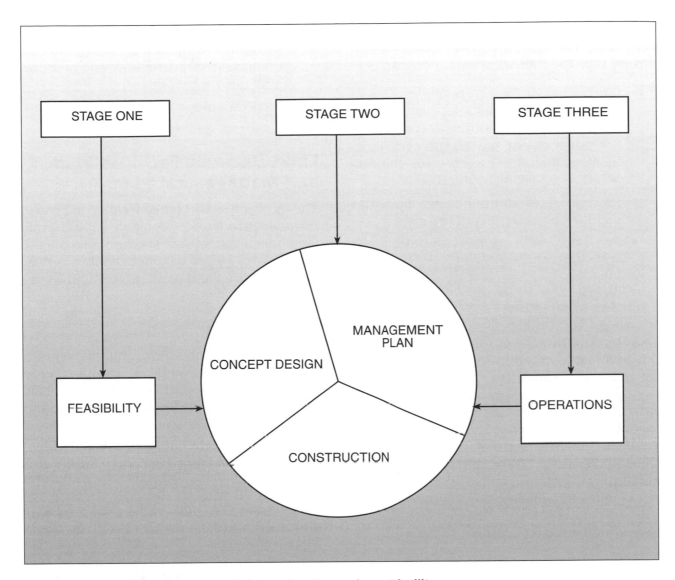

Figure 6.1   Project planning approach for a recreation and sport facility.

high priority. Wider community consultation at this stage can raise expectations that may not be able to be met. Therefore, community consultation should be left until the next stage when concept design and the viability of the project have been determined.

Details of usage of similar facilities in the vicinity should be researched, along with possible locations for the facility based on access by potential users plus availability and the price of land.

The following considerations are also included:

- Construction and operating cost estimates including budgets and cash flows.

- Sources of funds.

- Suggested management structure.

At this feasibility stage, there are opportunities to reconcile conflicting factors such as high capital costs against estimated income. Also, there are opportunities to modify the project, delay it until the conflicts are reconciled or cancel the project without too much cost involved.

Stage 2: Detailed Concept, Construction and Management

Having tested the feasibility in stage 1, it is now vital to bring together the physical development of the project with management so that future operations are maximised. The preparation of concept plans and a design should take the following into account:

- Integration of the physical elements of the project. This includes evaluation of costs and design options, accessibility to transport, pedestrian and cycle links to other facilities, access for the disabled and parking requirements.

- Production of an open space plan that includes landscaping of the site.

- Provision of a phased development schedule for the project.

A critical point in the development of the project is when tenders are received. If they are above the budget, it is still possible to abandon the project at minimal costs. After this point large expenditures are involved and the project is committed.

A good working relationship between the constructor and the manager can result in modifications at minimal cost while the construction is in progress. This ensures a smooth transition to the third stage of being fully operational.

Management plan options should be considered as part of stage 2 leading into stage 3, and should cover the following:

- Establishing a structure that will encourage maximum use and provide an agreed return on investment.

- Preparing a budget.

- Preparing an organisational structure that clearly indicates lines of responsibility.

- Developing an organisational chart for the staffing structure.

- Appointing a manager to allow concurrent interaction with the construction that will lead to smooth operations.

Stage 3: Operations

This involves the ongoing operation of the facility. It also allows the manager who should have been appointed in stage 2 a lead in time to implement the management plan that

- provides customer services that have flexibility to update and take into account seasonal variations with new possibilities for programs,

- monitors programs and activities, and

- evaluates and reviews the plan.

Links Between Facilities Plan and Management Plan

The most important consideration in project planning is to have thorough feasibility studies undertaken with a management plan in place either before or immediately after the detailed design and construction phases are undertaken.

Endorsement

The principle of obtaining endorsement for the project strategy by the proposer, local council and the appropriate state government agencies responsible for recreation and sport validates the implementation. This does not entail acceptance of any specific actions or recommendations nor does it commit any party to financial obligations. The advantage is that the strategy can be used in setting priorities, seeking funds and negotiating with sporting and recreation clubs and organisations.

Implementation of the Project

Whatever planning method is adopted, it is important that plans do not gather dust on shelves and become rapidly out of date. It is strongly recommended that a *process* rather than a static plan be encouraged. This means that an *implementation process* needs to be established.

Outcomes From the Implementation Process

The following outcomes should be expected from the implementation process:

- *Realistic objectives and principles* on which recreation and sport open spaces and facilities planning can be established.

- *Clear action plans, priorities or recommendations* for the development of recreation and sport facilities and open spaces at the local and regional levels within states and territories.
- *Ongoing communication* among all key organisations and agencies that influence the development of recreation and sport. This includes regional and local councils, state and territory government agencies and recreation and sports associations and clubs.
- *Specific feasibility studies* for regional and local recreation and sport projects.
- An investigation of *appropriate management structures* for recreation and sport facilities and open spaces at local, regional and state levels.
- *Review of procedures* to continually update both local and regional recreation and sport strategy plans.

Development of Recreation and Sport Construction Alternatives

Having completed needs and feasibility studies (referred to in chapter 3) and obtained the required financial support, it is necessary to decide on how to construct the facility.

Inevitably, differences and disputes will occur, usually because of changes in design and time overruns that also involve additional expenditure of hard-to-obtain money. Well-written contracts are vital to remove doubts on who is responsible for the work and conditions that apply within a specific time frame.

Construction Options

There are a number of options to consider.

In-House Design Team

Until recently, state governments and large councils had specialist departments or branches that designed, sometimes even constructed, the facility or at least supervised construction. The advantages of this method are that construction was under the direct control of the client. The disadvantages are that it takes years to build up experience in a specialist area such as sport and recreation facilities and no one authority has built enough of these facilities or kept up with the latest design practices.

Tendering and Negotiation Method

This is the traditional way construction is undertaken. Usually, the tender document is drawn up with the assistance of an architect using other specialists such as the quantity surveyor and subcontractors. Then, either a public tender is advertised or a 'selective tender' is invited from a number of firms chosen because of their capabilities in the construction of the particular type of facility.

The selection of the successful tender is usually based on the lowest price, but this may not always occur if there are doubts about the capability of the tenderer. For example, it may be wise to check out the financial viability of the proposed contractor with the appropriate industry body, such as the Master Builders Association[4] or its equivalent, and draw up an appropriate contract.

Specialist Recreation and Sport Consultants

There are now specialist recreation and sport planning and design consultants who can put together teams of experts for constructing a specific facility. This is a cost-efficient advantage when building expensive aquatic facilities and indoor stadiums with special requirement for playing surfaces such as velodromes or basketball, netball or tennis courts. One disadvantage in using specialist consultants is that due to the growing competitiveness among consultants, tight margins do not allow time for consultants to adapt the proposed facility to suit the client's specific needs. You may get a standard version of a facility that has already been built in another location. A lack of originality in design can therefore occur.

Lump-Sum, Fixed-Price Method

This construction method obligates the contractor to complete the work for an agreed amount and usually within a specific time frame. This does not mean that cost plus additions are not entirely avoided, because there may be alterations that only become apparent during the course of construction, but they can be minimal if the documentation is tight. It may be possible to agree on a target cost with the possibility of a bonus to the contractor if the target is met or it could be agreed that the contractor shares a proportion of the shortfall.

Lump Sum, Rise-and-Fall Method

This protects the contractor against the effect of inflation after the tenders close. It is not a fixed price but a price based on building costs current at the time of tendering. Therefore, it is important that the budget for the project takes into account likely increases based on cost and price index movements and the speed of construction. Care needs to be taken with the method of calculation of the rise-and-fall clauses.

Design-Build Method

There is a growing view that even a very competent design team is not able to give an accurate estimate of cost and time until a tender is obtained. Also, some design teams tend to be overly optimistic about the tender prices; they seem to underestimate tender prices.

With this method, the design team and the builder work together to produce a design and cost for the client. Because both design and cost are in the one package, for a predetermined price, the final cost is not subject to variation. While costs are controlled, any changes to the design can be expensive unless a very tight brief is agreed to at the beginning. This method is helpful when there is an urgency to complete a facility with standard features as a package. Highly specialised buildings such as swimming pools and other aquatic facilities need customising to suit local conditions and contractors are sometimes pressured to cut corners if faced with unusual situations outside their knowledge or the contract.

Cost-Plus Method

With this method, the client agrees to pay for the cost of the actual work, plus a fee to remunerate the contractor for organising and overseeing the work. Usually, this is on a percentage basis (say, around 10 per cent) or a fixed fee. This is sometimes called a 'do and charge' method. There are a number of drawbacks to this method, the major one being that the contractor does not price the work under competitive conditions so there is an incentive to keep the costs up, if the fee is a percentage of the cost. An independent administrator, if appointed, adds to the overall costs of the project, but cost-plus ensures that the client gets a guaranteed product according to the specifications including such items as wind- and weatherproof facilities and other environmental services.

Schedule of Rates Method

This is a variation on the cost-plus method. The tenderer submits reasonably accurate final costs by multiplying the provisional bill of quantities by the schedule of rates for overheads, mark-up percentages, site establishment, etc. Dealing with variations can be a complicating factor, but there is an Australian Standard[5] that has a schedule of rates contract plus a bonus for early completion of work.

Project Manager

In large projects over $1 million, there is a need for on-site 'project management' or a 'construction manager' whose main task is to exercise control over the project from beginning to end. The manager is responsible for cost controls, quality assurance, security and dispute resolution and time spent on the job by the various contractors and subcontractors. The appointment of a project manager allows the architect freedom to negotiate changes in design while the project manager gets on with the task of efficiently meeting tight schedules and satisfying the inevitable changes introduced during the construction phase. It can be seen that this and other methods previously described are gradually replacing the architect as project manager particularly when cost-plus or design-build methods are adopted. The choice to use an architect is largely determined by the construction option selected.

Fast Tracking Method

This is a method of delivering a completed facility sooner than using the traditional methods. Fast tracking can include construction management or elements of design-build methods. Extra costs sometimes are incurred by wastage, but these are compensated for by savings of time and therefore cost.

Design

This section concentrates on providing some practical designs for a range of indoor recreation and sport centres; aquatic facilities; children's playgrounds; skateboard facilities; and walking, cycling and horse trails. It is not intended to imply that the following facilities and designs are suitable for all purposes; they only assist to clarify thinking and avoid many elementary mistakes in design through using wrong assumptions. These designs should be modified in the light of the needs analysis and the other planning processes suggested in the previous chapters.

Before concentrating on the designs, it is timely to be reminded of some common mistakes that have been highlighted by the Queensland Department of Tourism, Sport and Racing and the New Zealand Hillary Commission:[6]

- Poor location relative to where users come from.
- Inappropriate space allocation within the facilities, i.e. the expected use changes and the design was not flexible enough to meet changes in programs.
- Built for a single use that often means underutilisation.
- Inadequate activity areas to attract potential users.
- Poor presentation of facility; not attractively presented; not user-friendly.
- Poor internal layout of facilities in relation to each other. Poor designs such as control areas that compromise security of facilities and toilets in wrong places.
- Inadequate attention paid to disability and wheelchair access to building with poor gradients from the curb to the building and internally to amenities such as showers and eating areas.

INDOOR RECREATION AND SPORT CENTRE DESIGNS

The following layouts (figures 6.2-6.13) are for guidance only; there is no perfect layout to meet all situations. Each project will have its own criteria that will need to be taken into consideration.

Retractable seating.

Acknowledgement:
Recreation Hall, University of California
Parkin Architect.
Reproduced from *Arenas*,
Sports Council, London

LOCAL ONE-COURT CENTRE

Dimensions: 34.75 m × 17.07 m × 8.00 m. *Note:* No space has been allowed for spectators, circulation or warm-up area.

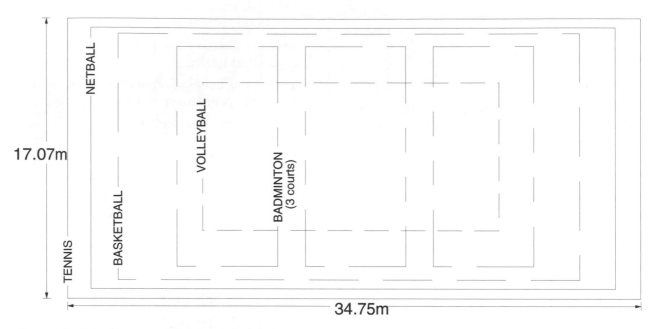

Figure 6.2 Local one-court centre dimensions.

This size hall will accommodate the following popular activities for recreation (including the required safety run-off, if any):

1 netball court: 32.00 m × 16.75 m × 6.70 m

1 basketball court: 30.00 m × 17.00 m × 6.70 m

1 tennis court: 34.75 m × 17.07 m × 8.00 m

1 volleyball court: 22.00 m × 13.00 m × 6.70 m

1 badminton court: 16.44 m × 8.54 m × 6.70 m

2 badminton courts: 16.44 m × 15.86 m × 6.70 m

3 badminton courts: 16.44 m × 23.18 m × 6.70 m

4 badminton courts: 16.44 m × 30.50 m × 6.70 m (side by side)

No allowance has been made for spectator accommodation or for timekeepers, reserve players, team officials, etc., because being for recreational purposes only, this additional space may not be necessary.

LOCAL TWO-COURT CENTRE

Dimensions: 34.75 m × 36.00 m × 8.00 m.

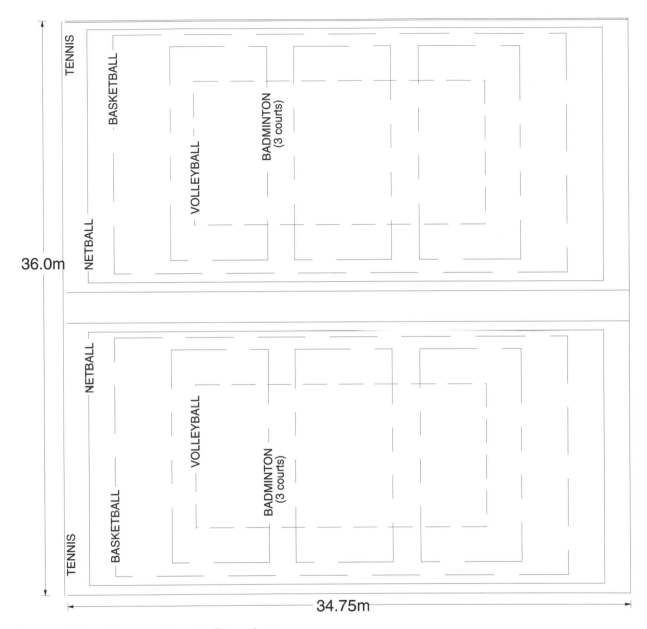

Figure 6.3   Local two-court centre dimensions.

This size centre will accommodate the following popular activities for recreation:

2 netball courts: 32.00 m × 34.00 m × 6.70 m

2 basketball courts: 30.00 m × 34.00 m × 6.70 m

2 tennis courts: 34.75 m × 31.70 m × 8.00 m

2 volleyball courts: 22.00 m × 24.00 m × 6.70 m

4 badminton courts: 16.44 m × 30.50 m × 6.70 m
  (side by side)

8 badminton courts: 31.30 m × 30.50 m × 6.70 m
  (2 rows of 4 courts)

As with the single court, this two-court complex includes the required safety run-off. Remember that no allowance has been made for circulation around the playing area for supporters or others, and no allowance has been made for spectator accommodation or for timekeepers, reserve players, team officials, etc., because being for recreational purposes only, this additional space may not be necessary.

LOCAL ONE-COURT CENTRE LAYOUT

The minimum standard recreation court has been complemented with other minimal amenities for a facility this size. The total area is 56.75 m × 17.07 m for the building.

The car parking requirements will depend upon the location of the hall, e.g. can existing car parking facilities be utilised, such as those for shopping centres, schools, and roads? Car spaces are calculated as 2.5 m × 5.4 m each. The aisle widths are 6.2 m.

The building components for additional spaces are by using a basic two-metre module. These can be adjusted according to local needs.

The change room space has been designed to accommodate 12 people at any one time.

The creche has direct access to the storage area and also has its own toilets.

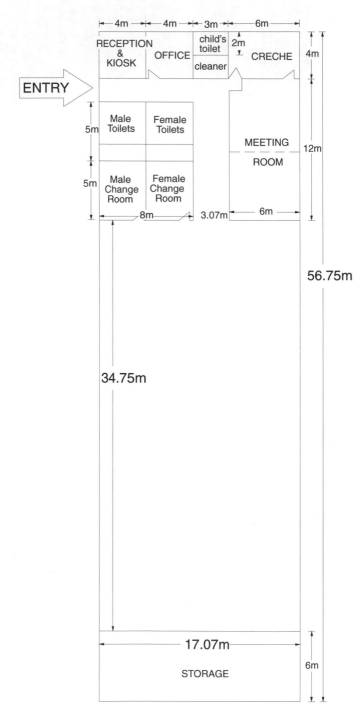

Figure 6.4   Local one-court sport centre layout.

LOCAL TWO-COURT CENTRE LAYOUT

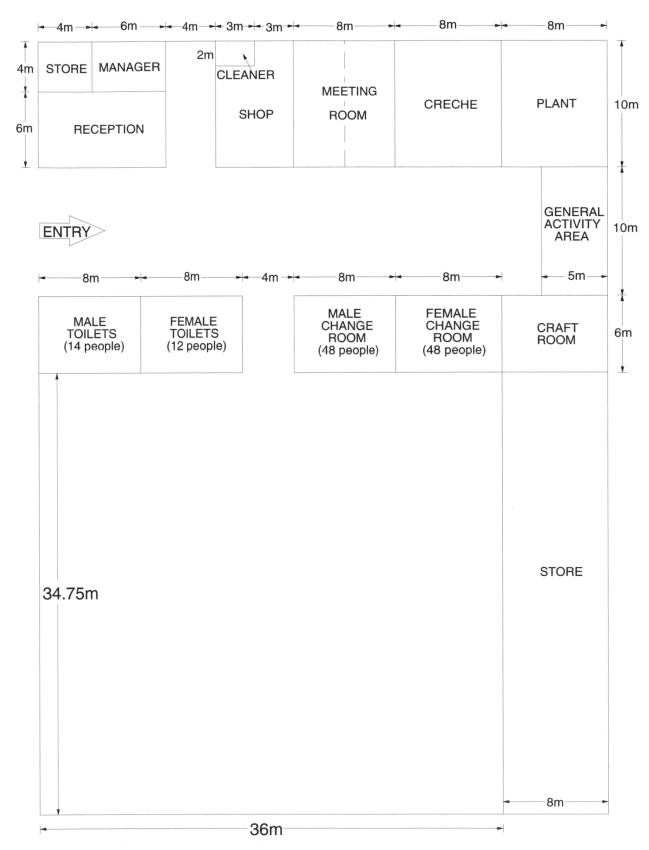

Figure 6.5   Local two-court sport centre layout.

REGIONAL ONE-COURT CENTRE

Dimensions: 39.00m × 22.10 m × 9.00 m. *Note:* No space has been allowed for spectators, circulation or warm-up areas.

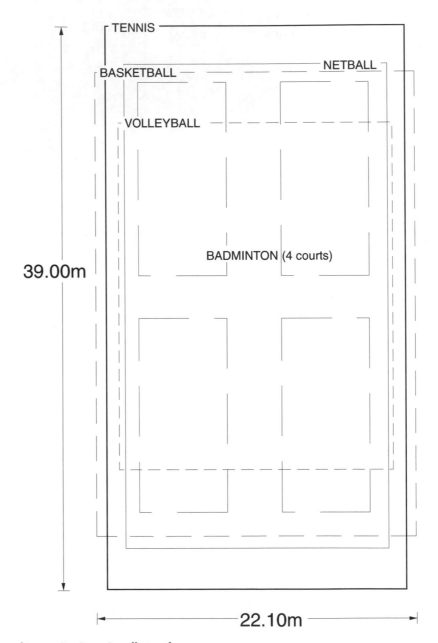

Figure 6.6   Regional one-court centre dimensions.

This size centre will accommodate the following popular activities for recreation:

1 netball court: 32.90 m × 17.65 m × 7.00–7.60 m

1 basketball court: 30.60 m × 17.60 m × 7.00 m

1 tennis court: 36.57 m × 18.29 m × 9.00 m

1 volleyball court: 26.00 m × 17.00 m × 7.00 m

1 badminton court: minimum: 16.44 m × 8.54 m × 37.82 m

4 badminton courts: 16.44 m × 37.82 m

REGIONAL TWO-COURT CENTRE

Dimensions: 39.0 m × 46.20 m × 9.00 m.

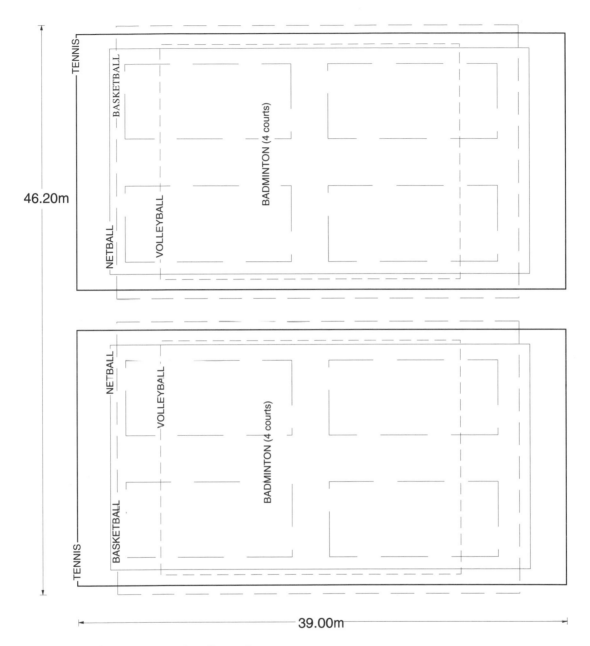

Figure 6.7 **Regional two-court centre dimensions.**

This size hall will accommodate the following popular sports for club competition:

2 netball courts: 32.90 m × 34.10 m × 7.00–7.60 m

2 basketball courts: 33.9 m × 30.60 m × 7.00 m

2 tennis courts: 36.57 m × 33.53 m × 9.00 m

2 volleyball courts: 28.00 m × 26.00 m × 7.00 m (side by side)

8 badminton courts: 16.44 m × 37.82 m

The dimensions shown for each of the sports includes the required safety run-off. Remember that no allowance has been made for circulation around the playing area for supporters or others, and no allowance has been made for spectator accommodation or for timekeepers, reserve players, team officials, etc. These requirements have been left to the discretion of the users and management.

REGIONAL ONE-COURT CENTRE LAYOUT

The minimum standard club playing area has been complemented with other necessary amenities for a facility this size. The total area is 63.00 m × 27.6 m for the building.

Car parking requirements will depend on the location of the sport centre, e.g. can existing car parking facilities be utilised, such as those for shopping centres, schools, roads, etc. Car spaces are calculated as 2.5 m × 5.4 m each. The aisle widths are 6.2 m.

The change room spaces have been designed to accommodate 25 people in each room with flexibility.

The first-floor seating will accommodate 360 people including circulation space (6 rows of 60 seats). The lounge area, approximately 20 m × 14 m can be set out with tables and chairs for refreshments.

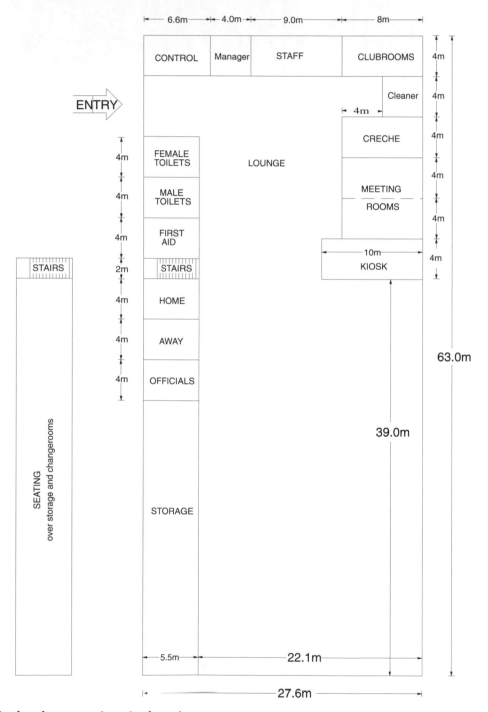

Figure 6.8   Regional one-court centre layout.

REGIONAL TWO-COURT CENTRE LAYOUT

The creche can be designed to be self-contained with its own toilets and storage.

A suitable two-court hall as shown has a total area of 101.80 m × 73.60 m × 9.00 m.

Changes to the building design allow for alterations to the plan. These can be adjusted to local needs.

Change rooms in the two-court hall can accommodate 100 people at any one time.

The seating capacity in the two-court hall is for 1,500 people in the main area and 440 people in the training and warm-up hall. The seating in the main arena is ideal to cater for those people with disabilities.

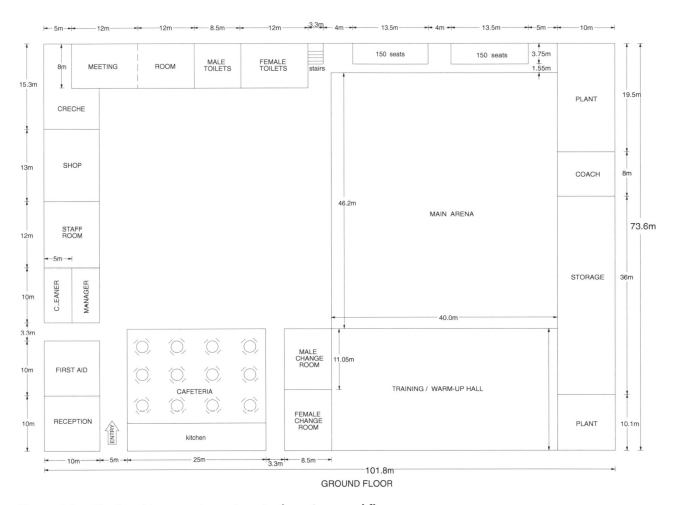

Figure 6.9a   Regional two-court sport centre layout: ground floor.

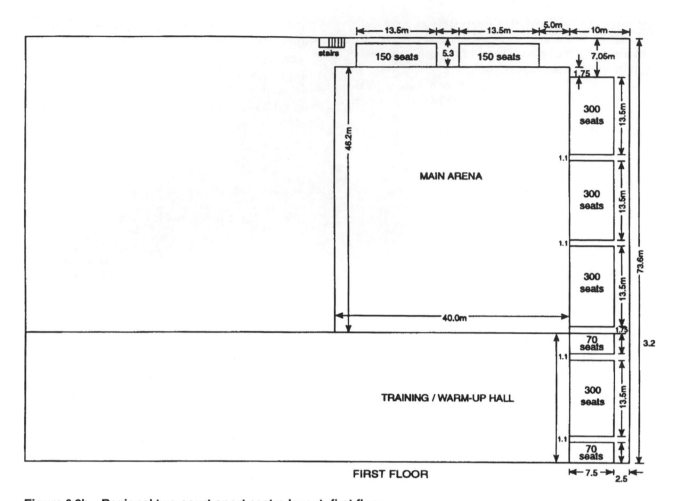

Figure 6.9b   Regional two-court sport centre layout: first floor.

INTERNATIONAL ONE-COURT CENTRE

Dimensions: 40.00 m × 25.00 m × 12.50 m. *Note:* No space has been allowed for spectators, circulation or warm-up areas.

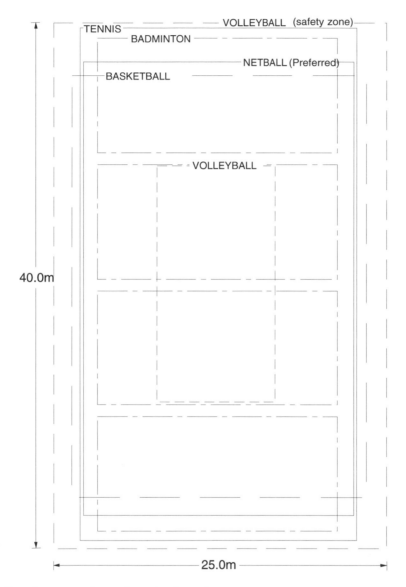

Figure 6.10   International one-court sport centre layout.

This size centre will accommodate the following popular sports for major competition:

1 netball court: 33.50 m × 20.00 m × 7.60 m

1 basketball court: 32.10 m × 22.10 m × 7.00 m (min)

1 tennis court: 39.00 m × 20.73 m × 9.00 m

1 volleyball court: international: 40.00 m × 25.00 m × 12.50 m; national: 26.00 m × 17.00 m × 7.00 m (min)

1 badminton court: 18.00 m × 10.50 m × 9.10 m (min)

2 badminton courts: 18.00 m × 18.60 m × 9.10 m (min)

3 badminton courts: 18.00 m × 26.70 m × 9.10 m (min)

4 badminton courts: 18.00 m × 34.80 m × 9.10 m (min)

INTERNATIONAL TWO-COURT CENTRE

Dimensions: 40.00 m × 54.20 m × 12.50 m. *Note:* No space has been allowed for spectators, circulation or warm-up areas.

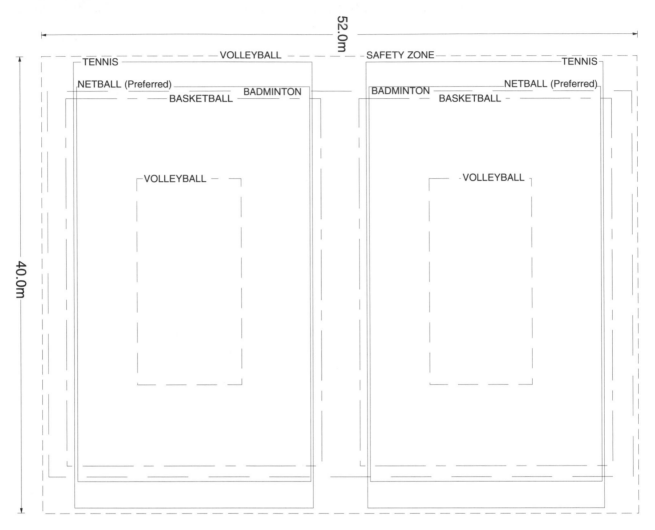

Figure 6.11 International two-court sport centre layout.

This size centre will accommodate the following popular sports for major competition:

1 gymnastic competitive area for artistic and rhythmic: 33.00 m × 54.50 m × 9.00 m

2 netball courts: minimum: 33.50 m × 38.50 m × 7.60 m

2 basketball courts: 42.15 m × 32.10 m × 7.00 m

2 tennis courts: 39.00 m × 41.50 m × 9.00 m

2 volleyball courts: international: 40.00 m × 47.00 m × 12.50 m; national: 26.00 m × 34.00 m × 7.00 m

6 badminton courts: 18.00 m × 51.00 m × 9.10 m

12 badminton courts can be accommodated by setting out two rows of six courts.

Major Recreation and Sport Centre

The dimensions shown for each of the sports includes the required safety run-off. Remember that no allowance has been made for circulation around the playing area for supporters or others. No allowances have been made for spectator accommodation or for timekeepers, reserve players, team officials, etc. These requirements have been left to the discretion of the users and management.

The dimensions for volleyball to be played at the international level are the determining factor for the dimensions for one-court sport centres. If the intention is not to play volleyball at the international level in a particular centre then the dimensions for that centre can be reduced to the size of the next sport, or sports, for which the centre will be designed. The same applies to the two-court centre.

MAJOR ONE-COURT CENTRE

The minimum playing requirements for major tournament competition in one-court centres is complemented with the other minimal amenities for facilities of this size (see figures 6.12a and 6.12b).

MAJOR TWO-COURT CENTRE

Dimensions: 28 m × 15 m × 7 m (minimum). Safety zone: 2.05 m (minimum). One side 3 m clear space for officials.

For recreational use, the playing dimensions are standard but the height can be reduced to 6.7 m.

Note: All line markings are 50 mm wide. The boundary lines are outside of the playing zone.

For Miniball for children 10 years and younger, the court size is the same as for seniors but the basket is lowered to a height of 2.44 m.

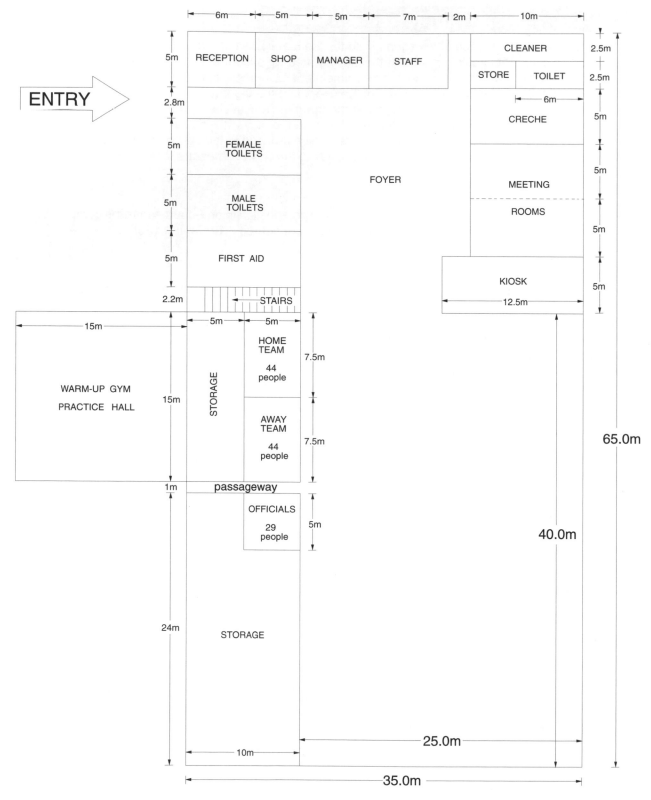

Figure 6.12a Major one-court sport centre layout: ground floor.

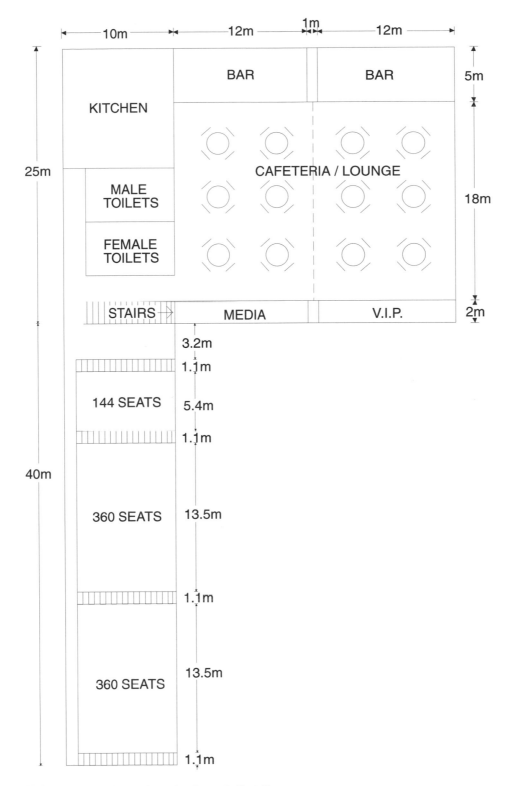

Figure 6.12b   Major one-court sport centre layout: first floor.

A suitable one-court centre can be accommodated within an area of 65.00 m × 50.00 m × 12.50 m. Each change room in a one-court centre has been designed to accommodate 44 people with flexibility between the two rooms and 29 people in the smaller (officials) change room.

A creche can be designed to be self-contained with its own toilets and storage.

The seating capacity in the one-court hall is for 360 people.

INTERNATIONAL TWO-COURT CENTRE LAYOUT

A suitable two-court centre as shown in this manual has a total area of 65.00 m × 89.90 m × 12.50 m.

The change rooms can accommodate 414 active participants plus officials at any one time.

The creche can be designed to be self-contained with its own toilets and storage.

The seating capacity in the two-court centre is for a total of 7,470 people plus ample seating accommodation for VIPs and media on the first floor. The viewing accommodation at ground level in the main arena is ideal to cater for spectators with disabilities.

The car parking requirements will depend upon the location of the sports hall, e.g. can existing car parking facilities be utilised, such as those for shopping centres, schools, roads, etc. Car spaces are calculated as 2.5 m × 4.0 m each. The aisle widths are 6.2 m.

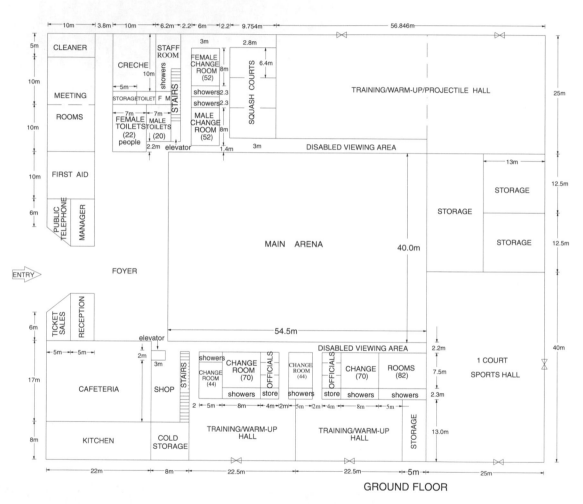

Figure 6.13a   International two-court sport centre layout: ground floor.

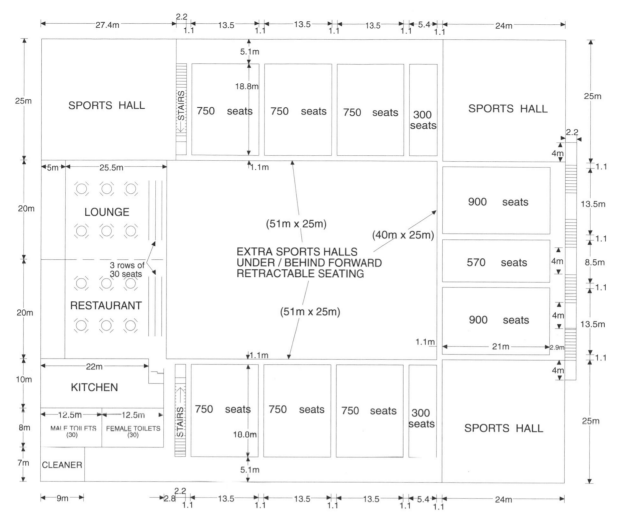

Figure 6.13b   International two-court sport centre layout: first floor.

CREATIVE DESIGNS FOR AQUATIC FACILITIES

Rick Bzowy, a leading design architect, provides this part on the architectural design and planning of aquatic facilities.

The last decade saw an enormous growth in the development of recreation and aquatic facilities around Australia. Today's aquatic centres are composed of an infinite variety of individual aquatic components designed to suit a range of sport, health and fitness, and recreation programs.

Purpose of the Design Guide

The purpose of this design guide is to outline the architectural principles governing the design of some major types of components within an aquatic centre. These principles must be carefully explored in the context of the overall functional brief, the available capital funds and the intended operational principles of the facility.

Appropriate Designs for Aquatic Facilities

The following outlines serve as an introductory guide to the nature of the aquatic components and the architectural design skill with which they must be brought together in order to create a viable and thriving facility. Appropriate designs for aquatic facilities vary considerably from one community to the next. Issues such as demographic location, population level and density, surrounding competitor facilities and user program needs are comprehensively researched in predesign feasibility analysis, which subsequently creates an overall functional brief.

In the development of this functional brief, aquatic components are then selected in response to the perceived demand for a range of activities and programs.

In determining the most appropriate balance of aquatic provision for any individual facility, this range of potential aquatic components is prioritised to provide a viable facility.

The Design Process

The design of aquatic components is a complex, many-layered decision-making process involving all manner of disciplines. Architects must work closely with both client and management throughout the design process to ensure that the final design of the aquatic components responds to specific program needs and operational forecasts.

A number of contributing parties must be involved in this decision-making process. The consultant team must integrate a variety of disciplines, supplementing aquatic architecture with sound engineering practice in service areas such as water treatment, air handling and acoustics, as well as building engineering and cost planning.

Feasibility Analysis

The preliminary determination of the functional needs of an aquatic facility is established through the preparation of an analytical feasibility study, exploring the strategic, operational and architectural issues relevant to an individual client and community.

The exact scope of aquatic spaces and components, and the balance between formal and leisure water, is developed from a combined analysis of individual program needs, functional priorities, operational objectives and, of course, available capital budgets, all developed in the context of the planning, architectural and engineering parameters.

The resultant functional brief is then measured against the implications of both expenditure and income projection, as drawn from the projected visitation levels.

The comparison between the anticipated capital cost of the intended design solution and the operational outcome is then analysed through a cyclic process of comparison and modification, until the required balance between the operational outcome and the available project budget is achieved.

The position of this balance will vary between aquatic projects, ranging from the minimal requirement of a break-even operation, through to a client-determined level of financial surplus.

Typically, the principal outcome of a feasibility analysis is to give a clear planning and architectural direction for the aquatic facility, accompanied by a confident projection of the business and financial structure.

Management Principles

The management principles by which the facility will be operated are of considerable importance to the architectural design phase, as they have a critical bearing on the functional balance of the design and layout of the facility with the financial outcomes of the operation.

Management principles are discussed at the end of this chapter. An excellent description of management models is also provided in *Provision of Public Aquatic Facilities*.[7]

Master Planning

In determining the nature of the provision of aquatic components, it is important to consider a long-term view of the future of the facility to identify how and where recreation and sport needs may vary in the future.

While it may be impossible to predict the trends of the future, it is critical that any aquatic facility has the opportunity to be able to expand to suit a flexible range of future contingencies.

Facility Planning

There are a number of critical planning relationships within and around aquatic components.

These include clear circulation patterns for patrons and staff around all pools, as well as clear space for all manners of equipment movement and distribution, which must not interfere with the aquatic activity areas themselves.

Effective space planning is also important to allow clear supervision lines for the requisite number of pool supervisory staff in order to ensure patron safety with complete visibility over all water spaces.

Not only is this necessary for the wellbeing and enjoyment of the patrons, it is also essential in ensuring that poorly designed aquatic layouts do not create a need to compensate with additional pool staff, threatening the financial viability of the operation through excessive staffing costs.

Sufficient space is also required for a variety of viewing areas, from informal relaxation seating, through to formal arrangements of tiered seating for sport viewing.

As with any well-thought-out facility, the issue of patron safety must remain paramount in the consideration of aquatic component planning.

Relationships such as the proximity of water areas of varying depths, circulation patterns to and from amenities, and the distribution of patrons and their activities by age and aquatic experience must be clearly considered to avoid any potential hazards.

A range of secondary activity areas and peripheral elements such as food and beverage areas, relaxation lounges and so on, must also be assembled in the context of the overall aquatic layout and circulation plan.

Architectural Detailing

From a technical standpoint, the issues of architectural detailing within an aquatic centre are quite complex. The corrosive nature of the aquatic atmosphere must be addressed with expertise and care. Other detailing considerations include issues of surface finish, aquatic glare and acoustics.

Detailing must be cost effective, yet must also offer an uncompromising response to the provision of patron safety and comfort, as well as offering maximum durability and minimal maintenance requirements in the selection of materials and finishes.

These elements of architectural responsibility must come together to provide the aquatic centre user with a strong expression of contemporary architecture, one which encourages repeat patronage within an amenable, comfortable environment, in facilities that contribute to the broader responsibility of architectural excellence.

Aquatic Design Objectives

The principal objective of an aquatic centre must be to provide all pool patrons with a safe and enjoyable water experience. In order to achieve this objective, a number of support objectives must be adopted and adhered to throughout the design process.

The design team must collaborate with both client and management to confirm the principal objectives for the development of any aquatic centre. These objectives create an agreed schedule against which all design decisions are measured.

The final architectural form and urban impact of an aquatic centre, the balance between its commercial and community opportunities and the principles by which it is to be operated will rely on adoption of a comprehensive series of objectives against which any conflicting priorities may be weighed.

The following is an outline of key objectives that should be considered throughout the determination of an aquatic centre design.

Development Objectives

- Site boundaries cannot be exceeded; centre designs must maximise and complement use of available site areas.
- Overall designs must respect the surrounding urban context.
- Long-term master planning must allow opportunities for expansion.
- Provision must be made for vehicular access; car parking must be considered as a function of the surrounding civic circumstances.
- Strong relationships must be established between the site and urban vehicular distribution.
- Centres must have easy access by bicycle, car and public transport.

Cultural and Social Objectives

- Centre designs must encourage access for all people, providing components that enable users to have a valuable and enjoyable experience.

- Centres must maintain affordable access to all, particularly those on low incomes.

- The variety of aquatic components must attract people of all interests and abilities.

- Aquatic centres must provide for individual cultural and multilingual group requirements.

- Centres must be flexible to adapt to future community cultural and leisure needs.

Design Objectives

- Aquatic centre components must be fully integrated.

- Centres must aim to be operational 365 days of the year.

- All facilities and programs are to be accessible to the disabled.

- Centres must be easy to manage and control to encourage effective management and minimise recurrent management expenditure.

- Design and fit-out must be easy to maintain and energy efficient.

- Designs must create minimal environmental impact whilst satisfying the previous criteria.

- The architecture must recognise and adopt best practice principles in design.

Financial Objectives

- Centres must at least operationally break even, or strive to record an operating surplus.

- Operational budgets must allow for required building, plant, fixtures and equipment maintenance and must reserve annual funds towards maintenance provision.

- Established capital budgets must not be exceeded in design and construction.

- Plant, services and fittings must be designed to minimise or eliminate operational shutdowns, as well as associated customer effects of closure.

- Design layouts must optimise staffing numbers and be efficient to control patrons.

- Components must be assessed against their capacity to generate usage and revenue.

- Ongoing operating and maintenance costs must be minimised.

Aquatic Design Principles

A number of general principles apply to the design and development of aquatic components.

Aquatic Component Areas

Actual areas of the pools are determined by a balance between the financial parameters of available capital budget and the desired operating result, the program requirements and the general intent of the overall facility.

Access Equity

Equal access for disabled patrons is essential in any aquatic development. The manner in which this is provided throughout the building is sufficiently covered in relevant building standards and codes.

However, access into actual water areas for the disabled is far more complex and not as sufficiently covered in any design guidelines. Access to water spaces for disabled patrons is typically either through shallow graded water or directly into deeper water with some form of mechanical assistance such as a hoist. The exact nature of provision must be discussed with the community, the client and any specific interest groups as part of the design process.

Water Depths and Gradient

As overall aquatic areas are being established through analysis of cost and program needs, pool gradients and depths must also respond to a variety of program needs. These vary from facility to facility and must also embrace issues of patron safety as well as functional suitability.

Visibility and Supervision

Simple rectangular formal pools such as 50-metre and 25-metre pools offer the easiest visibility lines for supervision across water. With the increasing use of free-form pool designs associated with elements such as landscaping and furniture layouts, maintaining clear sight lines must be well thought out.

Water Temperature Requirements

A number of different aquatic activities require particular attention to specific water temperatures to suit intended programs. Principally, these will involve a different assessment for formal aquatic areas for activities such as lap swimming and competition, as distinct from leisure pools and supplementary components such as spa and hydrotherapy pools.

This becomes a critical parameter in the associated decision of separate treatment systems, which can add significantly to both initial capital cost and long-term operating cost implications. These distinctions are further created by differences in statutory requirements for a number of these aquatic components.

Combination Pools

Current trends towards maximising the use of available capital funds mean that individual aquatic areas are increasingly being brought together into some combination of aquatic activity areas that require water at a similar temperature and can host a diverse range of programs that do not interfere with each other.

Aquatic Components

The following is an outline of some of the main aquatic components to consider:

- Formal pools
- Diving pools
- Leisure
- Learn-to-swim pools
- Play pools
- Supplementary elements

These various types of aquatic components will be defined in terms of scale, size and detail and will be likely to offer a blend of formal water areas for competition, areas for health and fitness programs, and leisure water, principally for recreation, with the ability to accommodate some specific program activity.

The balance between these different aquatic components will vary to suit the individual needs of the client and community.

The overall market position of the facility will also determine the scale of aquatic components, varying from local municipal facilities through to regional complexes, as well as larger venues for state, national and international use.

Formal Pools

These are typically either 25-metre or 50-metre pools, rectangular in profile (see figure 6.14). Depths and widths vary from facility to facility. Overall proportions are governed by the standards advocated in the handbook produced by the Federation Internationale de Natation Amateur (FINA), which is the world swimming body.

Pool depths may vary according to the nature of programs to be run, as well as the approach of management, client and community. Within a community facility, pool depths may vary from the accepted minimum of 1.10 metres, through to maximum depths up to 2.00 metres.

The deeper end may be increased to incorporate some deeper-water programs such as water polo, synchronised swimming and underwater hockey. These latter functions will also be governed by the available pool width.

To create a consistent level for a range of programs, a 50-metre pool and, to a lesser degree, a 25-metre pool may have the pool floor gradient divided into some segments of horizontal floors and some intermediate graded areas.

The principal program function of any formal pool is typically a combination of lap swimming, competition swimming and limited

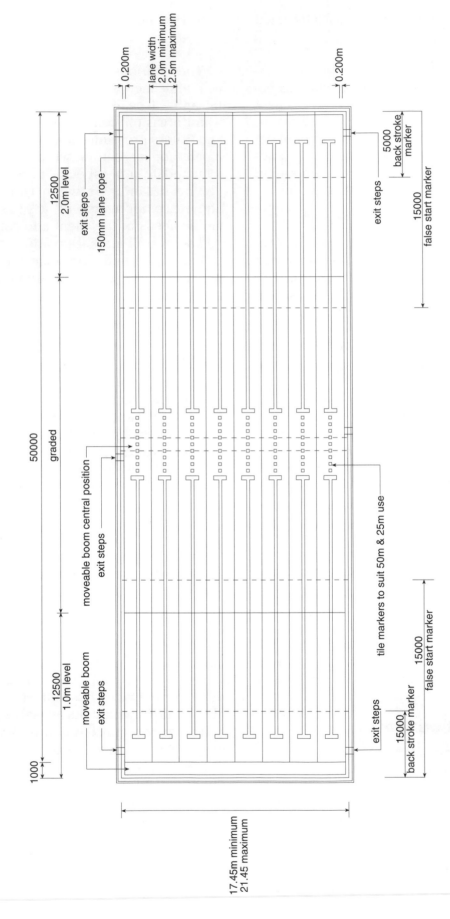

Figure 6.14   Dimensions for a formal pool (conforms to FINA standards).

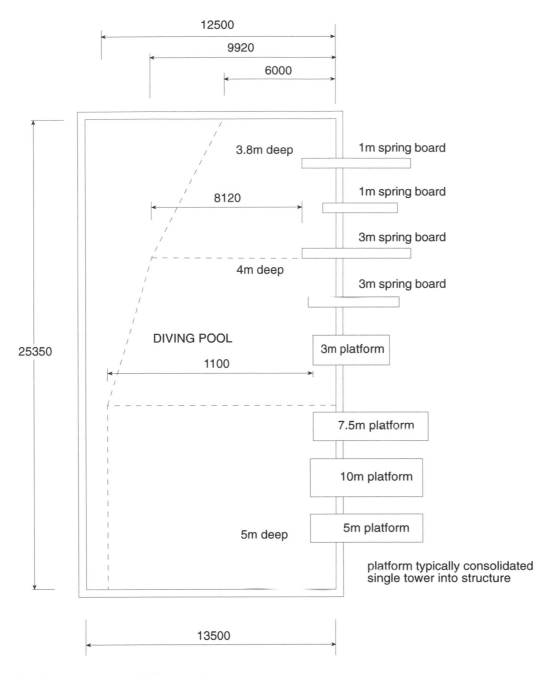

Figure 6.15 Dimensions for a diving pool.

recreation. Some teaching programs are run in the shallower pool ends. While the overall priority of the pool must take precedence, the modern aquatic centre must offer a range of programs to create a viable facility.

To provide maximum long-term flexibility, although FINA recommendations are likely to form the basis for the overall pool proportions and depths, related programs will create a number of specific influences.

Issues such as the number of lanes and their width, will also vary from one facility to the next. Typical lane profiles in community aquatic facilities run to eight lanes, with elite sport facilities running up to ten and occasionally twelve lanes. Lane widths for community pools within which lap swimming is to be a priority should be at least 2.40 metres, although competition pools can reduce lane widths to 2.10 metres.

An automated mobile boom can increase the flexibility of programming in 50-metre pools. These booms can configure the pool into a number of sizes, the most common being a straightforward division into two 25-metre pools.

Diving Pools

With the emphasis on the provision of viable aquatic facilities, diving pools complete with full tower and spring board facilities are increasingly being relegated to either regional or, more typically, state and national facilities.

However, at these high-profile facilities, overall viability is no less critical. Consequently, the principles of maximising program flexibility are still important. The provision of a diving pool should therefore consider the incorporation of the maximum number of supplementary activities such as water polo, underwater hockey, synchronised swimming and SCUBA training.

Their level of provision must also be carefully assessed to offer balanced opportunities for all activities. These needs will vary, dependent on the combination of competition and training required for each activity. See figure 6.15 (previous page).

Leisure Pools

Typically, leisure pools will involve an integrated mix of aquatic components for a range of activities, including swimming, general recreation and programmed activity (figure 6.16).

Water depths may vary from zero through to 2.00 metres, subject to operational preferences. Water temperature is typically warmer than that of a formal aquatic area such as competition and lap pools.

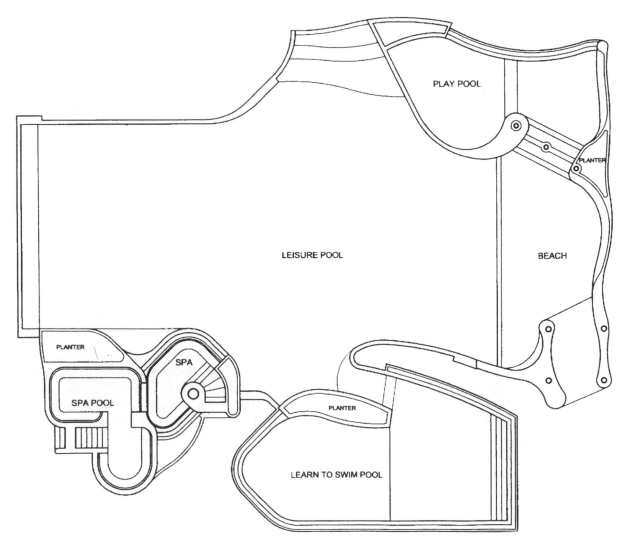

Figure 6.16   Layout for a leisure pool.

Layouts of leisure pools vary considerably from one centre to the next, with the general layout determined by the nature of integrated leisure components. Increasingly seen as a central component to a viable aquatic facility, the leisure pool is effectively a free-form body of water that incorporates a range of recreation components, in water depths suitable for water play and recreational swimming, if so desired.

Only design expertise and capital and operational budgets limit the diversity of components. A leisure pool can be saturated with a variety of play components and structures, as well as an assortment of water movement features. These must be carefully selected and coordinated in order to provide aquatic areas that can be easily supervised and that offer patrons a safe, yet exciting and stimulating, recreation experience.

The principal criterion in providing a well-laid-out and thoroughly supervised facility is the provision of elements that do not obstruct critical sight lines.

The number of principal components within a leisure pool will typically be limited to one or two major elements and a number of selected features to support the overall theme.

Of the major elements, principal components tend to comprise some combination of wave pools, water slides, and moving, or rapid, rivers.

Wave Pools

As with all elements, these vary in scale and size. Principal design decisions relate to the width of the wave generation area, the overall length of the body of static water and the maximum water depth.

A wave pool typically comprises a graded pool floor with a 1.80-metre-deep wave-generation area as a minimum depth requirement for the development of a suitable wave. A series of wave chambers can be programmed to create a variety of wave patterns, as well as variety in the strength and size of the resultant wave. This means that wave motion can be introduced for quiet program times, as well as for more boisterous activity.

The pool floor is uniformly graded, at a gradient no less than 1:14, preferably 1:17 if space allows.

The extent of beach area is defined by the overall parameters of pool gradient, wave size and overall pool length. Beach areas offer the multiple benefits of a graduated access point for children, as well as offering access for the disabled along a graded floor.

The overall wave pool can be supplemented with a variety of fountains, geysers and moving water features.

Fountains and Geysers

These water elements add considerably to the recreation and fun nature of an indoor aquatic facility. They can be incorporated into the pool concourse area, into the surrounding landscaping, into the pools themselves, and even suspended from ceiling areas over the pools.

The size, strength and exact nature of the water features is endless in variety. They can also be integrated with a range of fibreglass play sculptures, which can vary in size from simple round sculptures set into the pool floors, through to large sophisticated sculptures in the guise of fantasy theme elements.

These elements can be assembled for individual applications by designing with readily available technology. Alternatively, numerous manufacturing organisations produce a range of purpose-made water play components, from simple water cannons, to complex play sculptures that offer a range of interactive water play equipment.

The key issue in their selection, arrangement and location in and around pools is that of safely adding to the recreation and fun experience.

Any new designs or ready-made equipment to be used must be carefully considered to ensure that the provision of excitement and stimulation is done with complete patron safety as the principal concern.

Water Slides

The modern water slide is removed from any necessary interaction with an area of swimming pool water.

Water slide flume designs, these days typically fully enclosed, involve sections of 'run out' flume. Essentially, the enclosed water slide gradually becomes horizontal in its final sections, forming a safe, level, run-out channel from each slide for the individual slide user. The length of these is dependent on the overall gradient and length of the slide.

As an example, a 12-metre tower with a graded slide length of some 80 metres will run out to a horizontal open flume, fixed to the level concourse, of around 6 metres. The architectural advantage of this system is that the feature is wholly independent of pool water areas and the slide can therefore be more flexibly located within an indoor aquatic complex.

From a safety perspective, only one individual patron exits a slide at any one time, eliminating the risk of collision and simplifying supervision.

Slide diameter sizes vary. Some offer patrons the ability to use inflatable tubes as part of the ride. In major theme parks, these may be assembled in banks of several slides. Within an indoor aquatic centre, a typical layout may comprise two adjacent slides of different excitement levels.

Future planning may provide for additional slide rides of varying size and gradient to be added.

Rapid Rivers

The term refers to a body of moving water along which patrons can be propelled at a variety of speeds, subject to the use of pressure-driven water creating an artificial current.

A river can be used as a stand-alone feature, or it can be integrated into the design of a leisure pool, since the temperature of the water is likely to be the same. Water depth should be no more than 1.20 metres to 1.30 metres, allowing patrons the safety margin of being able to stand, if necessary, during rapid moving-water programs.

The rivers can also be used to float a variety of elements such as foam sheets or inflatables in some of the gentler moving-water programs. As with wave pools, a free-board area above the level of the water is necessary in order to contain the splashing water. However, since these water channels are typically quite narrow, perhaps no more than 1.80 to 2.10 metres, supervision by staff into the channel along its full length is critical in the planned layout.

Islands and Bridges

If space permits, areas of dry concourse can be provided as islands within pools. These can add significantly to the amenity of a facility by allowing patrons the ability to sit and watch people from within the pool area itself.

Functional uses can include kiosk seating areas, lounge areas and so on. These are then linked back to the main concourse with bridges, which overpass water areas.

However, the notion of solid structures within pool areas must be carefully assessed in the light of supervision issues, such as pockets of water area that may be difficult to see into easily, or that may be partially obstructed from easy sight lines. Figure 6.16 offers an example of a leisure pool layout.

Learn-to-Swim Pools

These pools are laid out to offer a limited range of water depths, typically in the range of 0.60 to 0.90 metres.

Although a free-form edge can be incorporated to integrate a learn-to-swim pool with an overall aquatic interior theme, at least two sides should be square to facilitate teaching. A number of specific design features should be incorporated to ensure that sufficient flexibility exists in the planning of the aquatic space to accommodate a number of concurrent programs for different age and skill levels.

To maximise flexibility in class levels, each end of the pool should offer a level of uniform depth at both 0.60 and at 0.90 metres. Across a pool size of 20 × 10 metres, at least 5 metres at each end could be dedicated to a uniform depth, with the intermediate area uniformly graded. Where budgets permit, nonobtrusive leisure features can be built into learn-to-swim pools to improve their flexibility in recreation programming.

The provision of a stepped entry along at least one, and preferably two, sides to the pool is important as a teaching aid. These entry areas should be supplemented carefully with features such as entry handrails.

In close discussion with management, a range of lane rope anchors can be distributed around the pool perimeter and in the pool floor. These facilitate the layout of a number of different configurations of class size with lane ropes, as well as for the occasional attachment of inflatables to supplement teaching activity with some recreational elements. Figure 6.17 shows a sample layout of a learn-to-swim pool.

Toddler and Play Pools

As an overall plan form, these pools can be a wonderful opportunity to create elements of water fantasy and play, provided supervision sight lines are not compromised. Overall size should be no less than 50 to 80 square metres to allow a variety of users to play at the one time, without appearing to be overcrowded.

It is also important to recognise that, almost without exception, this age group will be accompanied by one or two adults in the water. Adult safety must also be a consideration.

These pools can provide a range of water depths, more in the 0.10-metre to 0.30-metre depth range, with the provision of a beach entry if readily achievable. The floors should preferably be horizontal; any gradients to the pool floors should be absolutely minimal.

Integrated recreation elements must recognise the sensitivity of the young and very young. If well designed, water movement elements can create a healthy, fun and safe introduction to water.

Elements such as balustrades and perimeter barriers should be designed carefully to balance the safety issues of the young patrons, as well as recognise their likely use by adults. Screening and separation from deeper water areas must be carefully considered.

Integrated seating elements are also useful to allow adults a close interaction with the activities of the children. See figure 6.18 for a sample layout of a toddler's play pool.

Supplementary Components

The following components for aquatic facilities can also be considered.

Variable Depth Floors

Where flexibility in water depths is critical for a range of programs, but the opportunities for building and water areas are minimal, operable floors within a pool offer a diversity of water programs at a considerable number of depths, within one pool. In a modern, multipurpose aquatic facility, a number of different water areas are often already present, combining leisure and formal water programs.

Operable floor systems are costly. In practice, the number of variable depths any pool will be run to must therefore be weighed against the cost economies and operational benefits of building a separate body of water.

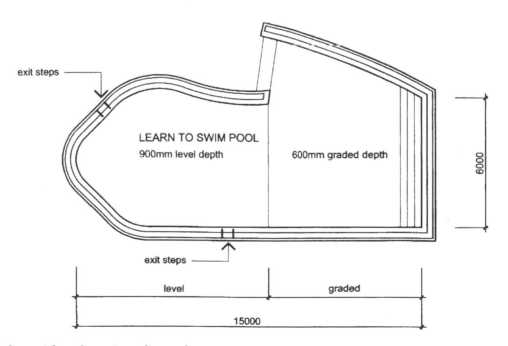

Figure 6.17   Layout for a learn-to-swim pool.

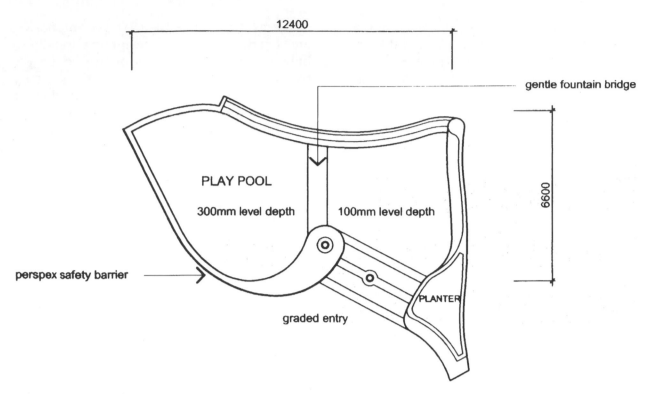

Figure 6.18 Layout for a toddler and play pool.

Health Suites

In an aquatic environment, the provision of a health suite area is often considered a desirable adjunct to recreation and fitness programs in the total centre.

A health suite can incorporate a range of components subject to community demand and may include spa pools and hydrotherapy pools. Some of the nonaquatic components may include consultancy rooms for services such as massage, physiotherapy, and so on, as well as steam and sauna rooms. These can be designed to create an integrated and relaxed environment that complements the indoor aquatic facility.

Site-constructed spa pools are preferable to domestic fibreglass units, which may not possess the longevity required for constant public use. The layout and proportions of the spa pools may vary from large open areas to a series of intimate and connected seating areas.

Hydrotherapy

What makes a hydrotherapy pool different to a spa pool is the dedicated provision of open, still water for a variety of therapeutic and rehabilitation programs.

Although the water area is typically rectangular, the use for other programs is limited, since the nature of a hydrotherapy pool is the use of quite warm water. In some instances, spa pools and hydrotherapy pools can be combined as a cost economy. However, careful analysis must take place to ensure that neither program opportunity is compromised.

Plant Areas

Central to the operation of an aquatic facility is the design and layout of a suitable plant room for a range of functions. Water treatment of individual aquatic components, air handling, and service functions of the overall facility are all integrated in a variety of service areas.

Subject to the final configuration of aquatic activity areas, as well as in response to external issues such as vehicular access, noise and visibility, plant areas may be a combination of distinct areas located either centrally or broken down into individual areas around the facility.

Examples of Good Planning and Design Practice

The following photos are examples of good practice in planning and design from Australian states and territories. If further information on these projects is required, see the photo credits.

Life Saving Australia provides good safety practices at Sydney's Bondi Beach, the site for Beach Volleyball events at the 2000 Summer Olympic Games.

Permission to reproduce this photograph has been granted by Surf Life Saving Australia, Australia's leading aquatic safety organisation.

In South Australia, railway land unsuitable for other purposes makes an ideal site for the new state-of-the-art athletics stadium. This is a gateway project to the city of Adelaide from the international airport.

Gary Edwards Aeriel Portraits, Henley Beach, South Australia.

This is the home of the North Queensland Cowboys competing in Australia's national rugby competition. The facility was formerly a racecourse. It now boasts totally integrated players' facilities and hosts major concerts, conferences and sporting events.
Photo by Cameron Laird.

The Northern Territory has the Micket Creek international standard shooting complex that attracts a wide range of shooters and events. It Is situated in a typical outback location near Darwin.
Jan Waddy, Manager, Arafura Games, Northern Territory Government.

The Waves Leisure Centre in Victoria provides the latest indoor aquatic technology including a wave pool, geysers, bubble jets and sprays as well as a formal pool and fitness facilities.
Waves Leisure Centre, City of Kingston.

Tasmania offers some of the best outdoor recreational experiences in Australia. This is a view from the top of Mount Geryon from Walled Mountain in the Cradle Mountain National Park.

Supplied courtesy of Tourism Tasmania.

In Western Australia, the Leeming Recreation Centre and Senior High School offers an example of community/school use. The facility consists of a sports hall, performing arts area, function room squash courts, playing fields and hardcourts, swimming pool, spa and sauna.

Ashley Wilson, Facilities Project Officer, Ministry of Sport and Recreation, Western Australia.

Tuggeranong Skatepark in Canberra, Australian Capital Territory, is a purpose-built facility that provides a range of degrees of difficulty for participants in this growing sport and recreational activity.
Rick Rand, Bureau of Sport, Recreation and Racing, Australian Capital Territory.

The Anchorage marina at Port Stephens in New South Wales was previously a boat building and repair facility for boats plus a slipway. Excellent community consultation led to the developers significantly modifying their project so that a win-win resulted in a 90-berth marina and 80-room, five-star resort with conference facilities.
Photo used by permission of Anchorage Marina, Port Stephens.

Stadium Australia is the centrepiece for the 2000 Summer Olympic and Paralympic Games. It is the largest outdoor venue in modern Olympic history. In the background are facilities at Homebush Bay, Sydney.
News Limited, Australia.

Storage

Ask any facility manager about storage and the answer will inevitably be 'not enough'. Yet storage is critical to the well-ordered functioning of aquatic facilities. The modern facility hosts such a diverse range of programs that storage is no longer simply for lane ropes, but for all manner of activity equipment, from small-scale elements such as kickboards and fins, through to large inflatable structures and rubber mats. All need to be carefully recorded and assessed to provide well-sized storerooms located as close as practicable to the aquatic activity areas themselves.

Water Treatment

A significant technological aspect is related to water treatment and circulation, since all aquatic features demand the highest public standards in purity and cleanliness.

Numerous chemical treatment systems exist; their suitability for any application is dependent on factors of cost, temperature, volume, turbulence and, of course, the exact nature of public interaction intended.

Principal water treatment systems based on familiar methodologies such as chlorine, ozone and ultraviolet filtration should be carefully weighed against ease of maintenance, suitability to the purpose and, critically, their cost-effective lifespan.

Supplemented with a variety of filtration options, a well-developed system can almost become self-managing with the incorporation of computerised monitoring systems. These constantly assess all aspects of water quality and movement and vary in the level of automatic and corrective measures constantly taken to maintain clarity, temperature and circulation criteria.

Past Does Not Equal the Future

From the late 1980s, the Australian approach has expanded into the integration of leisure aquatics. New facilities around the country are embracing the concept of leisure water as integral to the overall amenity and attractiveness of facilities, as well as adding to the bottom line.

Components such as moving water systems, wave pools, indoor water slides, and so on, had become an integral part of the architectural design palette in the establishment of new aquatic developments. As we move through the pragmatism of the 1990s, the momentum for continued growth and development appears to have stalled.

A formula approach has begun to creep into aquatic architecture; if it works for one client it will work for the next. With some rare and notable exceptions, the interest in and development of individual facilities is steadily being eroded into a cloning of current concepts, to the detriment of progressiveness in design and operational thinking.

Yet each successive aquatic development should demand a greater level of distinction in the consumer marketplace.

While the overseas experience of excess and extravagance is not necessarily one to follow, the development of leisure aquatics in Australia has stagnated. The provision of indoor leisure aquatics should be concerned with the provision of a leisure experience and an exciting and stimulating series of aquatic activities rather than the selection or rejection of one or two principal aquatic components.

Design thinking at this level considerably misses the point of leisure aquatic architecture. Informed leisure aquatic architecture and engineering deals with an experienced and enthusiastic approach to the principles of water movement, rather than simply a shopping list of components which have (or have not) worked for other facilities.

While the overseas experience can be considered overly extravagant, particularly in the context of locally available budgets, their continued development has at least involved an appreciation of aquatic principles rather than the repeated use of a common approach.

In the pursuit of innovation, the role of aquatic architects and engineers is increasingly dependent not only on an experienced knowledge of water as a design medium, but on a deeper understanding of the subtleties of water movement, in order to continue to surprise, stimulate, entertain and pamper.

This design responsibility must be equally shared among staff, clients and operators to continue to seek site-specific means of entertaining the public with safe, rewarding, stimulating experience and still leave them with a little of the sense of mystery and wonder of our relationship with this most fundamental of elements.[8]

CHILDREN'S PLAY FACILITIES

The following play space development model and facility design guidelines were created in order to illustrate the elementary factors required to establish an area specifically for children's play.[9] It is advisable that a long-term approach to planning be established, otherwise resources may be spread too thinly on each project, resulting in superficial experiences and facilities that are underutilised. The four principal features of any play space development are an active equipment-based play area, an active nonstructured play area, an imaginative and creative play area, and an adult and caregivers area. An optional fifth component is a special features area. See figure 6.19 for an example of a play space development model.

1. *Active equipment-based play area.* Play equipment has historically been the dominant factor in playground provision. However, play equipment should complement the remainder of the play environment rather than be the only play feature in an area. Play equipment aids children's development by providing them with purpose-designed structures on which they can balance, climb, jump, swing or run. The use of such equipment also assists in the development of social skills such as sharing and cooperation.

2. *Active nonstructured play area.* This is an open space area that should not be confused with formal sport requirements. The essence of such a space is to encourage and allow activities to develop spontaneously among the children. These areas often appeal to older children as a meeting place or socialising area or for informal ball games. Features such as cricket nets or a basketball ring set in isolation should be located on the perimeter of these areas with consideration given to the impact on the surrounding environment.

3. *Imaginative and creative play area.* This is often the most neglected aspect of play provision and it requires sensitivity to develop the possibilities for such an area. Some areas, however, simply need to be left in their natural state. Establishment of this area is usually inexpensive and requires only enthusiasm, commitment, time and labour. The natural environment lends itself particularly well to this element of play provision. This area usually appeals to younger children and creates an attractive environment in which

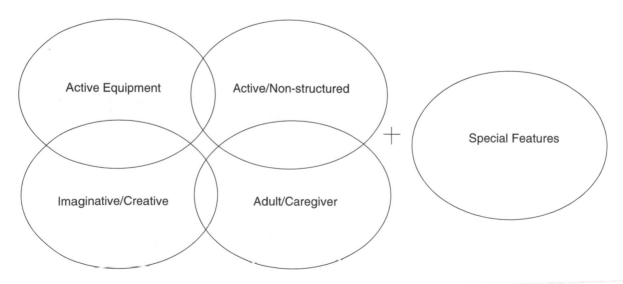

Figure 6.19 Play space development model.

adults can congregate. Many of the features are not specifically covered by Australian Standards.[10]

4. *Adult and caregivers area.* Adults and caregivers accompanying children to play areas require a comfortable area where they can oversee activities should they choose not to participate. The inclusion of such areas in playgrounds may result in longer periods of use by families or adults and caregivers with young children. Increased adult presence in playgrounds can also reduce problems such as vandalism and is also an important factor in reducing the occurrence of accidents.

5. *Special features area.* This is an optional component which may be included in the play space.

Although these areas are not essential, such features as a rollerblade or skateboard ramp or a BMX track can discourage children from practising their skills in less acceptable locations. Other special items that may be included are

- some sporting facilities,
- an open air theatre,
- a rotunda,
- a maze,
- a swimming pool,
- a lake, and
- a waterfall or some feature equipment.

Five Steps to Play Space Planning

The Play Space Development Model is used to plan the development of new, or the redevelopment of existing, play spaces. The following is a list of the planning steps that should be undertaken to achieve a balanced design.

Step 1: Inventory

Prepare a plan identifying

- boundaries, area, fencing;
- natural features, landscaping, existing trees and shrubs;
- existing equipment, soft-fall areas;

- existing services and facilities, toilets, water fountains, lights;
- access and pathways, dimensions, gates, etc.; and
- any other existing feature that relates to the site development, its current use or relationship to its surrounds, i.e. surrounding land use, roadways, signage, etc.

Step 2: Bubble Diagrams

Using the four or five features of the Play Space Development Model, arrange bubbles, allocating the various areas designated for different activities (equipment, non-structured, imaginative and creative and adult and caregiver and special features if deemed appropriate). Take time, consider and modify. This step represents the essence of how the reserve will be developed and is by far the most important step in the planning process.

Community consultation should occur first at this stage and as much publicity as possible should be given to the project. You should be prepared to rework the concept and compromise where necessary. Remember, it is far easier to alter the bubble diagram than the working drawing or the finished development.

Step 3: Wish List

Make a list of items you, the local community or other users would like to see in each bubble, that is, particular play items, specific trees, landscape features, etc. Do not feel constrained by practical considerations. This stage is fantasy!

Step 4: Time Line

Highlight the items that are achievable immediately and that would most benefit the children and then prioritise those that need to be deferred into an achievable time line.

The planning for many projects may stop at this point. If suitable staff can direct operations on site with a creative flair then a working drawing need not be prepared.

Step 5: Drawing

This stage is optional though good practice. A working drawing may be required for planning approval or as a construction guide; it can also be used to publicise the project and is particularly effective if seeking to 'sell' an idea to councillors or the public.

Note: Leave a copy of the plan and time line in an appropriate place for future reference.

Playground Facility Design Guidelines

There is a tendency to think of children's playgrounds as just swings, slides and round-a-bouts. Successful play areas, however, require other facility considerations.

Future inspection and maintenance of the facilities must be an essential consideration when designing playgrounds. Elaborate and complicated equipment and poor access for maintenance purposes could prove costly in the long run. The following facilities for playgrounds are listed under a number of sub-headings.

Site Works

Site works can be divided into two categories: hard surfaces and soft-fall surfaces.

Hard surfaces should be used only for the provision of access, for example, pathways, areas for some ball games, wheeled toy areas and decorative purposes. *Hard surfaces should not be used beneath equipment.*

There are a range of natural soft-fall surfaces such as varying grades of wood chips and many artificial surfaces to choose from. Soft-fall should be used under any piece of equipment that might cause an injury if a child should fall.

Landscaping

Variety and diversity of landscaping are essential requirements when planning for children's play.

Natural Play Spaces

It is widely recognised that children find much of the play equipment available today challenging for only short periods of time. Some studies suggest children tire of it after 10–15 minutes. It is further suggested that much of the child's imaginative play takes place with elements other than equipment.

It is no secret that children find natural elements, such as creeks, trees, shrubs and rocks, a far more stimulating environment than many of our manicured, irrigated and very formal municipal parks. This does not mean that there is no place for play equipment. Children will always be attracted to it and it fulfils many needs but it must not be supposed that it will provide for our children's total play requirements.

Children's Needs Versus Providers' Needs

An honest appraisal will reveal that providers often put their needs above the play needs of children. For example, how often do threats of litigation override a child's legitimate need for challenge and risk in his or her environment? Furthermore, how can children learn competence if they have not learnt to manage these elements? Playgrounds are often developed as a statement to the community rather than being based on children's needs. Perceived management problems relating to vandalism and antisocial behaviour often prevent the inclusion of many desirable features in local parks.

The real needs of children and the community must be put first when planning our play spaces, parks and gardens.

Remember that the sun is now recognised as contributing to long-term health problems in the form of skin cancers. Landscaping to accommodate the climate, in conjunction with the provision of large shade trees or dense smaller shrubs, can provide a haven from extended exposure to the direct sun.

Ancillary Items

The following ancillary items should be considered.

A variety of *seating* should be provided for both children and adults. If possible surround some seating by low planting so that children have privacy but can be observed. Climatic conditions should be considered. Some seats should be located in play areas used by toddlers and young children, for example, near sandpits to encourage a longer stay by adults.

Attractive childproof *fencing* with self-closing gates should be considered for use around the perimeter of areas designed specifically for young children or in areas located close to heavy traffic.

Some children and adults visit playgrounds by bicycle and provision may be made for *bicycle racks* adjacent to the play space.

On large playgrounds, consideration should be given to providing *toilets* with access for children and adults with disabilities and *shelter* from the sun and the rain. Shelters could be in the form of a large roof without sides. Appropriate planting should also be considered. Provision should be made for *drinking water.*

A wide range of *litter bins* are available. These should be aesthetically designed to fit into the environment and large enough to meet the needs of the users. They must be emptied regularly.

Children with special needs are often neglected when designing playgrounds. The principle of access for all children should be adopted. Provision should be made in accordance with the Australian Standard.[11] The following guidelines should be considered to provide for children with disabilities:

- Vehicle access and drop-off points should be provided with ramps as recommended by Australian Standards.
- Gates should have an opening width of at least 900 millimetres and there should be sufficient space around the gate to manoeuvre a wheelchair.
- If toilets are provided, they should be accessible for children and adults with mobility difficulties.
- There should be access for people with mobility difficulties around the area and between the equipment, and the surfaces should be nonslip, firm and stable.
- Care should be taken not to socially isolate children with disabilities from their nondisabled peers.
- Equipment selection and its layout should take into consideration children with specific disabilities.

Safety

A number of safety issues must be considered at the planning and design stage.

The Australian Standards have not been written as a document to restrict planners and designers but as a guide to the concepts involved in the provision of safe playground equipment. The spirit of the Standards is that children's play spaces should not contain unacceptable nor imperceptible hazards for the children using the equipment. The Standards are guidelines only.

There is a growing community concern about child abuse or molestation and attention is drawn to the following priorities for meeting parental and community fears. A playground should

- provide seats or shelter for parents or supervisors to encourage them to stay in the area;
- be situated so that it can be seen from adjacent houses and streets;
- be located in a manner that enables it to be publicly supervised by passers-by, park officials and neighbourhood watch schemes;
- in some situations, have restricted or controlled use; and
- in certain areas should be closed at night.

Try to retain the essence of why these areas exist and remember that planning and design guidelines should meet children's needs and not the preconceived ideas of well-meaning adults.

WALKING, CYCLING AND HORSE RIDING TRAIL DESIGNS

Walking, cycling and horse riding tracks are very much a part of most recreation and sport strategy planning. The demand for designated recreation trails and routes that cater for walkers, cyclists and horse riders have been steadily increasing as leisure time has become more available in the community. Trails are becoming popular as recreational activities as they require little preparation or equipment and are cheap to use. The following sections offer suggested guidelines for these facilities.

Environment

The planning and design principles for walking, cycling and horse riding tracks should strive for ecological sustainability. Where possible, track development and long-term use should have minimal impact on the environment as well as complementing the area they pass through. Linear parks or linked networks to open space can be used for dual-use paths for both walkers and cyclists. In addition there may be opportunities for separate horse riding areas in designated areas.

Opportunity

In many urban and rural areas there may be opportunities to establish recreation tracks for walkers, cyclists and horse riders. Open spaces such as parklands, adjacent watercourses, disused or unmade roads and rail corridors and existing paths can all be examined when planning recreational trail networks. If there is sufficient space and funding, the establishment of dual-use paths (DUP) with connecting loops should be examined so people have the choice of walking or cycling for a short period of time or for a whole day.

General Design Principles

Once established, a trail will become an important feature in the area, so any trail development should be in harmony with its surroundings and cater for needs of the potential consumers. The following features should be considered when planning a trail:

- *Climate.* If the area is hot and dry, there should be efforts made to make the trail more pleasant by providing water and planting trees for shade and shelter. On long trails, huts may be necessary to relieve fatigued trail users.
- *Flora and fauna.* Trees should be established or featured to improve the trail users' experience. The vegetation should provide habitat for birds and animals.

- *Topography.* Trails should be established to take advantage of landforms. Viewing areas across hills and mountain ranges and attractive corridors along river valleys can all enrich the route for users of a trail system.
- *Local history.* Contacts with local people will give trail developers an opportunity to incorporate historical information and features along a trail. It may even inspire the development of a theme for the trail. The development of an identifying name and symbol or logo will help in the marketing and promotion of the trail. Often, service clubs such the Rotary or the Lions are prepared to provide funds and assistance in establishing and maintaining local trails.
- *Available materials.* In many areas numerous materials and expertise can be employed to develop a trail. Infrastructure and materials can often be purchased very cheaply in local areas adjacent to the trail being established. Using local businesses and tradespeople can help develop local pride and ownership.

Walking Trails

When developing a trail, the following points should be considered:

- Consultation with the local community should be undertaken to identify the issues concerning the establishment of a trail.
- Development and management plans should be prepared that consider the budget, time lines, maintenance and future issues for the trail.
- Attractions (scenic, historical, physical challenge, etc.) must be featured in or along a trail to provide interest for users.
- Close access to public transport routes will increase the trail use.
- Separation from vehicle traffic especially in busy urban areas will reduce risk.
- Walkers travel at fairly low speeds and therefore require fewer design require-

ments to other trail users (cyclists, horses).

- Appropriate signage should be made indicating lengths, times and gradients of trail, trail direction changes, interpretation, trail layout and maps, warnings to traffic and trail users of road and trail crossings.

- The surface preparation should be able to withstand frequent use all year without being too hard. Asphalt can be a hard surface to walk on over extended periods.

- Risks should be managed to minimise the potential for accidents and injury by users.

- Consideration should be given to closures for certain local conditions and seasons, e.g. fire ban period, land management (tree felling in forests, lambing season, etc).

- Where possible, loop walks and networks should be established to provide choice for walkers and use of existing tracks and minor roads.

Infrastructure for Walking Trails

The following infrastructure is suggested for walking trails:

- Provision for people with physical disabilities wherever possible, including ramps, handrails, adequate car parking.

- Rest stops incorporating benches or seats, drinking water, shelters, picnic areas and toilets may need to be considered particularly along well-used trails.

- Gates and stiles should be readily negotiable by all users.

- Soil compaction by walkers or disturbance of paths by horses can bring about water drainage problems.

- Growth of trackside vegetation can lead to long-term maintenance, so the preliminary work while determining the route of a track is an important environmental consideration.

Long Distance Walking Trails

Long distance walking is a popular and challenging recreational activity that should offer broader experiences for participants, catering for overnight stops. It enables the planner to include changing landscapes and attractions along its route.

These trails should link with others or provide loops and link routes that return participants to their vehicles or link with public transport and incorporate towns, services or features of interest. The provision of accommodation within a day's walk such as huts and camps or existing local facilities must be considered. Linkages to public transport may be established in trail development to enable users to utilise a trail in one direction.

Because the trails will inevitably extend through several local government areas, close consultation between the authorities must be established. There is an opportunity to give the trail some distinctive identification markers and checkpoints to differentiate it from local and regional trails. As with local trails, an identifying name and symbol or logo will help in the marketing and promotion of the trail. For example, in South Australia, the Heysen Trail (named after one of our early landscape painters) is recognised nationally and internationally for its diversity of walking experiences.

When developing recreation trails, the specific needs of user groups should be given priority and people with disabilities can be catered for on some sections of a long distance trail. A trail management authority that oversees the responsibility for maintenance and development should be established.

Trail Markers

Trail markers may be provided at intervals that allow trail users to find their way in adverse weather conditions. Spacings of markers will depend on trail definition, intersections, vegetation cover and topography. Where the trail is well defined—for example, 4WD track—a spacing of up to 500 metres would be sufficient. Markers should be placed to indicate a change of direction such as at a track junction or where the direction is unclear.

All direction markers should be placed in a position where they clearly show the correct route from both directions. When marking along a track, keep markers on one side of the track if possible. Markers should be located no farther than one metre from the track.

The use of markers along trails requires the development of a long-term management and maintenance program. If budgets are tight, consider using maps that indicate clear checkpoints if markers are not a viable option. The use of markers can be costly in the initial development of a trail and will require regular checking and maintenance. Some trail users on remote ill-defined trails will rely on markers rather than using maps, which can lead to problems if markers are missing, vandalised or poorly maintained.

The walking trail corridor and immediate area is generally left in a natural condition, but occasionally some trimming of projecting branches and bushes is necessary. As a general rule, the scrub should only be cleared to a metre in width and 2.1 metres in height.

Any trees larger than 100 millimetres in diameter should not be cut down; the trail should instead being directed around them. Ideally, the walking path should be cleared to a width of at least 500 millimetres. Projecting limbs, bushes, logs, debris, large stones and saplings should be cleared sparingly to a width of one metre. Logs greater than 200 millimetres but less than 400 millimetres in diameter may be left across a trail to retain character.

Cycling Trail Development

With the development of lightweight, robust, multiple-geared and multipurpose cycles, more people are undertaking cycling for fitness and pleasure. As cycling increases in popularity, safe and convenient routes and trails may need to be established.

Before a cycling network is established, consideration must be given to which group of cyclists will be using the trails. In some areas a cycling network can be utilised by a number of different cycling groups. Listed below are some cycling groupings:

- *Recreational.* Use their cycles for enjoyment and leisure on a casual basis. They prefer quiet, safe backstreets or cycling paths and often combine cycling trips with family activities. Users have a cross section of available cycles including BMX, mountain bikes, hybrids, tourers or road bikes.

- *Sports.* Competitive riders who may use purpose-built tracks or a designated road route. In training they may ride along roads or cycling paths. Normally ride lightweight, narrow-tyred racing bikes.

- *Commuters.* Use cycles as a means of transport between work and home or to other regular activities. These riders prefer short, direct routes and may combine roads or cycling paths in their journeys. This group may ride hybrids, mountain bikes, road bikes, tourers or racers.

- *Health and fitness.* These riders often combine cycling within their fitness training regimes. They will often cycle a regular predetermined route, which may combine roads and cycling paths. They may ride tourers, hybrids, mountain bikes or racers.

- *Touring.* Riders that undertake long distance rides usually for an extended period (one day or more). They may use a trail network or the quieter, rural road networks on touring, mountain and hybrid bikes.

Cycling Network Development

Most towns and cities have numerous road and street networks that could be developed into routes for cyclists. Where possible, quiet backstreets which link minor arterial roads with cycle paths should be incorporated into a local cycling strategy. Opportunities should be investigated for developing cycling paths away from vehicle traffic routes if possible.

In many areas the walking track network may be widened to facilitate the building of dual-use paths. If a dual-use path is under consideration, appropriate signage, centre lines, comfortable two-way directional passing, clear oncoming vision and wide lanes for passing must be developed.

The recommended minimum width for a well-used dual-use walking and cycling path is 2.5 metres. *The Guide to Traffic Engineering Practice—Bicycles—Part 14* produced by Austroads[12] gives the details of correct track widths, signage and other requirements for the establishment of a cycling path.

Ideally, the shoulder or verge of a path should be kept clear of objects and vegetation to a distance of at least 1.5 metres to provide a run-off area for pedestrians or cyclists. Wide-open areas along a path will provide further opportunities to avoid traffic problems.

The surface material for this path will vary depending on use and location. Ideally, a bituminised, concrete or paved surface is preferred in high-use urban areas. Although costly to establish, such surfaces will withstand high use for an extended period (20+ years). This surface will also enable centre lines to be applied to delineate traffic. In Australia, the rule is keep left, pass on the right and this rule should be reinforced in any information brochures or on signs along the trail at appropriate intervals.

When designing a trail for cyclists, determine what speeds are safest particularly if there are other users. This will need to be considered when determining sight lines near corners to enable safe stopping distances or adequate warning times.

Cyclists may require bicycle racks at key locations such as rest areas, towns, attractions and service centres adjacent a trail network.

In rural areas or on minor tracks, the existing road surface may be used or a path may be surfaced with a compacted material such as quarry dust or rubble. Often, a local surfacing material is widely available and in common use.

Horse Riding Trails

Many urban fringe and country areas are home to numerous horse riding individuals and groups which are keen to find safe, long distance routes away from vehicle traffic for riding. In many areas, these opportunities are becoming more difficult to find.

The existing road network is not a safe option for horse riding, as many motorists do not exhibit caution when approaching horse riders.

If possible, quiet, low-use roads, disused rail corridors or undeveloped road reserves should be investigated for the development of a horse trail network.

Due to their large size and different trail surface requirements, horses should be separated from walkers and cyclists wherever possible. This will necessitate the development of separate bridle paths away from dual-use paths (DUP). In many areas where a DUP has been established, there should be a wide enough verge to develop an adjacent, but separate bridle path.

Many trails can be made to accommodate horse riders with minimal problems.

Unlike cyclists, horses do not require hard surfaces but in some cases they may require special surface treatments. The key to minimal damage and maintenance is the preparation of a good base for the horse trail.

Once the trail route is determined, it is necessary to provide good horizontal vegetation clearance (over two metres) and vertical vegetation clearance (over three metres). Trees and shrubs should be pruned flush with the trunk.

Horses require a good sight distance for oncoming traffic of at least 30 metres. See figures 6.20 and 6.21 for recommended tread widths.

SKATEBOARD FACILITY PLANNING AND DESIGN

Skateboarding is not a new recreational activity; it goes back to the 1930s and 40s when, as a Victorian skateboard publication says, 'kids attached roller skates to a flat piece of wood and tried to ride them down a steep slope. Some suggest that skateboarding evolved from a scooter, with the vertical steering system removed.' [15]

In 1958, the skateboard as it is known today was produced and since then the technology has continued to improve with the accompanying sophistication of skills and competitions. Today skateboarding has been described as 'urban acrobatics' and it is now also considered a sport with a high degree of skill and its own local and national competitions. It is likely to continue to be popular with

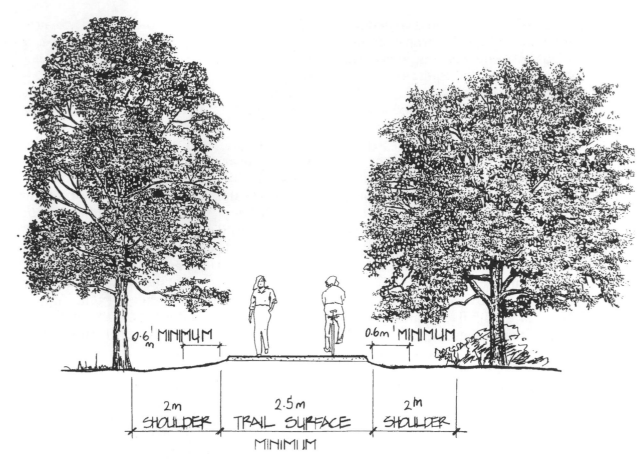

Figure 6.20   Recommended single tread width for a riding/walking trail.[13]

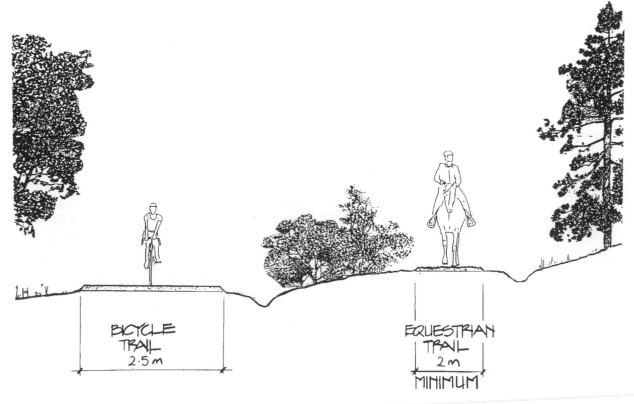

Figure 6.21   Recommended double tread width for a riding trail.[14]

a growing number not only of teenagers, but also older participants in veteran competitions that cater to those who enjoy retaining their interest and skill levels.

The facilities for skateboarding are suitable for other disciplines such as in-line skating and BMX bikes (see section on definitions on page 132).

General Planning Criteria

There are many sources of information on skateboard techniques and design of bowls, ramps and other facilities as well as information on events and equipment. The Internet has thousands of sources for purchasing personal gear from skateboards to clothing with a surprising emphasis on safety advice for what some people consider a high-risk activity. Also, local councils and skateboard outlets are sources of information about this growing sporting and recreational activity.

Construction of particular ramps, bowls, platforms and other obstacles are well documented on a number of Web sites, but there seems to be a lack of information on overall facility development at local, district and regional skateboard levels. The following criteria apply to all skateboard facilities.

Location

Evaluate potential sites keeping the following in mind:

- *Potential usage.* A demographic analysis and a needs assessment is important (see chapter 3 for planning methodology).
- *Size of site.* It should be large enough for skateboard activities at local, district, regional or state levels.
- *Access to public transport.* Most of the users will be teenagers. If it is a local- or district-level facility, safe access by foot or bicycle is important. Consider locating near or on linear paths.
- *Drainage* of the site.
- *Location.* Facilities should be separated from neighbours to avoid potential noise and nuisance problems.

Safety

Safety and other amenities are important elements and the following design features should be addressed:

- Safe spectator areas
- Low-maintenance site
- Adequate sight lines of the area for observation of activities
- Protective netting or barriers around pieces of equipment to guard against falls and to impede flying skateboards
- Walkways a safe distance from equipment
- Emergency access
- Seating
- Exposure to wind and the elements
- Shade areas
- Drinking fountains

Consultation

Professional and other assistance is required and there needs to be input from the following:

- An architect preferably with experience in designing skateboard facilities to plan the layout of the site.
- A landscape architect may be required to make sure the site is user-friendly and meets a number of environmental requirements such as noise abatement and access issues referred to in the specific criteria.
- Council planning regulations and approval processes.
- Skaters who can assist with the design of ramps, bowls and other obstacles.
- Safety experts who can take into consideration public and personal safety issues and liability risk.

Other Considerations

Adequate lighting should be provided to allow for night activities, particularly for facilities catering for district and regional usage. At least the issues of lighting should be addressed, such as noise and light intrusion on neighbours.

Take into account facility orientation to face north or south and not east/west as the rising and setting sun will make it difficult for skaters to see on difficult aerial manoeuvres.

Definitions

The following definitions of skateboarding and other activities as well as the equipment components that make up a skateboard facility will assist planners and designers to understand the nature of their use when referring to the diagrams that follow. More detailed information on construction can be found in the publications referred to at the end of this chapter.

Skateboarding

Skateboarding started with sets of skate wheels mounted to wooden boards. The technology of the wheels took a giant leap forward with the use of polyurethane wheels.

In-Line Skating

Sometimes known as rollerblading, in-line skating involves a number of single wheels attached to a boot, similar to a skate blade. Some of the activities cover recreational, speed, in-line hockey and freestyle or aggressive skating.

BMX Bikes

'BMX' stands for Bicycle Motocross. These bikes are a modification of the traditional bicycle made to ride on dirt tracks or for doing manoeuvres such as jumps. They are made to handle challenging rough terrain. The following equipment components can be integrated into a local-, district-, regional- or state-level facility:

- Fun box: a platform box with various transition curved walls built around in a box formation.
- Beginner's area: a large flat area with small transitions consisting of various shapes depending on the design.
- Half pyramid: a three-sided box with slightly curved walls and a platform on top.

- Quarter pipe: a platform usually built above the ground. The curved side is usually a quarter of the circumference of a circle.
- Bank ramp: an angled wall with a curved bottom angle that can vary between 20 and 45 degrees.
- Hip ramp: two quarter pipe ramps off-set against each other.
- Vertical ramp: two curved sides connected by a flat section with a platform at either end. Recommended height approximately three metres radius with a third of a metre being vertical.
- Mini ramp: two curved sides connected by a flat section with platforms at either end. The height can vary from 1.2 metres to 1.8 metres.
- Vertical wall: a quarter pipe style ramp with an extended vertical side that is variable in length.
- Wedge pyramid: a four-sided box with walls tapered into a flat section on top.
- Spine: two quarter pipes placed back to back with no platform on the structure.
- Bowl: generally in-ground with rounded corners and sides. They can be various depths and shapes.
- Doughnut: similar to the bowl but with an additional raised plateau area like a platform in the centre.
- Capsule: generally sunk into the ground at various depths, it has parallel sides and a semicircle at both ends.
- Street obstacle: various pieces of equipment that resemble the types of street furniture in most cities, such as stairs, guttering, ledges, handrails and benches.

Local-Level Skateboard Facility

The design shown in figure 6.22 caters for neighbourhood skaters who can walk or cycle to the facility from nearby residential areas. It should be noted that the following layout can be modified and many local fa-

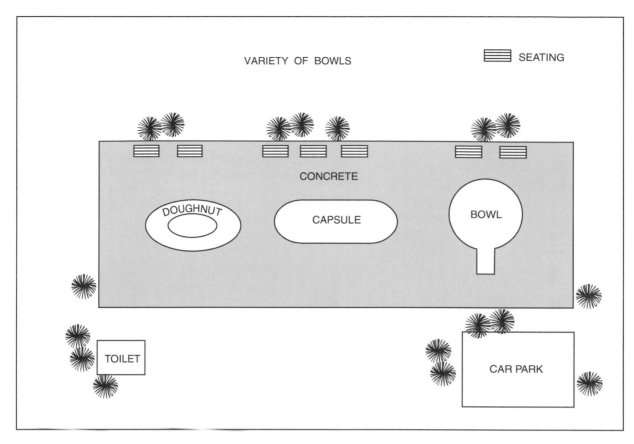

Figure 6.22 Local-level skateboard facility.

cilities may not have all of these equipment components.

The following criteria should be considered:

- Designing the facility primarily for street skaters.
- Providing a variety of ramps and obstacles for a wide range of skating experiences.
- Arranging equipment in such a way to provide continuous skating opportunities.
- Allowing space between pieces of equipment so skaters can use them individually.

District-Level Skateboard Facility

The following criteria should be considered for a district-level skateboard facility (see figure 6.23):

- Allowing for a larger number of skaters of all ages and capabilities than in a local-level facility.
- Locating the facility with access to public transport and safe bicycle routes.
- Designing each bowl differently to suit the style of skating.
- Providing a variety of bowls and ramps for beginners and more skilled participants.
- Constructing the bowls so that they can be ridden separately or continuously from bowl to bowl.
- Providing trees so that there are areas out of the sun for resting riders and spectators.

Regional-Level Skateboard Facility

The following criteria should be considered (see figure 6.24):

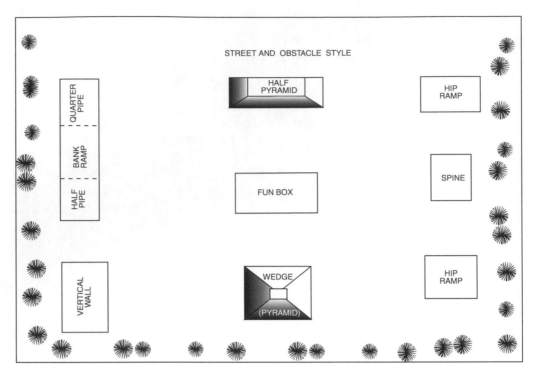

Figure 6.23 District-level skateboard facility.

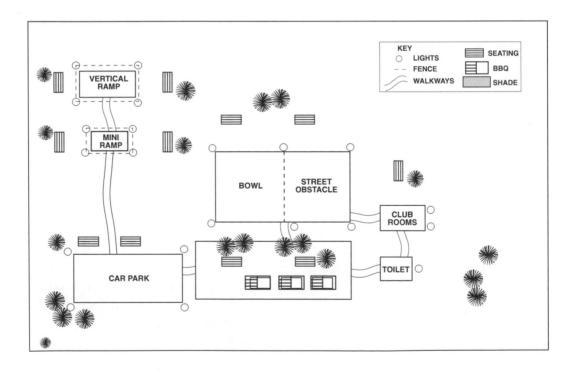

Figure 6.24 Regional-level skateboard facility.

- Allocating funds that provide the quality and diversity of the facilities constructed to meet wider skateboarding needs than those at local and district levels. This requires a commitment of substantial funds to provide an adequate regional-level facility. Consideration should be given for financial contributions from adjoining councils.

- Providing for a larger number of skaters than local or district facilities can, skaters with a wide range of skills and abilities.

- Constructing bowls with a number different transitions and heights as well as corners and hips.

- Combining the street obstacle and bowl to allow the skater to pass from one to the other.

- Providing amenities such as a drinking fountain and seating and barbecue facilities to encourage spectators and family activities.

State-Level Skateboard Facility

The top-level facility in a state or territory should be designed so it can conduct national and state competitions and open events to attract international-level skaters (see figure 6.25).

The following criteria should be considered:

- Providing sufficient funding to enable the construction of a facility that is identified the preferred site for top-level competition and use required for both sport and recreational users at all levels in the following categories: competition level participants; sports and recreational skaters; and skaters at various skills levels

- Locating the state-level facility in a central position with access to public transportation.

- Constructing a diverse range of ramps and obstacles suited for beginners through to the top skaters at state and international levels.

- Assuring that the facilities are suitable for all styles of skating, including skateboarding, in-line skating, sport skating, speed skating, recreational skating and freestyle or aggressive skating.

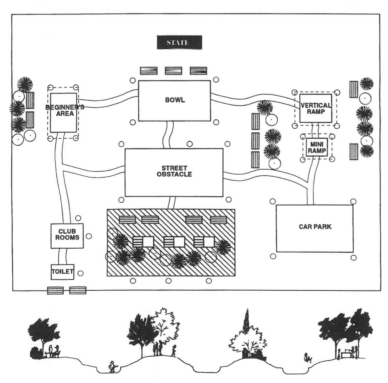

Figure 6.25 State-level skateboard facility.

- Constructing the equipment in such a way that each area is ridden separately, which allows for a more controlled environment.
- Installing lighting for night use.
- Creating a safe environment for users and spectators with adequate fencing.
- Making the area user-friendly with adequate spectator amenities, landscaping, shade areas, walkways, car parks, bike racks and toilets.
- Providing clubrooms with areas for meetings and organising purposes. They should also include toilets, showers and change facilities.

Funding of Skateboard Facilities

Because skateboarding is an activity that has grown out of using public areas by default, there has been a lack of dedicated facilities. Some public officials and community leaders hoped that skateboarding was just another passing fad that would fade away and therefore investment in expensive permanent facilities would not be necessary. The popularity of this activity can be gauged by the fact that during 1997–98 the number of Australian roller sport participants over the age of 18 years was 34,000. [16] These numbers do not record the teenagers who make up the majority of participants in these activities. Skateboarding is the sixth largest participatory sport in America with more than six million people involved. A better indicator of growth is the sale of skateboards and associated products that contribute to the growth of the recreation and sporting goods retailing sector.

Increasing examples of publicly funded skateboard facilities by the three levels of government warrant serious consideration of providing adequate skateboard facilities at local, district, regional and state levels through existing funding programs. A major task is to ensure that these funds are effectively allocated to viable projects, while also guarding against the duplication of existing facilities. The next section provides details of funding sources.

Indoor Facilities

A number of indoor facilities are being developed by both public and private bodies. A relatively cheap solution may be the use of old warehouses and industrial buildings but these are often in the wrong place in relation to access, pubic transport and safety. If the activity continues to grow, custom-built indoor skateboard facilities may be provided with funds from commercial sources to supplement the limited funds now available from public sources.

Managing Skateboard Facilities

To limit community conflict and often unfair criticism of skaters and their behaviour, a sensitive and cooperative approach to management of these facilities can be the difference between a facility that is looked upon as an asset or one that is seen as a liability to the community.

The Brisbane City Council Recreation Planning Unit [17] advocates the formation of community skate committees with the general public invited to become involved in the management of the facility along with a number of skaters. Their tasks are to

- suggest on-site selection;
- design input into plans of the skateboard bowls, ramps and other equipment;
- promote the facility;
- organise competitions and events;
- develop strategies to maximise the use of the facility;
- deal with complaints from nearby residents;
- take care of general park maintenance, including removal of graffiti; and
- conduct regular maintenance checks to ensure the site is safe and suitable for use.

Involvement of Young People

An increasing acknowledgment and awareness by government and community groups of the changing recreational needs of young people who are the main users of skateboard facilities is the first step. By involving them in the planning and design of the facility, then in the ongoing management, planners take a step towards gaining the confidence of youth in other community initiatives.

FUNDING OPTIONS FOR RECREATION AND SPORT FACILITIES

A strategic directions report in South Australia[18] produced the following funding options that have been slightly modified to be relevant to a wider audience.

Public Sector Funding

In the last decade, tight budgetary conditions in all sectors of government have led to a number of changes to the role, function and operation of government in terms of responsibilities for the provision of goods and services.

An area of government where the impact of these influences has been particularly evident is in the provision of community and economic infrastructure. The public sector has historically played a leading role in the provision and management of infrastructure with the government owning some 90 per cent of national infrastructure. To simply maintain the nation's $400 billion infrastructure base, let alone provide for new or upgraded needs, will require the expenditure of considerable public funds.

It is unlikely we will see a change in the culture of constrained public sector spending in the near future. Therefore, significant infrastructure upgrades or new projects may need to call upon nontraditional funding and delivery mechanisms.

States, territories and local governments have identified this trend and have been quick to investigate and test innovative methods of project funding and delivery. The following discussion profiles funding opportunities identified from consultation with government and private sector groups as they relate to recreation and sport facilities.

These options are assessed for their strengths and weaknesses and a way forward is proposed for further consideration.

Federal Government Funding

Since 1972–73 the commonwealth has been involved in recreation and sport facilities development, including aquatic facilities. In recent years the commonwealth has withdrawn funding for community recreation and sport facilities. A recent inquiry into the funding of community sport and recreation facilities[19] is an indication that the commonwealth is considering re-establishing a program to fund recreation and sport needs. It would be important that any funding provided by the commonwealth government for regional or national facility development be in accordance with the state and territory planning strategies.

State and Territory Government Resources

The state and territory governments have historically played an important role in providing funding for the development of facilities. This position is expected to continue into the foreseeable future with each state and territory having its particular grants programs for capital facilities.

Local Government Sources

Local government has traditionally funded the development of infrastructure projects (including aquatic centres) from three main sources: general rate revenue, loan borrowing and nonrate revenue. Pressures on these sources have seen the introduction of new sources or derivatives on established methods of financing.

Methods for Securing Funding for Capital Development

In the following section, older and newer methods of securing funding for development are outlined.

Rate Revenue

Competition for general rate revenues is likely to intensify in the medium term within Australia with local authorities prioritising project and recurrent needs to reflect community aspirations.

Aquatic centre projects seeking capital funding will need to demonstrate a business and a political case that gives a high or quick payback or evidence of community support.

While each funding case will be based on its respective merits, there is a greater potential for successful submissions among larger local authorities and those based in metropolitan areas than their smaller or regional counterparts. This is due to the greater revenue base of these councils and their capacity for discretionary spending. The impact of the importance of the political will as a means of overcoming financial constraints should not be understated.

The benefits of this approach are the use of readily accessible funds for defined purposes under normal budgetary processes of review, control and their lower cost to councils in comparison to loan borrowings.

Drawbacks include the use of scarce resources for projects yielding either a political or financial return that may be below that of competing needs.

Special Rates

Under certain circumstances, local authorities can apply special rates where there is a specific issue or project, a discrete community of interest, identifiable community benefit and evidence of political and community support.

While permitted under various local government acts, the lack of recent examples indicates the reluctance of local authorities to impose rate levies or surcharges. This reflects two issues: the difficulty in meeting the required parameters and community resistance to extra rate impositions.

Consultations within local government identified only limited support for this initiative, based on the difficulty in defining communities of interest that did not extend across council boundaries, and the lack of wider community concern regarding the condition of existing recreation and sport facilities.

While offering advantages of defining the budgetary requirement and at a lower cost than borrowed funds, the political costs of this approach need to be defined and clearly communicated. Project failure in terms of return on funds will also be more transparent with consequent risks and outcomes.

Loan Borrowings

Borrowing is an accepted method for local government to source funding for infrastructure projects.

The historical approach to borrowing involved accessing funds from the Local Government Financing Authority (LGFA) on credit foncier[20] terms where the interest rates were below those of the commercial market. This suited local government because projects were often for social or community infrastructure or involved activities whose returns were not of a commercial rate.

This position has changed in recent years with commercial lenders seeking local governments' borrowing business and councils responding with a reappraisal of these new funding sources.

An outcome of this new environment is the range of options available to local governments in securing loan borrowings. Low-start, indexed payments and interest-only methods are but a few of the alternatives available from the LGFA and its commercial competitors.

This has created new opportunities for innovative packaging of funding for projects, particularly where these developments have the capacity to generate returns and meet the debt repayment.

Against this backdrop, it is generally accepted that local government tends to adopt a conservative approach to financing. This reflects both historical behaviour and current perceptions among the community and elected members towards high levels of debt funding and repayment. There is a rule of thumb among local government financial managers that borrowing should not exceed 25 per cent of rateable income.

The opportunity to use loan borrowings for the development of aquatic centres is driven by a number of interrelated factors such as

- the council's rate revenue base,
- existing levels of borrowings,

- a forecast of project performance, and
- the cost and terms of loan funds.

The relative performance of these influences will determine the appropriateness of using this source.

Benefits of this approach will include the availability of larger lump sums for project works that would otherwise not be available through rate revenue, the cash flow benefits of interest repayments rather than one-off capital requirements and the transparency of funding costs associated with the project through the loan facility.

One disadvantage is the cost of funds and the requirement to manage the process in a commercially sustainable manner over a longer period of time. Another disadvantage is the political risks of projects that fail to match community or financial expectations. Finally there are the alternative uses of scarce funding for projects that generate better rates of return that could be applied elsewhere within the community.

Bank Guarantees

The provision of bank guarantees or underwriting of borrowed funds is a method that has historically been used by a number of local authorities for the improvement of sporting facilities.

Under this method, local governments borrow the funds and in turn on-lend to an organisation, for example, a sporting club that would be responsible for making repayments to the funder. The council has the option of foreclosure where the sporting group is unable to make repayments.

This approach has the benefit of enabling organisations with the closest contact to the project to manage the process using funding that is competitively priced. Drawbacks to this approach are the administration time spent by local authorities in managing the repayments and the downside risk of failure by the funded body.

Underlying this approach are similar factors identified in the loan borrowings section with the additional risk factor of the performance of the organisation whose activities have been underwritten.

Asset Sales

The use of revenue generated by asset sales (land and buildings, for example) is a method that a number of local authorities use in funding capital works initiatives.

In these circumstances, funds gained from asset sales are set aside in a capital fund for discretionary use in the following year's forward works. Whether this fund is used exclusively for specific recreation and sport facilities or as part of a broader recreation plan or infrastructure program is the subject of consideration by the council and the community.

Benefits of this approach are that there is a forward plan that can be developed based on expected sales activities, planning can be flexible to reflect specific requirements and there is discretionary capacity within the decision-making process.

Disadvantages include the short-term focus of such funds where the size of the revenue base is subject to real estate market conditions and the continuity of the political process.

Separate but Incorporated Bodies

Local government legislation usually provides for the incorporation of separate bodies for the purpose of undertaking specific activities. Examples of such bodies in South Australia include the West Beach Trust and waste management and environmental health bodies.

The establishment and continued operation of these bodies is a political process involving the clear definition and allocation of rewards and risks between the involved parties. In effect, they are joint ventures between local governments and relevant parties on a development, management or operating basis.

Separate but incorporated bodies are useful vehicles for facilities involving a cross-council catchment or where a facility is located near council boundaries.

This option can also be considered where councils commit to the management and development of a package of facilities, for example, recreation and sport facilities such as recreation centres, reserves, tennis courts.

Drawbacks associated with this process include the unclear definition and allocation of risks and rewards, the political risk of financial failure, the lack of direct council control, the management of partners' expectations and requirements and the need for ongoing funding.

Benefits are the reduced financial and political risk associated with sharing of costs, the improved planning and management process involving cross-council thinking, and improved economies of scale for the project's management and operation.

Future Opportunities: Revolving Fund

Discussions within the Office for Recreation and Sport have identified the prospect of a new 'revolving fund' method being developed subject to government endorsement. The revolving fund model is a derivative from the grant-based Sport and Recreation Fund with the primary difference being that the funds are made available on a soft-loan basis.

Funding for this program in the first instance could be in the form of an allocation to be managed by a government agency such as the Office for Recreation and Sport. The designated agency could distribute it to local authorities seeking funding assistance for the capital development of recreation and sporting facilities.

Applications could be received from both regional and local centres where relevant considerations (such as ability to repay and a facility operating plan) are satisfied.

Initial views are that the funds would be repaid by local government on either an interest-only or interest and principal basis over a defined time frame.

The proceeds from these repayments would be used to service other loan applications so that, over time, the fund becomes self-sustaining rather than a drain on the public purse.

The key attribute of the program is the servicing of demand for projects that are not yet on a commercial footing. The finance can be considered to be 'seed funding' for the betterment of access to facilities and as a method of repositioning existing centres to achieve sustainable financial and facility profiles.

Nongovernment Resources

The private sector has historically played a limited part in the provision of recreation and sport facilities. This reflects the impact of factors including

- community attitudes towards the role of government to provide what are considered to be community services; and
- the provision of facilities for noneconomic reasons such as access to services, economic development, and social and community development.

The scenario has the potential to change significantly in the coming years due to policy changes that are encouraging the role of the private sector in the funding and delivery of community goods and services.

Rationale for Using the Private Sector

The rationale for using the private sector rests on a number of key economically driven principles such as

- improvement to the efficiency and effectiveness of service delivery;
- inability or unavailability of funds to develop facilities;
- time constraints to develop facilities; and
- net community benefit expressed in economic and noneconomic terms.

Underpinning these principles is a range of specific benefits and features of private sector involvement. These include

- reduction in the size of government;
- minimised impacts of projects on the public purse;
- improved risk management practices;
- better project management and lower administrative costs;
- greater responsiveness to the needs of users;
- more innovation in meeting and securing funding; and
- more flexible labour market arrangements.

Such efficiency gains could be reflected in either lower cost of designing, constructing and operating infrastructure or superior solutions to infrastructure needs.

Access to manage the joint venture relationship and project can either be given to an independent group or remain under the auspices of one of the partner organisations. Policy and management directions are undertaken by way of board members appointed by the joint venturers.

Distribution of surpluses and the contributions to losses are undertaken in accordance with the terms of the joint venture agreement that sets forth the rights and responsibilities for the duration of the project.

An advantage of this approach is that it provides a risk-sharing vehicle for local authorities and the private sector partners. In addition, skill sets can be matched and tailored to particular projects and resources identified and allocated for fixed time frames.

Drawbacks for this method are the initial selection process for partners; changes in the expectations and requirements of joint venturers; the potential requirement for additional funding to realise the opportunity, risk management and control planning; and political risks associated with partners.

Build-Own-Operate-Transfer (BOOT) Schemes

BOOT projects are an arrangement in which a private sector organisation agrees to build a public facility at its own expense in return for the right to operate the facility and charge users (often government-regulated) fees. At the end of the contract or concession period, ownership of the facility reverts to the public sector. State governments are increasingly entering into schemes of this type across Australia with some noteworthy projects, including Melbourne's City Link, the Sydney Harbour Tunnel and Sydney motorways.

Recent South Australian experiences in this field have involved education and sewerage treatment facilities.

Each state government has developed its own approach to BOOT schemes around the central core described earlier.

In South Australia, the Department of Treasury and Finance Act is the clearing-house for BOOT projects.

To assist proponents, the South Australian government has developed a series of parameters to guide the private sector's involvement. The general principles are as follows:

- A strategic fit with the government's overall economic, social and environmental priorities, strategies and plans.

- Cost effectiveness and economic efficiency criteria are based on the proponent's ability to demonstrate that, on a whole of life basis, the cost to the community is lower under the private sector option than it would be if the public sector were to undertake the project. This assessment will typically involve a comparative analysis to ensure consistency of service quality, price, time, risk apportionment and certainty.

- Technical and financial viability needs are to be clearly demonstrated by the private sector together with a positive track record of project delivery.

- Performance criteria will need to be clarified and specified on a broad needs basis to allow for innovation by proponents. Technical documentation from the public sector should concentrate on functionality and performance rather than preconceived technical specifications.

- Risk sharing between the parties must reflect a realistic assessment of benefit apportionment against strategic objectives. Private equity and the commercial benefits to be derived from the project must be commensurate with the level of risk assumed by the private sector. The level and type of risk to be assumed by the public sector must be resolved prior to the short-listing stage of a project.

- Liability must be quantified and transparent for both parties.

- Ownership of the project must be undertaken as a long-term exercise. While this does not preclude parties joining or withdrawing from consortia during the project life, the program does not seek to encourage the use of short-term construction finance packages.

- Industry development is a key outcome of the process wherein the local economy can benefit at no net cost from the introduction of new techniques, innovations, employment opportunities or the development of sustainable business enterprises with a view to export development.

- Commitment to the project needs to be clear and definite.

The key steps in the delivery process for BOOT projects involve the following:

- Project identification, which can occur from either the public or private sector.

- Registration of interest from the private sector, which occurs by means of a formal approach to the relevant minister and agency. After an assessment of the strategic fit of the scheme, and the availability of information within government to proceed, an approval in concept to proceed is granted with or without an exclusivity agreement.

- Feasibility analysis of the proposal, whether initiated by the public or private sector. This will involve a combined effort from the proponent and the sponsoring agency. Conflicts of interest in terms of information need to be clearly defined early in the process and responsibilities must be defined. The assessment will consider the economic and financial merit of the proposal, the potential impacts on government policies and how well it fits with the state's overall infrastructure strategy.

- Approval in principle, granted by the government subject to the findings of the feasibility process. The preferred approach of the government is that tenders will be called for projects. However, there can be circumstances where, due to confidentiality and intellectual prop-

erty reasons, the public sector can negotiate directly with proponents.

Future Funding Directions

The next wave of development for recreation and sport facilities will occur in an environment that differs markedly from that in which the current projects were conceived and developed. Key among these differences is the financial capacity of government. Availability of private sector participation is both a constraint and an opportunity that will need to be addressed when planning the future delivery of recreation and sport facilities.

Using private sector funding is expected to be limited in the short term due to the issues associated with supply-side constraints. These constraints include

- commercial viability of recreation and sport projects in the face of other potentially more profitable opportunities;

- concerns regarding the management of public-private projects and demand issues;

- level of need;

- costs of projects using private sector delivery; and

- political will to enter into partnership arrangements.

For the benefits of private sector participation to emerge, there is a need for both sides to develop an improved understanding of each other's needs and expectations through education and consultation.

MANAGEMENT OF FACILITIES

Owners of recreation and sport facilities are often local councils who may have more than one multipurpose leisure centre or large stadia under their care, control and management most likely built with public funds. Other owners of facilities include sports clubs such as football and basketball clubs with stadia for large spectator numbers. Privately owned facilities operate on a commercial basis by entrepreneurs who enter the industry primarily to make profits on their investments. They are interested in facilities such as fitness and health studios, bowling rinks, squash courts and swimming pools for teaching and coaching. Very soon all owners of recreation and sport facilities realise that building the facility is only a small part of making the facilities viable. It is the ongoing management of such facilities that can be the difference from owning a very expensive liability or a lucrative asset.

Management Styles

Whether to out-source management or maintain it in-house is debatable. Owners of facilities are interested in the management style that produces efficient operations within tight budgets that deliver acceptable services. Two management choices can be considered: in-house management and contracting out.

In-House Management

Most facilities are purpose built on the assumption that funds will be found to operate them. If there is specific sports focus on high performance, then management might be required to gear their operations to training times of athletes and these often clash with other more lucrative recreational use. Often community facilities have a requirement to provide facilities for individuals and groups with special needs who may not be able to meet the normal fees charged. A social justice component to these facilities involving concessions makes it more difficult but not impossible to meet budget obligations.

Some owners of facilities contend that managing the facility in house makes it easier to meet the needs of special groups in the community and management is more responsive to the original purposes for which the facility was provided.

Contracting Out

There has been an increasing trend towards contracting out to specialist managers to obtain greater efficiencies and economies. Advocates of contracting out would argue that a well-prepared contract can build in social

justice elements and determine who is to pay for them.

Examples of good practice can be found to support of both propositions. As Graeme Alder, Chief Executive of Leisure Australia, says, 'In their best form, private management and public management are generally as good as one another. To my knowledge, there is no evidence to suggest otherwise, however, on a situation basis I believe it can be argued that public management is more suitable where the owner requires more day to day control and private management is best where political interference is likely to frustrate the owner's desired outcomes'.[21] The political interference referred to is usually from minority groups, difficult residents or even councillors who can consume inordinate amounts of administrative time, both of the service managers and the owners of the facility.

Seven Components of Management

Management tools vary, but the aim is to provide a clear mandate and accountabilities under which to operate. Seven components of management are now briefly examined (see figure 6.26).

Develop a Strategic Plan

A strategic plan provides the guide to where the organisation wants to be after a period of time, usually three or five years. The rate of change now being experienced by many organisations, including those in the recreation and sport industry, suggests that strategic plans are now more likely to be for a shorter period with opportunities to review these documents if the circumstances demand.

Following are steps for developing a strategic plan:

- Review and evaluate past performances.
- Analyse the market to make sure that there is a demand for your products.
- As part of the previous step, define your clients.
- Consult widely with existing participants, potential customers, staff and any groups or individuals who can make a

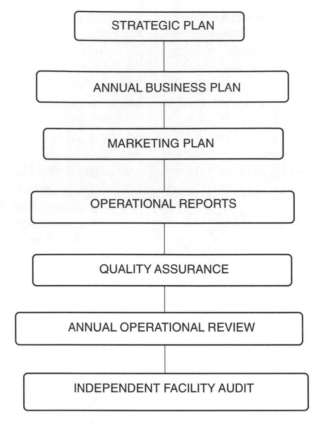

Figure 6.26   The seven components of management.

contribution to defining what they want from the service. Consultation techniques used should be nonthreatening and, as much as possible, free of bias.

- Prepare a vision or mission statement. This should be short and should summarise clearly the main purpose.

- Formulate policies which are overall statements of intent.

- Develop goals that can be translated into end results.

- Identify strategies that are the methods by which the goals will be attained.

Provide an Annual Business Plan

A business plan is usually for 12 months and it becomes the working tool to refine the strategic plan with step-by-step details of how the strategies in the three-year strategic plan are to be achieved.

In most cases, the policy-making body, usually the board, council or governing body, requires a monthly summary of how the policies

and strategies are being implemented. Staff members also use this business plan as a management tool to indicate the strengths and weaknesses in the organisational structure and adjust the human and financial resources as soon as possible. It is no use realising that there is a problem in the third year of the strategy plan and then making panic management decisions that are usually too late.

The components of a business plan are as follows:

- Goals and strategies in abbreviated form should be up front as part of the business plan.

- Actions are the means by which the strategies are to be implemented.

- Targets provide the board and staff with a guide as to how they are proceeding towards achieving the goal.

- Time lines for actions are important to keep both management and staff on track.

- Performance measures need to be established and agreed to so that everyone is clear about what is required. Performance measures will be discussed further under the sections on audit and operational reviews.

Prepare a Marketing Plan

Because most recreation and sport facilities compete for the time of their participants against many other interests, it is important that constant marketing is undertaken to retain current users, encourage new participants and educate the community about the facility.

The characteristics of a marketing plan are

- flexibility to meet the inevitable changes in the program as the year unfolds;
- constant updating of the promotional activities;
- regular marketing analysis to make sure that the promotions are reaching their target groups;
- marketing intelligence (that is, know your markets);
- a detailed, well-funded promotional plan with clear forecasts and measurable targets;
- monthly reporting of marketing activities to the board; and
- clearly identified staff responsibility for each promotional activity.

A successful marketing plan should focus on the four Cs (community, customers, competition and clients[22]) and have a monitored sales system that includes

- phone enquires that offer free visits,
- tours of the facility,
- membership follow-ups,
- a promotional calendar of events,
- trial periods,
- feedback mechanisms to gauge the effect of the marketing plan,
- customer-retention statistics, and
- measurement of the sales system.

Detailed Monthly Operational Reports

Most management committees or boards meet monthly. At these meetings they should receive detailed monthly operational reports on each program, which summarises

- statistics of attendances in percentages against that predicted figures;
- financial information against budget estimates;
- achievements measured against what was what was set down as achievable;
- priorities as determined in the business plan (these could be in percentage terms); and
- wherever possible, the manager or relevant staff responsible for specific programs.

A Certified Quality Assurance System

There is a difference between how courts of law view standards as opposed to guidelines when determining the standard of care in negligence claims. Obviously, the adoption of standards approved by a reputable body hold more weight in law.

Some recreation and sport facilities and programs are adopting certified quality assurance standards approved by Standards Australia and New Zealand ISO 9001:1994 and 9002:1994.[23]

Quality endorsement is compliance with specifications and meeting customer expectations.

Note: these standards are not specifically designed for recreation and sport programs or services, but they can be adapted to meet the use of leisure centres and similar operations that deliver less tangible products and services.

Standard 9000-1 covers guidelines for selection and use of programs and services while 9000-2 deals with generic guidelines for application of 9000-1. Having to meet standards set by an independent body is a powerful incentive for quality performance. Other incentives are quality audits that include training of staff, open inspections, corrective and preventive actions, and maintainance of quality records and statistics.

The fact that there is a commitment to writing down what is done, then having it checked by an outside authority, provides an incentive for maintaining high standards of programs and services.

Annual Operational Review

It is important to continually monitor the facility performance against the needs and expectations of the users.

To obtain an objective comparison with other similar facilities can assist in the delivery of high standard performance across a number of indicators. A fee for service is offered by a nonprofit organisation called CERMS (The Centre for Environmental and Recreation Management at the University of South Australia).[24] After six years of benchmarking of performance indicators, CERMS offers their clients confidential information on how facilities compare in terms of

- national trends(over the last three years);
- industry categories (aquatic, dry venues, golf and outdoor sport facilities);
- internal comparisons over time; and
- criteria-based best-practice indicators.

One of the major benchmarking facets is the use of objective, measurable data as reference points. Provided that the reference points or indicators are important to the goals, needs and requirements of a particular organisation, they can be a valuable addition to the whole decision-making process, giving an organisation quantifiable measures to focus on.

Facility reviews serve two purposes. First, they enable managers to establish, monitor and manage the customer-stakeholder-managerial relationship by way of cost-effective, nationally relevant performance indicators of operational effectiveness, including efficiency and customer service quality. Second, they enable a determination of appropriate levels of service for the target population.

Consider Introducing an Independent Facility Audit

An independent facility audit provides an independent check on the centre against predetermined standards. This type of audit can be done in house by a manager or person who is not on the staff of the centre, but who knows the quality standards set by the organisation.

Leisure Australia[25] use the following criteria in what they describe as a close examination and analysis:

- Quality and efficiency indicators
- Progress on business plan outcomes
- Facility presentation (the cleanliness, standard of maintenance and services)
- Risk management
- Management systems
- Labour audit
- Financial performance
- Centre promotion
- Programs and services

The results are graded as (U) unsatisfactory, (N) nonconformance (minor) which means that they can be brought up to standard without too much effort, (S) satisfactory, (G) good and (E) excellent. These gradings are carried out once a year and require a day on site and a day to write the report.

Following is a collection of the most prevalent mistakes made in recreation and sport facility planning, design and management. It may be useful to planners, entrepreneurs, management committees and financial backers of projects.

- Failure to carry out a needs analysis to determine if the recreation or sports facility is *really* wanted.
- Planning the facility without deciding on the type of management structure, e.g. in-house or out-sourced.
- Manager and key staff not involved in the building design.
- Poor project brief of what was required (no market analysis before the centre

was built on who the customers are and what they want).

- Lack of user-friendly atmosphere (staff motivation on service delivery not part of their on-the-job training).

- Financial constraints leading to design cutbacks . Usually the first thing that suffers is the provision for storage and space for socialisation such as foyers and refreshment areas.

- Poor staff recruitment.

- Management tools such as an effective corporate plan, business plan, marketing plan and various audit procedures both internal and external.

REFERENCES

1. Office of Recreation and Sport [1998] *Queensland Sporting Facilities Plan—A Needs Analysis,* Queensland Government, Department of Emergency Services.
2. LRM Australia [1992] *City of Elizabeth Recreation and Sport Recreation Plan,* City of Elizabeth and the Department of Recreation and Sport, South Australia, p. 41.
3. Thompson, John [1992] *Planning to Get It Right the First Time,* AUSF Conference.
4. Standards Australia [1995] *General Conditions of Contract for Design and Construct, AS 4300-1995.* Canberra: Standards Australia.
5. Standards Australia [1986] *General Conditions of Contract, AS 2124-1986.* Canberra: Standards Australia.
6. Department of Tourism, Sport and Racing (Queensland) and Hillary Commission for Sport, Fitness and Leisure (New Zealand) [1994] *Getting it Right—A Guide to Planning and Developing Sport and Recreation Facilities.* Queensland.
7. Hassell Pty Ltd and Nicholas J. A. and Associates [1997] *Provision of Public Aquatic Facilities,* Local Councils in South Australia and Department of Recreation and Sport, pp. 36–45.
8. Bzowy, Rick [1998] *Best Practice in Aquatic Facility Design.* In Australian Parks and Recreation, summer 1997/1998, pp. 22–23.
9. Office for Recreation and Sport [1998] *Playgrounds Manual.* South Australia.
10. Standards Australia [1993] *Design for Access and Mobility, AS 1428 Parts 1-4.* Canberra: Standards Australia.
11. Standards Australia [1993] *Design for Access and Mobility.* Canberra: Standards Australia.
12. Austroads [1993] *The Guide to Traffic Engineering Practice—Bicycles—Part 14.* Sydney: Austroads.
13. Ryan, Karen-Lee, ed. [1993] *Trails for the Twenty-First Century: Planning, Design and Management Manual for Multi-Use.* In the Rails-to-Trails Conservancy. Washington DC; Covelo, CA: Island Press.
14. Ryan, Karen-Lee, ed. [1993] *Trails for the Twenty-First Century.*
15. Sport and Recreation Ministers' Council [1990] *Skateboard Facility Planning—A Manual for Local Government.* Melbourne: Sport and Recreation.
16. Australian Bureau of Statistics [1998] *Participation in Sport and Physical Activities,* Catalogue 4177.0 1997-98. Commonwealth of Australia, ACT, Canberra.
17. Community Development Branch Recreation Planning Unit [1997] *Brisbane Skate Story.* Brisbane City Council.
18. Hassell Pty Ltd and Nicholas J.A. and Associates [1997] *Provision of Public Aquatic Facilities.* pp. 46–59. Adelaide: Adelaide City Council.
19. House of Representatives Standing Committee on Environment, Recreation and the Arts [1997] *Rethinking the Funding of Community Sporting and Recreational Facilities: A Sporting Chance.* Canberra: Australian Government Publishing Service.
20. A loan that is mathematically designed to reduce progressively the loan's balance to zero.
21. Alder, Graeme [1998] *Private Versus Public Leisure Management,* in Leisure Exchange Journal, Ministry of Sport and Recreation and the Leisure Institute of WA, p. 10.
22. Leisure Australia [1998] *7 Step Cellular Business Planning Technique.* South Australia: Leisure Australia.
23. Standards Australia and Standards New Zealand [1994] *Quality Systems—Model for Quality Assurance in Design, Development, Production, Installation and Services ISO 9001 and 9002.* Australia. Sydney: Standards Australia.
24. Centre for Environmental and Recreation Management [1998] *CERMS Performance Indicators Project.* University of South Australia.
25. Leisure Australia [1997] *Facility Audit Certificate.* South Australia: Leisure Australia Incorporated.

CHAPTER
7

Coastal Recreation Planning and Design

Australia's relatively unspoiled coastline attracts increasing numbers of people who wish to participate in a wide range of recreational activities. This chapter provides guidelines to assist planners, government policy makers and developers to meet the increasing demand for recreation facilities and services and at the same time preserve the coastal environment.

Human safety is a high priority in satisfying the requirements of coastal users and this is of equal importance when meeting environmentally sustainable development guidelines. Recreation can be a good environmental citizen and the coast offers opportunities to develop planning which protects sensitive natural features along the coast and at the same time caters for people who wish to enjoy a growing range of coastal recreation activities.

The aims of coastal recreation are first clarified, then some potential conflicts identified. Coastal recreation objectives and principles including an integrated planning process are then detailed, followed by a number of design guidelines for coastal recreation facilities such as marinas, boat ramps and recreational jetties. Detailed attention is given to describing 19 diversified recreation activities that impact on coastal planning. Effective management of recreation activities is an important key to good ongoing coastal recreation planning of facilities and services. The problems of risk management are also dis-cussed followed by three examples of good coastal recreation practice, concluding with some practical steps for coastal planners.

BACKGROUND

People are increasingly turning to the coast for enjoyment of a wide range of active recreational and sport activities. Statistical information indicates that a significant growth can be predicted in recreation facilities and services along the Australian coast. The development of guidelines will assist in meeting expected demand and will help avoid costly mistakes.

It is in the interests of planners, architects, environmentalists, developers, managers of facilities and officers of government agencies involved in policy setting to employ these guidelines.

THE AUSTRALIAN COAST

Australia is often described as an island continent. We are indeed fortunate to have a coastline that is relatively unpolluted and suitable for a wide range of coastal recreational activities.

The coast is the land within the mean high water mark and the mean low water mark on the sea shore and also contains the land area within 100 metres of the high water mark. It includes the sea within three nautical miles of the low water level and consists of estuaries, inlets, rivers, creeks and bays or lakes that are subject to the ebb and flow of the tide.[1] Its length provides some concept of the scope for recreation uses. If the coast is taken to consist of all areas within or neighbouring the foreshore, the length of the coastline within each Australian state and the Northern Territory totals 30,170 kilometres, made up as shown in table 7.1.[2]

USE OF THE TERMS 'RECREATION', 'SPORT' AND 'TOURISM'

By far the majority of leisure activities along the coast fall into the category of recreation. In the context of this chapter, sport is considered a subset of recreation while acknowledging that there is excellence in such sporting activities as swimming, surfing, yachting and other competitive and high-skill activities. When using the term 'recreation' some readers may wish to substitute 'community sport'. For more detailed definitions of recreation and sport including an understanding of their personal, social, economic and environmental benefits, see chapter 1 'Benefits of Recreation and Sport'.

Some planners interchange 'tourism' and 'recreation' because various definitions confuse rather than clarify the situation. There are differences, however. The primary characteristics of tourists are that they are non-residents or visitors spending a considerable part of their tourist experience participating in recreational activities. Another way of defining tourism is by identifying the distance travelled and the number of nights away from home. A distance of more than 200 kilometres from home or at least one night spent away from home is sometimes used as the criterion.

Governments often have their own definitions of tourism depending on the economic contribution tourists bring to their areas. For example, from the national point of view, tourists are those from overseas who bring new money into Australia. State governments suggest that tourists are visitors from interstate and overseas who bring new tourist dollars to the state or territory and local councils often consider tourists as those who bring economic benefits to their businesses regardless of where the visitors have come from.

Whatever definition is used, tourists enjoy the coast for a variety of reasons, which usually results in their participating in various active, enjoyable and socially satisfying recreational activities. Recreation or sport tourism is a growing market segment but by far the main users of the coast are local people or those who travel within a district or region to use coastal recreation facilities and services on a daily basis.

EXTENT OF COASTAL RECREATION ACTIVITY

Because the major population centres in Australia are concentrated on the coast, it is inevitable that the magnificent beaches and clean environment provide ideal opportunities for a wide range of coastal-based recreation activities.

Information on international visitor preferences suggests that '9% of visitors indicated that Australia's beaches were an influence in their decision to visit Australia'.[3] The same survey indicates that another 7 per cent of visitors were interested in nature-based activities including bushwalking and scuba diving which can also be beach activities.

No reliable data is available on the number of Australians who participate in coastal

Table 7.1   Length of Coastline Per State/Territory

State/territory	Length of coastline (kms)
Western Australia	10,100
Queensland	6,080
Northern Territory	5,030
South Australia	3,270
Tasmania	2,230
New South Wales	1,740
Victoria	1,720
Total	30,170 kilometres

recreation activities. Statistics from the Australian Bureau of Statistics focus on organised sporting and physical activities and do not represent the many other people of all ages who enjoy beach and boating activities in family or other social settings. Table 7.2 indicates that between 1993 and 1997 there was an increase in the number of Australians over 15 years of age who had a playing and nonplaying involvement in sport and physical recreation (but nonspectator involvement) of 164,900.[4 & 5] It can be assumed that there was an increase in coastal recreation activities as part of this overall increase.

Anecdotal information from sports and recreation associations suggests that coastal outdoor activities are likely to grow significantly over the next five to ten years. Careful planning strategies are required if the expected growth is to be managed without deterioration in the very coastal environment that attracts these recreational activities in the first place.

ECONOMIC IMPACT OF COASTAL RECREATION

Early settlement in Australia was along the coast, so the first housing in the major cities was developed there. Over the years, these once fashionable coastal areas have deteriorated, but as the demand for coastal recreation activities grows, local councils and state governments are recognising the economic importance of revitalising older coastal suburbs. This change of planning policy is shifting the centre of gravity of many Australian cities back towards the coast.

Three economic indicators are provided to demonstrate the importance of recreation.

Expenditure on Coastal Recreation Activities

A significant economic indicator is expenditure on transport, clothing and equipment by people in order to participate in their chosen recreation activity. These financial outlays flow on to the business community and to the local, state and national economies (see table 7.3).[6]

Employment Potential of Recreation

Another economic indicator is employment in businesses and services associated with the coast and marine sector.

Recent Australian Bureau of Statistics (ABS) figures indicate that for the 12 months ending March 1997, approximately 328,000 men and women over the age of 15 years were employed in recreation and sporting occupations.[7] Approximately half of these would be working full time, that is, at least 35 hours a week. There are no meaningful breakdowns of employment in recreation occupations associated with coastal activities, but a recent ABS publication indicated that 'Employment in the sport and recreation sector is higher than the following industries: Mining, Electricity, Gas, and Water Supply and Communication Services'.[8]

The many recreation and sport activities and services could not be offered without volunteers who give freely of their time and spend significantly on services and equipment to further their interests: they also generate jobs by assisting to provide coastal services and recreational activities. An ABS survey of volunteers indicated that 828,200 men and women were volunteers in sports and recreation over a year.[9] Many of these

Table 7.2	Involvement in Sport and Recreation 1993–1997		
Involvement	**1993**	**1997**	**Increase**
Males	2,660,200	2,824,300	164,100
Females	1,844,700	1,845,500	800
Total	4,504,900	4,669,800	164,900

Table 7.3   Expenditure on Selected Coastal Recreation Activities

Activity	Transport	Clothing and equipment	Total expenditure	Average per participant
Canoeing/kayaking	$ 4.4 m	$ 4.8 m	$ 9.2 m	$316.00
Fishing	$27.2 m	$49.3 m	$76.5 m	$629.00
Sailing	$ 8.2 m	$38.9 m	$47.1 m	$639.00
Scuba diving	$ 3.0 m	$23.5 m	$26.5 m	$964.00
Swimming*	$15.8 m	$10.2 m	$26.0 m	$101.00
Water skiing/ power-boating	$ 3.7 m	$26.8 m	$30.5 m	$936.00

*Includes swimming in pools, swimming classes etc.

would have been associated with coastal recreation activities.

Cost and Benefits of Coastal Recreation

Another measure of economic impact is using a cost/benefit analysis of coastal recreation on, for example, property values in the area.

A recent cost/benefit analysis of a northern coast beach protection strategy, 'yielded benefit-cost ratios of 28 to 1 at an 8 per cent discount rate (percentage of discount charged by banks or similar institutions) and has a net present value (properties at today's prices) of almost one quarter of a billion dollars'. That is, every $1.00 of public sector funds spent on beach protection yields $28.00 of benefits to the community.[10] Another report by the University of Adelaide indicated that the beach is worth an average of approximately $0.55m-$0.75m per kilometre per annum. This represents a total capital value of between $220m and $500m over 28 kilometres of coast (from Seacliff to Outer Harbour). American studies support the above approximate values of beaches and reflect that beachfront properties command much greater premiums than in South Australia.[11]

AIMS OF COASTAL RECREATION PLANNING

The Australian coast is under pressure from two different directions: those with strong commitments to conserve the marine environment and those who wish to encourage commercial activities such as petroleum exploration and production, aquaculture, fishing and tourism. Coastal recreation has both conservation and commercial elements. It is in the interests of those who use the coast for recreation to protect and conserve the very environment in which they enjoy their favourite pastime. There are also business opportunities that stimulate economic growth through direct and indirect employment in the recreation industry and sales of recreation and sports goods and services. Therefore, coastal recreation planning guidelines should have the following aims:

1. To provide through sound planning a diverse range of safe, healthy, vibrant and sustainable coastal activities that will contribute to the quality of life of present and future generations. From a recreational point of view, human safety is a prime consideration when planning access to the coast.

2. To encourage planners, developers and people concerned with the natural environment to establish a climate of cooperation to ensure that planning proposals are not biased unfairly towards the needs of any one interest group.

POTENTIAL CONFLICTS

Local councils and state and territory governments and the commonwealth government are giving increasing attention to the sustainable use of the coast. As the pressure for more recreation activities grows, inevitable conflicts will need to be addressed. An underlying theme of this chapter is that recreation can be a good environmental citizen by using planning practices that emphasise cooperation and not confrontation.

Areas of Potential Conflict

Following are some areas of potential conflict that require planning solutions:

- Who determines the opening up of untouched areas along the coast for recreation and sport use?

- What types of recreation and sport should be promoted?

- Who is responsible for determining if a coastal recreation activity or development is unsafe? As a consequence, who will be responsible if litigation arises?

- Should the recreation developments meet the needs of specific groups, and if so, which groups?

- Who decides on multiple use conflicts between for example, aquaculture and recreation use of land and sea resources?

- Who pays if the environmental quality controls affect the economic viability of the provision of recreation facilities and services?

- Do local, regional or visitor recreation needs take precedence?

- How do you control noise levels of some recreational activities?

- Who enforces recreational guidelines and controls?

Partnerships and Sustainable Recreation

Priorities have wisely been placed on coastal environmental issues because pollution and overuse threaten the future of the coast, which is one of our greatest natural resources and provides a livelihood to many people.

Partnerships with other coastal users that emphasise the sustainable use of both human and natural resources are essential. It does not make a great deal of sense to embark on coastal recreation planning in isolation from other initiatives now being developed at national and state levels by various government agencies.

COASTAL RECREATION OBJECTIVES AND PRINCIPLES

Objectives and principles are a practical way of focussing on the essentials for coastal recreation planning. Throughout this manual the use of 'objectives' refers to overall concepts that place recreation into a context. For example, the first objective places recreation within its coastal environment. Each objective is followed by more specific 'principles of development control' which are framed not to discourage development, but to be positive in providing an opportunity to add value to the coast through environmentally appropriate recreation development.

These objectives and principles are mainly derived from local council coastal zones requirements found in the South Australian Development Plan with additional material from other Australian states and territories, the commonwealth and overseas planning documents.

Objective 1: Coastal Recreation Environment

Wherever possible, natural features and coastal scenery should be retained within the recreation zone.

The development principles should be:

- To preserve and rehabilitate sand dune systems, wetlands and remaining stands of native vegetation and fauna in recreation areas or zones.

- To retain areas of high landscape and amenity value including stands of vegetation, exposed cliffs, headlands, hilltops, and areas, which form attractive backgrounds to recreation facilities.

- To ensure that all recreation facilities and services avoid erosion and interruption to natural coastal resources.

Objective 2: Recreation Access

Access by the public to the foreshore for use and enjoyment should be encouraged rather than diminished by the potential development project.

The development principles should be:

- To make the prime consideration for location not convenience of access, but safety.

- To enhance appropriate public access to coastal reserves and lookouts.

- To provide access wherever possible to recreation areas via public transport.

- To maintain safe and convenient vehicular, pedestrian and boating movements to the coast.

- To give priority to recreational projects that benefit and are used by the public and are not primarily for private interests.

- To locate shelters, boat ramps, public conveniences and kiosks in safe, convenient and accessible locations linked to the surrounding vehicular and pedestrian networks.

- To construct boardwalks and other walkways to protect sensitive areas and ensure the preservation of the beach and particularly sand dunes if applicable.

- To minimise vehicle access to coastal recreation facilities by providing well-designed and accessible walkways.

- To provide adequate car parks associated with recreation services and facilities located in such a manner that minimises their impact on coastal features. They should be drained, landscaped and preferably sealed.

- To introduce waste management controls of grey water, effluent and stormwater from built recreation facilities.

- To provide access to beaches by horses, dogs and vehicles based on guidelines which outline conditions of use. This issue is addressed later in the chapter.

Objective 3: Recreation Open Space Provision

Maintain and improve the recreational opportunities and open space character of the coast.

The development principles should be:

- To maintain the recreational open space character of the coastal area.

- To integrate built recreation facilities and services on the foreshore in such a manner that they enhance the open space provision.

- To encourage linear linkages in the form of walking and cycling trails as part of local and regional open space networks and corridors.

Objective 4: Recreation Planning

Recreation planning should be aimed at gaining public and government acceptance of a proposed coastal recreation facility or service through the adoption of a local and regional recreation planning strategy.

The development principles should be:

- To link local and regional recreation strategy plans to other coastal strategies and management plans.

- To involve people in the recreation planning process through community consultation at various levels.

- To provide recreation facilities related to demand that prevents the oversupply and inappropriate location of such facilities. Human safety must also be a prime consideration in deciding what is an appropriate location for recreation facilities.

- To undertake development of recreation facilities after proper and thorough justification of the benefits to the community.

Objective 5: Built Recreation Facilities

When developing built recreation facilities on the foreshore, consideration should be given to their location and aesthetics. If built facilities for life saving are needed, the extent, quality and appropriate location of such facilities should never be compromised in favour of other coastal development.

The development principles should be:

- To ensure high standard of design with respect to scale and external appearance.

- To build recreation facilities with as low profiles as possible along the foreshore.

- To design and site the recreation facility to minimise obstruction to coastal views from other dwellings.

- To provide maximum possible waterfront reserve between recreation buildings and the water by locating recreation buildings in such a position as to minimise potential damage from sea level rise or interruption of natural coastal processes.

- To take into account the visual compatibility of the recreation facilities in relation to the area in which they are located.

- To design dense recreation structures such as life saving buildings so that they do not cover more than 40 per cent of the site.

- To locate storage buildings associated with recreation facilities away from the coastline and screen them with native vegetation.

- To allow for future changes in sea levels that can be caused by global climate changes using nationally agreed most likely predicted rises when developing built facilities.

- To provide adequate reticulated domestic-quality mains water supply and common effluent drainage for larger recreation facilities such as marinas, tourist accommodation, change rooms, food outlets and jetty ancillary facilities.

- To construct recreation buildings with outside surfaces in natural colours to merge with the land- and seascapes.

Objective 6: Recreation Zones

To avoid a proliferation of recreation facilities and services that may encroach on sensitive coastal areas, compact development should be encouraged using designated recreation activity zones.

The development principles should be:

- To locate facilities requiring specific coastal functions in designated recreation zones where possible.

- To create recreation zones in areas that are accessible to the public, but not subject to sensitive environmental or commercial needs.

- To avoid creating recreation zones in areas that have a high hazard risk taking into account particularly rip currents that are the greatest danger facing swimmers. Other safety hazards such as beach storm tides, sand drifts and stormwater flooding should also be considered to minimise risk.

- To ensure orderly development within recreation zones that limit the size of the recreation zone to meet realistic needs of future requirements.

Examples of Recreation Zones and Other Zones

Some states and territories do not recognise recreation as a separate coastal use. In New South Wales, there are various classifications including tourist zones, but no recreation zones.[12]

An example of the interrelation of zones, including recreation zones, can be seen in figure 7.1, with information from the Western Australian Marine Conservation Reserves.[13]

It should be noted that the recreation zone encompasses tourism and recreational fishing as well as catering for a range of other recreation activities. The importance of a recreation zone is that it defines clearly what is *not included,* that is, commercial fishing and petroleum drilling and production.

Canadian Example

There is a move towards objective-based zoning in which users and developers meet the

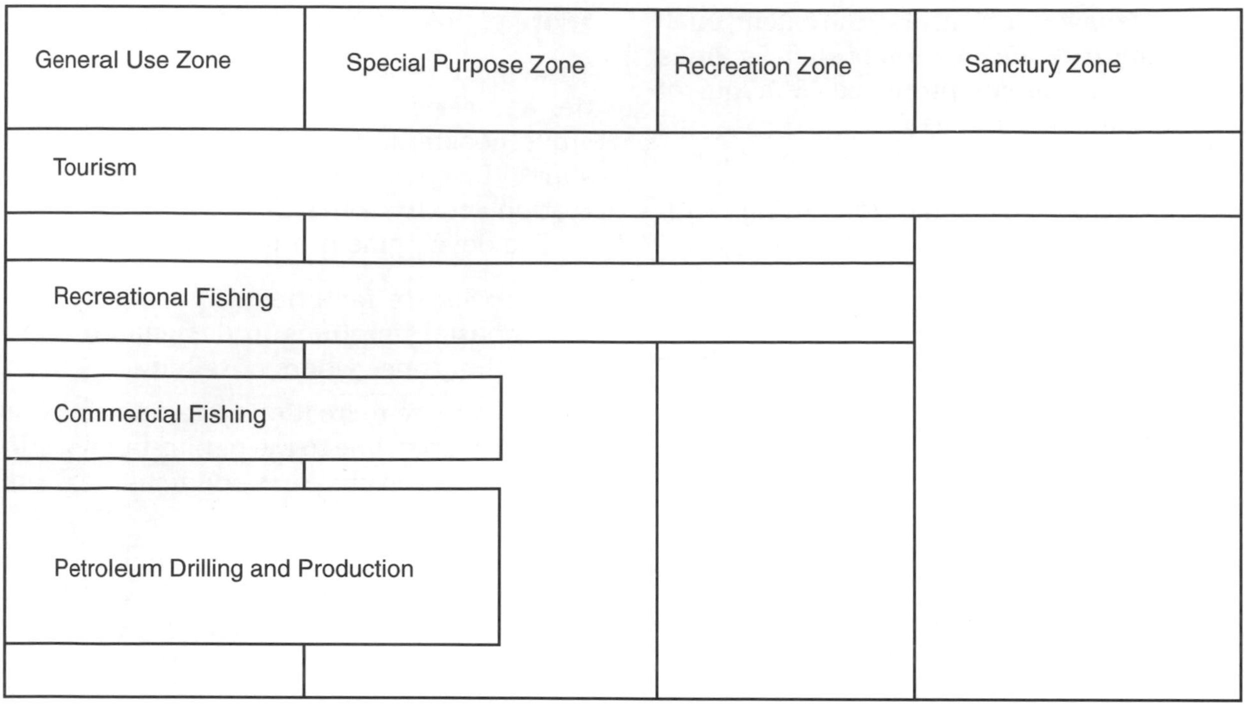

General Use Zone	Special Purpose Zone	Recreation Zone	Sanctury Zone
Tourism			
Recreational Fishing			
Commercial Fishing			
Petroleum Drilling and Production			

Figure 7.1   Possible zones and activities.

specific objectives of the zone thereby providing strength and direction.

Canadians have found that in the past, the development of government-formulated coastal zone management plans has met with limited success because these plans were not community driven.[14] Recognition needs to be given to local communities who are the best and most effective advocates for effective action leading to sustainable development. Although there are times when regional- and state-level priorities may seek to override local preferences, recreation and sports are often grassroots activities that are best developed from a strong local base.

PLANNING PROCESSES FOR COASTAL RECREATION

Various planning methodologies suggested for preparing local and regional recreation and sport strategy plans are outlined in chapter 4 and they can be easily adapted to prepare coastal recreation planning strategies. The recommended simple planning method in chapter 3 (figure 3.3, page 44) has been modified in figure 7.2.

This process delivers an integrating planning approach that protects environmentally sensitive coast and marine ecosystems and balances commercial, tourism and safe recreational use of the coast.

INTEGRATED PLANNING

Because coastal recreation is about people, the management of effective recreation programs and facilities requires an integrated approach understood by those who have had input to the process. A diverse group of service deliverers ranging from life saving clubs to jet ski operators to boating organisations should be involved.

Planning in recreation and sport is now demanded by communities as well as sports clubs and associations who wish to be involved in decisions on the location and design of their local facilities, including those on the coast. There are wider environmental issues for recreation facilities along the coast that are not easily understood at the local level. Every effort should be made to interpret complicated concepts and focus on how best to implement the project from a practical point of view while allowing wider inputs

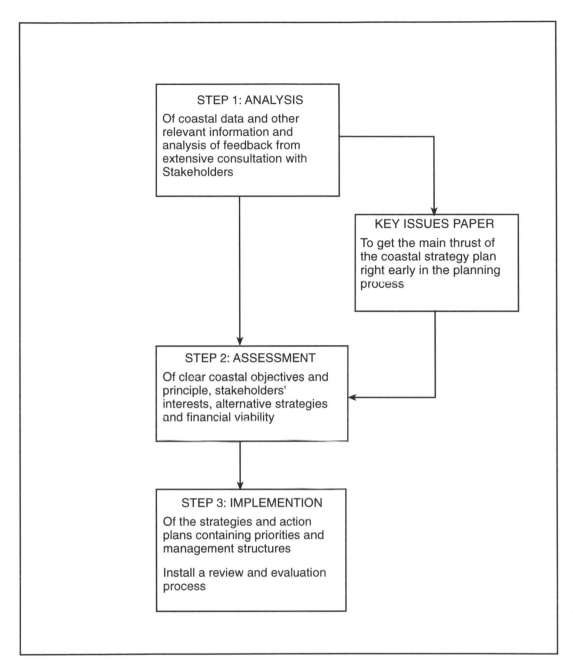

Figure 7.2   Three-step coastal recreation planning process.

from regional, state, national and international sources into planning.

In this context, the word ''integration'' means the provision of all necessary and relevant information from various sources in order to make objective decisions on coastal policy and development at local and regional levels.[15]

Local and regional planning involves varying degrees of information sharing across agencies. Many local councils and states and territories are developing local and regional plans for tourism, community services and recreation and sports that have coastal elements: these need to be brought together. Recognition of the urgency to come to grips with the complexity of coastal and marine environmental problems demands a more formal approach to integrated planning across a number of agencies to share knowledge and resources.

Figure 7.3 depicts how this integration works in practice as overall legislative and policy inputs are injected into the three-step

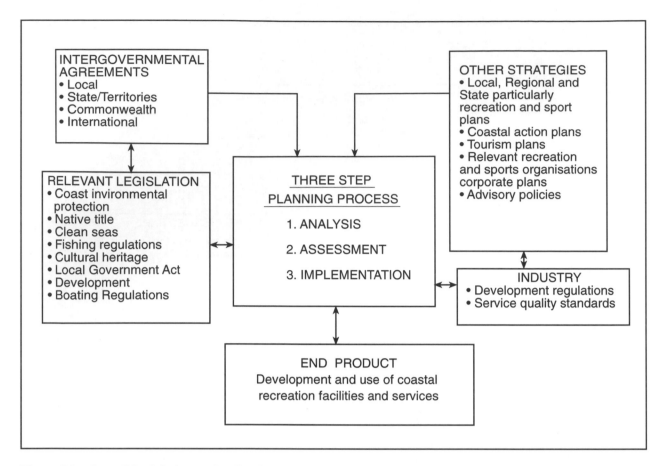

Figure 7.3   Overall legislative and policy inputs.

planning process at various stages. Emphasis is placed on the recreation planning components.

Components of the Model

The following components of the model explain an across- government-agencies approach for integrating coastal recreation planning.

Inter-Governmental Agreements

A rationalisation of government responsibilities is occurring to avoid duplication and achieve efficiencies. Increasing 'across-government' agreements are likely between the commonwealth, states/territories and local councils. For example, the provision of recreation and sport facilities requires funding agreements between various levels of government. Similarly, the 'Active Australia' program is primarily a government policy framework

to encourage participation in physical activity by all Australians. There is also broad consultation with the major industry sectors of sport, community recreation, fitness, outdoor recreation and health.

Other Strategies

Contents of other local, regional and state strategies are important not only to avoid the duplication of gathering the same information, but to tap expertise that can add value and credibility to the planning process. Local and regional recreation and sport planning needs to be linked to other strategies for tourism, health, education and community sportss and recreational organisations.

Relevant Legislation

Because the coast is a sensitive environmental area, many legislative and statutory acts and regulations are involved. For example, coast protection, clean seas legislation and boating and fishing regulations under various titles operate in all states and territories. Other relevant legislation could include native titles, cultural and heritage, and local government planning acts. These are not exhaustive: they point out the diversity of where to look for relevant legislation related to coastal recreation.

Industry

Recreation facility development and service provision are now subject to quality standards. Planners, architects, engineers and the building industry have advice on ethical practices that can be valuable in the development of coastal recreation facilities. As the sport, recreation, outdoor and fitness sectors of the recreation industry grow, industry associations are being formed to establish standards of service delivery. For example, there are boating and cycling industry associations in all states and territories.

End Product

Following step three 3, which involves the implementation of the planning process, there should be a measurable end product. If this is a built coastal recreation facility, the product is tangible, but often, recreation delivers services that are much more difficult to measure.

SITING AND DESIGN GUIDELINES FOR BUILT FACILITIES

Architects, engineers and planners who have training in other disciplines often develop recreation facilities. This section attempts to highlight those recreation elements that might be missed when locating and designing built recreation facilities along the coast.

Use of Existing Recreation and Sport Strategy Plans

Development along Australia's beaches is not new. In the past it has been somewhat haphazard, but now these developments can be linked to an existing planning framework or strategy at the local council level or state/territories planning at the regional level. To avoid duplication while obtaining economies of scale, these existing planning structures should be combined to achieve a recreation plan. Wherever possible, local and regional recreation and sport plans should be the primary tools to determine priorities for the provision of coastal recreation facilities and services.

Guidelines for Siting of Facilities

Following are guiding principles for recreation facilities along the coast:

- Locate facilities, if possible, within existing recreation activity zones.
- Take into account the inherent hazards of a specific coastal area and how these will impact on public safety. Provision of life saving resources in recreation zones can then be determined.
- Link with other regional services and facilities on the foreshore.
- Provide access to public transport.
- Develop sustainable coastal recreation facilities by having consideration for their size, type and location.
- Protect and enhance natural, landscape, and archaeological or cultural features of the site.
- Link to appropriate foreshore facilities for public use such as food and other services that provide for maximum public benefit and diversity of recreational experiences.[16]

Design

Because these recreation facilities are in a coastal setting, careful consideration should be given to the following:

- Determining the level of life saving resources that are needed to ensure that all due care is administered from the point of view of legal liability.
- Visual aesthetics of form and size. Sensitivity to the coastal environment will

ensure that the built facilities are not obtrusive but compatible.

- Recreation facilities that provide opportunities to demonstrate good practices in energy and water efficiencies.

- Facilities that have a minimal or preferably no long-term impact on the natural, heritage and cultural values of their location.

PLANNING AND DESIGN GUIDELINES FOR SPECIFIC COASTAL RECREATION FACILITIES

Specific guidelines for marinas, boat ramps and recreational jetties are provided because they are the major built facilities associated with recreation and sport along the coastline. These are not intended to be comprehensive because there are sources mentioned in other chapters to provide more details on planning, design, construction and management.

These are the first steps in testing the feasibility of the project. Detailed requirements for a particular proposal require advice from professional architects, engineers and planners with coastal environmental experience.

Marinas

Marinas are basically boat parking facilities, sometimes with ancillary repair capabilities. They vary in size and often obtain their economic viability from either housing or resort motel/hotel accommodation. Sensitive preparatory planning is required to make sure that the particular marina meets statutory and other requirements. The Anchorage Marina and Resort in Port Stephens has been successfully developed and serves as an example of good practice that is referred to later in this chapter.

Some marinas may need an accommodation component to make them viable and they are therefore primarily a tourist development project. The publication *Coastal Tourism—A Manual for Sustainable Development* [17] sets out more detailed guiding principles of plan-

ning, design, construction and operation of tourism facilities.

Key planning and design features of marina development are:

- A feasibility study that concentrates on an environmental impact statement which is mandatory in some states and territories and meets council and state government statutory requirements.

- Consultation with community groups who may either be in favour or antagonistic to the marina proposal.

- Sensitive design principles stressing landfill conservation techniques, sound waste management strategies and preservation of water quality in and around the marina, and the height and colour of the buildings so that they fit into both the land- and seascapes.

- High-quality construction techniques and the use of materials that will withstand harsh coastal conditions in conformity with relevant government legislation and regulations pertaining to the coast.

- Costing and financing projections of the project.

- Safety and management procedures up front to assure authorities that boating users comply with docking regulations, hazard identification, navigational issues, waste disposal, vessel repairs and maintenance.

- Ongoing staff training and monitoring procedures to create an awareness of emerging environmental problems. (Chapter 6 provides further information on management.)

Recreational Jetties

Around the Australian coast there are many jetties built originally for commercial purposes. These were the life blood of many small settlements before train and road transport was developed.

Today the majority of the jetties are used for recreational purposes. In addition their existence adds life and character to the communities in which they are located. Local and regional history is enriched by the stories associated with how communities have been built around these assets. This adds to the pride of a community and can attract some interest from outside the area. As far as tourism potential is concerned, jetties do not in their own right attract visitors. Their main economic potential is to assist local businesses by encouraging expenditures from tourists and visitors.

Jetties are important landmarks and provide a range of recreational activities such as fishing, sightseeing, swimming, berths for small boats and a reason to take an enjoyable stroll. It is not likely that new jetties for recreational use will be constructed in the future. Jetties significantly influence beach behaviour patterns of people. By just being there they act as a focus for many other beach activities. Therefore, the following planning and design guidelines should be considered:

- No jetty should be closed, demolished or significantly altered without full consultation with the community.

- A needs analysis should be undertaken as an element in a coastal recreation and sport strategic plan. See chapter 3 for more details on recreation and sport planning methodology.

- An immediate user survey should be undertaken to assess the potential of jetties as a recreational facility.

- Some jetties have significant historical importance and they may already be listed on a heritage register.

- Ownership of the jetties is an important consideration. At present, jetties are owned by the relevant states and territories. They are sometimes leased under a variety of agreements to local councils.

- Public safety requirements need a high priority. Most jetties are overengineered for their recreational requirements. For example, in South Australia, it is recommended that jetties be upgraded to a recreational standard of 30 per cent of the original design.[18]

- The structural safety of jetties needs to be assessed and public liability risk assessments undertaken.

- Costs to upgrade jetties and then ongoing maintenance should be addressed.

Boat Ramps

Boating popularity is increasing and, as a consequence, the demand for boat ramps is also growing. This requires identification of adequate, safe launching and retrieval facilities along the coast. For example, in South Australia, a four-knot speed limit applies around boat ramps in defined waters.[19]

Contrary to the general opinion, suitable locations for boat ramps are difficult to find. The following specific issues will assist in identifying a suitable site:

- A user survey to determine the need and the types of boats that will use the proposed ramp.

- Design standards that allow boats to be launched directly from a trailer with appropriate water depth at the toe of the ramp.

- Protection from severe weather conditions.

- Minimal impact on the environment.

- Local acceptance of the ramp proposal or objections.

- Accessibility to the proposed site by an all-weather road.

- Acceptable interesting destinations by sea for boat owners and visitors to explore.

- Availability of additional land for trailer and car parking, secured if possible.

- Sufficient site area for rigging, ramp queuing and manoeuvring of trailers.

- Sufficient ancillary facilities such as toilets, water supply for washing down boats, rubbish disposal, telephone access for emergencies and flood lighting.

- Knowledge of wave patterns, tidal movements and currents so that the proposed ramp is not silted up or eroded.

- An understanding of the cost of safe launching conditions and the possible need for breakwaters or groynes if the ramp faces the open sea.
- Council and other statutory planning requirements.

COASTAL ACTIVITIES: RECREATION AND SPORT

Increasing numbers of people will choose Australia's relatively unpolluted coastal beaches as destinations for a wide range of coastal recreational and sporting activities, whether planned or unplanned. If planners and policy makers are to cope with the anticipated expansion of coastal recreation and sport activities, they need to understand something about these activities and their potential impact on the various beaches and marine locations.

Understanding Recreation Users

Most recreation users are responsible and want to ensure the coastal resources they use remain unspoilt. It is much better to work with these users so that their activities have a minimum impact on the environment. Developers, industry groups with interests in the coast, managers of recreation and natural resources and tourist operators need to understand the environmental issues specific to coastal areas and establish a cooperative planning framework through integrating recreation with other coastal requirements.

This approach involves 'a non-sectoral approach to the management of coastal resources. It must consider the environmental, natural resource, socioeconomic, political and geographic dimensions of the zone in a multi-sectoral framework'.[20] The examples discussed next include both informal and organised activities and they are by no means exhaustive.

Safe Informal Recreational Beach Activities

Sightseeing, strolling along the beach and foreshore, playing in the sand or in playgrounds, paddling in the sea, walking along the beach, swimming, admiring the views, having a cup of coffee or ice cream are all acceptable recreational beach activities that require varying degrees of infrastructure.

It is incumbent on coastal planners to take these activities into consideration when planning for the safe use of the beaches. All beaches have the capacity to be dangerous and it is a dilemma for planners to decide whether to encourage the use of the more dangerous beaches by locating public facilities such as parking areas, barbeques, children's playgrounds and seating and walkways in areas that increase the potential for accidents. After all, there is also a duty of care to those who choose activities at dangerous beaches. It is critical to undertake a coastal safety assessment to identify clearly the types of hazards that may be present before planning any type of development that will attract recreational users to the coast. One of the valuable services offered by Surf Life Saving Australia is a beach assessment through their Beach Safety Management Program.

By understanding the nature of beach currents, wave formations and hazards such as reefs and rock formations that are partly exposed, it is possible to avert possible accidents by planning recreation and sport facilities in safe areas. On new or green-fields housing sites near beaches, it is possible to plan access to beaches and provide public facilities to minimise public risk. The link between land use and water and public liability judgements given against local councils make it clear that the courts are increasingly looking towards appropriate land allocations that minimise public risk. They expect coastal planners to 'influence the location and movement of people along the coast to increase public safety at the beach into policy and action'.[21]

Coastal Walks, Cycling and Horse Riding

A stroll along the beach is one aspect of coastal walking. Walking along cliffs provides elevated and spectacular views and in some areas where there are suitable cliffs, trails along the cliffs provide popular coastal activities. Defined coastal trails also can be used for recreational cycling and horseback riding. However, careful thought needs to be given to safety aspects, and in the case of horseback riding, a dedicated trail is recommended.

The following planning and design issues that should be addressed:

- Stability of the cliff for safe walking.
- Clarified land ownership. There could be some areas that are not surveyed accurately and cliff erosion over the years can lead to wrong assumptions on who owns the land.
- Trail surface compatible with its surroundings requiring minimum maintenance.
- Regular rest stations preferably with access to water.
- Disposal of waste.
- Public liability and risk assessment.
- Adequate signage.

Recreational Fishing

In 1992, 1.1 million Australians participated in fishing activities.[22] This is by far the most popular recreational or sporting activity.

In order to continue to enjoy the experience of recreational fishing, it is essential to make sure that the natural fish stocks are sustainable in the long term.

The fishing code of practice adopted by the Recreational Fishing Advisory Committee in Western Australia emphasises catching fish only for oneself and family not for sale or financial gain; helping to conserve fish breeding stocks by returning excess and undersize fish alive to the water; and taking old fishing line, plastic bags and other rubbish to a bin for proper disposal.[23]

Safety education of recreational fishers is an ongoing task. The Australian Sport and Recreational Fishing Confederation understands and emphasises to its members safety standards and the need to conserve fishing stocks. It is more difficult to educate the majority of people who fish as individuals or with mates. They are generally not part of an organised body that has standards of behaviour aimed at protecting the fishing environment. The task to educate should be shared between local councils and state and territory governments. As a last resort, legislation on recreational fishing issues may be necessary at commonwealth or state and territory levels.

Other planning issues that need to be considered are:

- Providing access tracks and camping areas to avoid environmental damage.
- Recognizing any restrictions on fishing such as catch limits, minimum sizes and marine reserves where *'No Fishing is allowed'* by adequate signage or easily accessible brochures.
- Developing interpretive and education programs for fishers, which includes safety and knowledge of the location of life saving resources.
- Providing fish-cleaning and rubbish facilities in high-use areas.
- Providing public access to shore-based facilities such as piers, jetties and wharves wherever possible.

Rock Fishing

This is one of the most dangerous sports in Australia.[24] Lives are lost by fishers being swept from rocks by waves and falls into the water. Yet, danger is probably the reason some people participate in this activity. A mix of adventure and the attraction of the almost limitless choices of fishing spots along the coast, often in isolated places, add to the attraction of this activity. This makes it difficult to provide safe access and built facilities.

Rock fishing has increased in popularity in recent years because it is a relatively inexpensive activity with only a rod and bait as the basic requirements. Since very few rock fishers belong to any organised fishing clubs, some ways of reaching nonmembers need to be explored to emphasise the need for safety education and advice on weather conditions that could minimise risk.

The following planning and design implications for rock fishing are identified in a National Water Safety Strategy.[25]

- Provide a roving (weekend) patrol of rock fishing locations using motorised rescue craft.
- Install 'guardian angel rings' or emergency outpost alarms.

Swimming

Australia's relatively moderate climate, sandy beaches and unpolluted water encourage people to swim at beaches. The beach for most Australians is synonymous with swimming. Although many people go to the beach for the purpose of 'having a swim', their skill levels vary with the majority simply seeking to enjoy a beach environment with an occasional venture into the water. Yet almost all who use the beach indicate that swimming is their preferred beach activity. It is one of the most popular reasons people go to the beach. In 1995–96, just under one million people participated socially in swimming compared with 281,000 organised swimming participants.[26] These statistics include those who swim in fresh-water pools, rivers, lakes etc., but the majority of swimming is along Australia's coasts.

Knowledge of planning and design can contribute to safe swimming. Some examples follow. By providing public facilities such as toilets, change rooms and commercial outlets for food and drink at safe beaches, planners also can discourage access to the use of areas where there are dangerous rips, rocks and hidden tidal reefs. Encouraging the use of safe beaches will help keep inexperienced swimmers from getting into difficulties.

An example of good planning and design is to use the knowledge of beach and tidal formations when planning and designing new housing areas along the coast. Access to estates can be designed in such a way that provides access to beaches in safe areas. Another way to promote safe swimming is to identify the level of life saving resources required to protect beach users, even in relatively safe locations. This may be as simple as choosing to arrange housing, shops and conveniences at the safer end of a beach. Safety education is an important part of planning and design. The next section on surf life saving takes up this issue in more detail.

Surf Life Saving

There are 7,098 beaches with individual characteristics around Australia and 65 per cent are already used for recreational purposes. Only 10 per cent of these beaches already used for recreation purposes are considered developed.[27]

A code of practice has been adopted by Surf Life Saving Australia on beach management practices which provides guidelines on how to conduct their activities including recreational and sporting events to ensure that they have minimum impact on dunes and surrounding coastal and marine environments.

Surf Life Saving Australia aims to reduce public risk on beaches through the development of a database providing comprehensive, standardised and scientific information on all Australian beaches. This database will provide information on the following:

- Location.
- Physical characteristics.
- Access.
- Facilities.
- Usage.
- Rescues.
- Physical and biological hazards.
- Level of public risk under various wave, tide and weather conditions.

A beach hazard rating has been developed which scales beaches according to surf zone topography, water depth, wave heights and rip currents. This information is invaluable for planners looking to design housing and community amenities in such a way that residents and visitors to beach areas are encouraged to use safe beaches.

Requirements for surf life saving facilities should be determined by an estimate of the level of hazards at the beach. Minimum requirements should include the following:

- An estimate of the expected number of club users.
- Storage areas for rescue, training and beach equipment.

- A first aid area.
- An area for training, meetings and seminars.
- Space for socialising (This could include licensed and bar facilities permitted by some local authorities.).

State Life Saving Centres can provide further information on the Australian Beach Safety Management Program.[28]

Surfing

Australian beaches offer some of the best surfing conditions in the world. Anecdotal evidence from Surf Australia suggests that the growth in surfing is between 20 and 30 per cent over the last four years in both participation and sales of products.

Surfing is an individual sport or recreation aimed primarily at seeking and riding the best waves wherever they are. Individual preferences and diverse locations combined with a culture that favours freedom 'to do their own thing' provide planners with particular challenges to meet the needs of this growing sporting and recreational activity.

Most serious surfers have an ongoing interest in maintaining low-impact access to the beaches. This means that minimal built facilities are required such as boardwalks, car parks, basic public toilets, showers and change rooms.

Members of various surf clubs are encouraged to participate in skills training that emphasises safety principles on the beach and in the water. Environmental education is also considered essential to beach activities and enhancing wave-riding opportunities that do not adversely impact on near-shore ecosystems.

As more competitive aspects of the sport are developed that attract significant prize money because of television and media coverage, there will be more emphasis on providing venues with access and facilities for the public. Most of these facilities are temporary, but as competition circuits for events are consolidated, there will be a requirement for planners to provide more permanent public and competitor facilities.

Windsurfing and Boardsailing

Windsurfing and boardsailing have the same facility requirements as sailing and, in Australia, formal windsurfing events are conducted from sailing clubs.

Informal recreational events held by windsurfers at local beaches do not use additional facilities other than those already in place at the chosen venues. These include public car parks, toilets, showers and change rooms.[29]

Sailing

There are many classes of yachts catering for those who wish to participate as competitors or enjoy recreational sailing. The requirements for facilities vary considerably because there are many different classes of yachts and their size will determine to a significant extent the sophistication of the facilities required to service their activities. Yacht clubs along the coast usually require the same facilities as a typical community sport club plus other specialised areas listed next. Club facilities include:

- A clubhouse to cater for members and guests.
- Office accommodation.
- Communication facilities, telephone, facsimile, computer, photocopier etc.
- Showers, toilets and change rooms.
- Board room and meeting areas.
- Entertainment area.
- Catering facilities, canteen with kitchen, cooking appliances, cold room etc.
- Bar facilities.
- Adequate adjacent car parking shared where possible.

The specialised facilities needed depends on the nature of sailing events conducted by the club and the type of sailing or motor vessels owned by the club or its members. The following are most important:

- An elevated observation area for fleet safety and race management.

- Secure and preferably undercover secure boat storage for rescue and race management.

- A radio room for communication with rescue boats.

- Storage for buoys, tackle and flags.

- Underground power lines to club facilities, because there are hazards in overhead lines when rigging sailing boats.

- Undercover, secure boat storage for club sailing boats (up to 12 boats) and preferably additional storage for members to store their boats.

- A wash-down area with water supply for cleaning boats and rescue craft.

- On-site workshop facilities.

- A mooring area or marina berths for larger yachts.

- A boat rigging area adjacent to the clubhouse.

- Access to the water via ramps, slipways and launching cranes.

- Access to the beach for vehicles to launch and retrieve boats.

Power Boating

As cheaper and more reliable boats come on to the market, recreational boating is becoming more accessible to a growing number of people who once could not afford to own a boat. Advances in technology have led to quieter motors and a user-friendlier product. Planners and designers should keep the following boating requirements in mind:

- A network of locations that offer safe, interesting destinations and safe harbours or good launching and retrieval facilities in environmentally sensitive areas.

- Navigational aids and marker buoys as well as rescue facilities.

- Infrastructures that will minimise environmental impacts such as adequate toilets, waste disposal and rubbish collection.

- Commercial facilities that complement marine services industries and encourage recreation and visitors, including foreshore facilities for refreshment and recreational activities as part of recreation zones.

- Fuel facilities.

Water Skiing

There are several water skiing disciplines including slalom, knee-boarding, ski boarding and barefoot skiing requiring relatively calm waters. Unless coastal areas are well protected they usually are not suitable for regular water skiing. Owners of expensive ski boats prefer calm conditions in which to operate and fresh water minimises damage to their engines and other gear caused by salt water. Lakes, reservoirs and rivers are often preferred to coastal areas unless estuaries or protected waters are available.

Water skiing is an inherently dangerous activity and serious accidents can and often do happen. Therefore, safety is a paramount consideration for the driver, skier or skiers and the observer who is the vital communication link between the skier and the driver. A great deal of consideration needs to be given to the permitted and prohibited zones or areas set aside for skiing. Many skiers who do not belong to a club may not be exposed to the need for disciplined use of their craft and consideration for others using the coast. As part of the planning process, publications that include clear safety principles and guidelines for the boat operators as well as a code of conduct should be readily available.

Most of the planning and design requirements for water skiers are similar to those for power boating mentioned earlier. In addition, water skiers require the following:

- Zoned areas that are clearly marked and separate from other users or, if this is not possible, clear access and exit channels through the zoned areas.

- Locations away from residential areas. Although boats have increasingly efficient silencers, they are still noisy and therefore they should be located well away from residential areas. If this is not possible, strict times of operation are required. Planning should include negotiations with all the parties concerned and strong consultative expertise is required with particularly good negotiating skills.

- Set times for water skiing. Under no circumstances should this activity be allowed after sunset or before sunrise.
- Boat launching facilities that protect the shore and allow beach starts for skiers.
- Access to spare equipment and repair facilities close to the designated skiing area.
- Grassed areas adjacent the skiing location for barbecues, toilets and changing facilities; a children's playground; and access to at least a limited range of food services. A strong family involvement is a characteristic of water skiing and this should be reinforced as part of the planning process.
- Competition venues require public access, amenities either temporary or permanent and viewing areas for spectators.
- Safety information readily available and reinforced through regular public education campaigns.

Beach Volleyball

For years beach volleyball has been a low-key recreational activity requiring not much more than a net and a marked-out area of beach. Now that it has won Olympic status, tournaments are often televised attracting a growing spectator audience.

Even with this change of status, beach volleyball facility requirements remain relatively minimal: spectator seating and courts and ancillary equipment for judges, officials and teams can be demounted after use. Some beach areas are now designated venues with permanent posts and good viewing areas.

Planners and designers should keep in mind that areas set aside for beach volleyball tournaments will attract spectators. There-

fore, the following facility requirements should be considered:

- Car parking and other traffic management.
- Additional toilets, change rooms and showers (could be temporary).
- Requirements of television and media (temporary).
- Food and other commercial services.
- Environmental protection considerations related to the beach area where the volleyball facility is located.

Personal Water Craft and Jet Skiing

The popularity of personal water crafts or jet skis has increased steadily since it was introduced a little more than a decade ago.

Controversy surrounds their use because of safety considerations. The South Australian Government introduced legislation that applies a four-knot speed limit for personal water craft along the metropolitan shoreline and in the off-river areas of the River Murray. This speed limit applies within 200 metres of the shoreline and on-the-spot penalties apply.[30]

Another controversial issue is excess noise levels and their impact on the environment including disruption of wildlife and water pollution from the two-stroke engines. Steps have been taken by the manufacturers to reduce the noise levels of engines by introducing more efficient silencers.

An education program through brochures issued with each craft purchased can provide at least basic rules and codes of behaviour. Some key extracts taken from a voluntary code introduced in South Australia emphasise the need for adequate planning to make it practical for the following safety requirements to be maintained.[31]

- If there is a designated PWC (Personal Water Craft) or boat-only launching and retrieving area, use it.
- Respect the rights of all users of recreational waterways and boat launch

facilities, both on public waters and on adjacent private property.

- Give all other vessels adequate space (keeping below four knots within 30 metres of other craft).
- Observe no-wake zones.
- Be especially aware of swimmers and other craft near the shore (keeping below four knots within 30 metres of swimmers).
- Avoid environmentally sensitive areas, especially those that are sign-posted.
- Take particular care when refuelling. Avoid fuel spillage. Dispose of all containers.
- Keep to a safe speed. Realise that equipment, ability, weather and wave conditions, and especially other vessel traffic should determine speed. Keep a sharp lookout especially when turning. In case of emergency, volunteer assistance.
- Pay close attention to the noise made by the jet ski and be aware of how others on boats and ashore react to that noise. Take appropriate action if noise is a problem.
- Ensure that registration label and numbers are displayed in accordance with the regulations (numbers clearly visible from 50 metres).

Local councils and other government bodies can react to complaints about jet skis in a variety of ways including restrictions, bans, fines or warnings. These methods although useful are less effective than developing a planned approach aimed at maximising environmental and safety factors while still allowing appropriate use. It is in the interests of manufacturers, retailers, users of the craft, government and the community to plan for this activity in a cooperative way.

Following are some planning and design considerations:

- Conduct a user study of jet skis in the region or along the coastline in question based on the number of hours of operation.

- Obtain jet ski accident statistics.
- Consult with jet ski sales outlets and users.
- Provide designated jet ski areas or zones.
- Introduce slow-speed and no-wake zones near shore.
- Make travel at idle speed mandatory within 200 metres of the shore.
- Charge registration fees to support the employment of wardens or appropriate officers to strengthen the on-water law enforcement and inspections capability. This needs to be a state and territory or regional seaside council decision.
- Provide compulsory education programs including safety-driving procedures that must be taken before users can obtain a jet ski licence.
- Limit speeds to 50 kph and mandate the wearing of personal flotation devices.
- Separate swimmers and surfers from users of skis.
- Require hirers of jet skis to provide adequate instruction.
- Review the use of jet skis in shallows because of safety and noise-abatement implications.

It should be noted that while the use of personal water craft for recreational purposes raises concerns about safety and the environment that are reflected in the legislation and code of conduct discussed, there are other operations such as rescue and law enforcement along the coast that justify their use along the coast.

Clearly, their use is a growing recreational activity and if they are allowed to be sold, people will want to use them. Therefore, it is preferabley that they are used in planned locations and, if possible, supervised.

Hang Gliding and Paragliding

Coastal cliffs offer ideal locations for these activities. They are subject to air navigation and civil aviation regulations that limit their use particularly in proximity to air ports and flight paths.

The Hang Gliding Federation of Australia has an operations manual that details the requirements for safe flying and launching sites along the coast with adequate car parking close by. The following requirements for launch sites are important for planning purposes:

- Sites need to be negotiated with the landowners, either public or private, and approval obtained.

- Ongoing use of sites require the users to make sure that the cliffs are not degraded and that care is taken to prevent possible erosion by preserving the vegetation. (Rehabilitation of sites are often undertaken by members as a sign of good faith to the landholder.)

Land Sailing

This recreational activity is also known as land yachting. It can take place on any firm and flat surface including beaches. High-performance land yachts are capable of three to four times wind speed or up to 100 kph.

Being completely silent and powered by wind, they appeal to people who seek an adventurous activity and are concerned with conservation and the environment.

Even at high speeds, land yachts are relatively safe. Their wide base and low centre of gravity make them quite stable. In addition, participants wear seat belts and helmets.

Not all beaches are suitable for this sport, and there is a need to acknowledge that these craft are similar to go-carts in the way they can spin out and slide into turns causing some beach damage.

Organised clubs include public liability coverage as part of their membership fee, and club members take a responsible attitude to beach care.

Facility requirements include the following:

- Access to car parks adjacent to the beaches. In most cases the land yachts can be carried on the roof rack of the family car.

- Public toilets and change facilities.

- Large flat beaches such as tidal flats.

Triathlon

This sport is growing in popularity and it will be a part of future Olympic Games. Some coastal areas offer an excellent environment for the swimming, cycling and running sections of this event. Triathlons are likely to attract increasing numbers of spectators to beaches and surrounding areas making this a recreational experience. The competitors enjoy the support of spectators, but the staging of these events requires effective planning.

No permanent facilities are required, but the following factors need to be taken into account in choosing a suitable site for triathlons:

- Sensitivity in choosing the site must combine sea and land locations where the environment is fragile. Remember that if there are many competitors in the event covering the same circuit, the wear and tear on the fragile beachfront land can be significant.

- Coastal sand dunes should not be used for training or as part of the course.

- Road surfaces for the cycling section should have no speed humps, roundabouts or significant volumes of traffic. The running section should be on a path or roadway with a hard, all-weather surfaces.

- Water conditions need to be suitable for the level of participants. Beginners should not be required to deal with strong rips or heavy surf.

- Entry and exit points to and from the water should have a sand surface that does not damage the feet of competitors.

- Ease of access to the water for participants in the swimming section.

- Provision of adequate bike parking facilities for participants in the cycling section.

- Parking provision for spectators.

- Convenient toilets and change facilities for competitors.

- An undercover area for registrations and presentations that also has access to power for amplification.

- A suitable transition area that allows for the changeover from cycling to running.

- Traffic controls that minimise the conflicts of runners and cyclists who will use the same roads as motorists. All parties should adhere to traffic regulations.

- Location or scheduling of the event should be at a time when amplification and other noise levels will not affect unduly the residents.

- Adequate rubbish disposal facilities.

Rock Climbing

Half the fun of going to the beach is scrambling around on the rocks. Some take rock climbing seriously and enjoy the challenge of mastering a rock face, then the thrill of abseiling down a cliff face. Public liability for accidents along rocky areas of beaches is a growing problem and councils will be required to take all due care in provision of a safe environment for both informal and more formal rock climbing activities.

Usually, organised rock-climbing groups or clubs have had some instruction through an accredited course. Nevertheless, safety considerations are important. Planners should consider the following requirements for both the informal recreational rock climbers and the experienced rock climbers:

- Carry out a risk assessment of the areas to avoid possible public liability claims.

- Encourage the use of only designated areas that are well sign-posted with appropriate warnings for inexperienced rock scramblers. In popular public areas, people like to watch experienced climbers, so provision should be made for accessibility and shared use of coastal rocks in relative safety.

- Clearly identify existing paths to prevent erosion and damage to plants and animals.

- Provide vehicle access to the cliff faces wherever possible in case of accident.

- Remove climbing aids after the climb or, preferably, encourage a climbing place where holdfasts have already been installed.

- Locate suitable public toilets and rubbish disposal facilities at convenient places near popular coastal cliff faces. If this is not possible, climbers must carry out all rubbish. Disposal into the sea or littering rocks must be strongly discouraged.

- Provide adequate signage to cover safety, pointing out dangerous rock formations.

- Signage should also refer to matters such as avoiding trampling on plants growing on the rocks and cliff surrounds. Climbers should be educated to climb well away from nests so that bird life is not disturbed.

Scuba Diving

Most people who own equipment for diving have undergone some training in its use. There are many diving groups and clubs throughout the country. Spearfishing is a popular activity, but because of decreasing fish populations on coastal reefs and in other areas, there are many areas in which it is banned or strongly discouraged.

Sports diving as it is sometimes known can nevertheless be a high-risk activity and planners should consider setting aside areas that offer challenges for both the novices and more experienced sports divers.

A recent submission to the Environment, Resources and Development Committee of the Parliament of South Australia on the establishment of artificial reefs[32] highlighted two developing aspects of scuba diving.

1. Dive tourism offers both local and overseas sports divers the possibility of exploring both wooden- and iron-scuttled hulls. Apparently, decommissioned vessels are sometimes available and suitable as artificial reefs. These hulls can be used to train divers in safe practices by negotiating through vari-

ous sections of the sunken vessels. Whether there is agreement or not on the value of establishing artificial reefs, planners may wish to consider access by divers to wrecks along the coast as a facility for dive tourism.

2. Volunteer scientific sports divers can be an enormous potential benefit to the scientific community through performing various routine tasks on their behalf. By using sports divers, researchers are free to undertake additional work and valuable research funds could be stretched further. The type of scientific activities performed by volunteer divers could include monitoring projects and replanting seagrass. Although this is a somewhat new concept in Australia and there is some skepticism by the scientific community as to the ability of sports divers, it has been a long-established practice in Britain and Europe. Scuba associations in Europe have acknowledged the high standards of training in sports diving and some of these peak bodies are currently in the process of recognising sports diving qualifications for scientific diving.

Continuing growth in sales of scuba diving equipment indicates that the activity is very popular and people who purchase expensive equipment will obviously wish to use their equipment and go diving along the coast. It is up to the planners to designate scuba diving areas and specify the types of activities undertaken in these areas.

The following facilities are required:

- Access to public showers, toilets.
- Car parking.
- Easy access to the water from beaches or jetties.
- Access to areas of historical and marine interest such as historic wrecks and reefs with marine life.

Recreational Vehicles

Access to beaches by four-wheel-drives and trail bikes is often criticised but they are used as recreational vehicles and by professional fishers and four-wheel-drive tourist operators.

These recreational vehicles have the potential to severely damage the environment by leaving existing tracks through dunes and breaking down vegetation. In addition, the noise can disturb the bird life, other fauna and people who use the area.

Effective planning and design can designate areas where these vehicles can be used in a way that minimises the impact on the environment. Better still, by developing well-designed walking and cycling trails in sensitive areas, people can be encouraged to leave their vehicles in adjacent car parks.

Since recreational vehicle use of coastal areas is unlikely to diminish, it is in the interests of planners to clearly designate areas that can be used and educate potential users in responsible behaviour along the coast.

Walking Dogs on Beaches

For many people, walking dogs on beaches is an important recreational activity often linked to a personal physical fitness program. Local councils with coastal areas to manage are faced with a potentially highly volatile situation dealing with the 'of rights to beach' access for people with or without dogs.

A recent survey of residents of an urban beach in metropolitan Adelaide indicated what is probably a typical reaction to the conditions under which walking dogs on beaches should or should not be allowed.[33] The results of the survey were:

- Should dogs be allowed on beaches: 8% dogs banned; 92% dogs allowed.

- Leashing requirements: 44.8% dogs leashed at all times; 53.2% dogs leashed only during specified times; 2.0% no comment.

- Special area for dogs: 47.6% agreed with allocating special beach areas for dogs; 36.4% disagreed with allocating special beach areas for dogs; 16.0% no comment.

In the case of this local council, specified times were 9.00 A.M. through 7.00 P.M. October through March during daylight saving. At other times, dogs needed to be under 'effective control.'

It would appear that dog owners are increasingly under pressure to take responsibility for their dogs' behaviour and hygiene on beaches. This will involve education of owners and a rising level of enforcement.

Instead of fines, most people can be inspired to do the right thing if they are assisted with simple directions and suitable facilities. For example, some councils are providing dispensers at strategic places along the beach with bags on which instructions are well marked. These dispensers called 'Pooch Poo Bags' are one way of allowing the exercising of a dog on a beach in a more environmentally acceptable manner.

Exercising Horses on Beaches

Councils near racecourses may be faced with trainers wishing to exercise horses on beaches.

Exercising racehorses on beaches is distinct from recreational horse riding on beaches. Trainers and riders usually exercise early in the morning;, therefore, they are off the beach at times of intense use and do not interfere with other users. Safety considerations are minimal because both trainers and riders are highly skilled. A tradition of early morning horse exercise can add character to a local beach range of activities causing minimal environmental impact. A safety issue of access to beaches by horses is important. Provision of an area for horse floats or bridle tracks to allow individual horse movements to and from beaches should be given consideration.

The question of recreational horse riding on beaches at other times should be assessed along with other uses, balancing the need for such activities, safety factors and environmental impact.

Bird Watching

This is a legitimate recreational activity and there are a large number of Australian coastal areas attractive to bird watchers.

As is pointed out in the Coorong RAMSAR Management Plan, problems associated with disturbing the birds may be alleviated by the development of a number of bird hides in key locations which could be used to monitor

populations (through voluntary sightings returns) and provide information and education sources.[34]

Commercial Beach Recreation Concessions

Commercial recreation operators provide services such as the hire of sports and recreation equipment as well as the sale of food and drinks. If not strictly controlled, they can detract from the beach experience.

Information on conditions for beach commercial operations is difficult to obtain because of commercial confidentiality. Some coastal managers are revising their policies as pressures mount to limit intrusive selling. There are also concerns that excessive commercial activities can lead to the degradation of the beach natural ecological systems.

The following principles can assist in developing more transparent policies for the operations of beach commercial concessions:

- Ensure that the new commercial recreational activity can demonstrate a demand for service with clear benefits to the coast users.

- Clarify the competency of the operators and the level of training required for water, land and air activities.

- Minimise built facilities or permanent locations that limit people using the beach for recreation.

- Consider other competitors who may be affected by beach operators.

- Provide clear access points for equipment to the beach and specific times of operation to limit disturbance to beach users.

- Ensure that all electrical installations if required are approved and tested with underground services wherever possible.

- Detail responsibilities of the operator for waste and rubbish removals.

- Clarify legal liability and insurance obligations.

- Safeguard the natural character and amenity of the area from the encroachment of obtrusive commercial activities.

- Control advertising and promotions so that they intrude as little as possible on beach users.

MANAGEMENT OF COASTAL RECREATION

There should be a strong commitment to community consultation when developing local and regional recreation and sport strategies. Throughout earlier chapters there are many references to methods of obtaining effective community consultation. Planners need to be sensitive to the need to involve people in identifying what coastal activities, facilities and services they require. Consultation should also include a definite acknowledgment of the resources required to maintain both services and facilities with adequate ongoing management structures.

Establish Sport and Recreation Forums

A method of involving people in management in South Australia is the establishment of Sport and Recreation Forums. It is suggested that these forums could be extended to considering the needs for viable coastal recreation.

These forums are organised community groups having a common interest in developing sport and recreational-based activities within a community. They are an important method of involving a wide cross section of people in coastal recreation planning. These forums have the capacity to increase community awareness of coastal and marine recreation issues through working with recreation and sports organisations, existing agencies such as Coast Care or Coast Action Community Program, local coastal environment groups, local councils, tourist organisations and state government departments.

Training

If quality recreation services are to be delivered along the coast, constant attention is necessary to the ongoing training of volunteers and employed personnel.

Use of Volunteers

The strength of recreation to a large extent rests on a strong volunteer involvement. Each state or territory has in place Volunteer Involvement Programs (VIPs) [35] aimed not only at providing training in a wide range of management skills, but also at recognising the value of volunteers.

Training opportunities can be extended through VIPs to include some of the skills required by those involved in coastal recreation services.

Employed Personnel

The recreation industry has Industry Training Advisory Boards (ITABs) in all states and territories that conduct regular training needs analyses that take into account relevant coastal recreation requirements. Through the ITABs, both short-term and more extensive training is aimed at the following:

- Enhancing marine and coastal management and technical skills.
- Strategic business management and planning.
- Aboriginal heritage and consultation.
- Asset management.
- Marketing and public relations.
- Integrated coastal planning.

Tertiary training is available in recreation, tourism and environment disciplines at universities and technical and further education institutions. Appropriate coastal recreation training in marine management should be provided for those employed in coastal recreation.

Awards for Excellence

Annual awards for excellence could be a method of highlighting the importance of coastal recreation and lifting standards of service delivery. Awards could be given in the following suggested areas:

- Innovative recreation activities on the coast.
- Professionalism and excellence in coastal recreation.

- Community and volunteer contributions.
- High-quality service from commercial recreation initiatives.
- Excellence in recreation building and design.
- Initiatives for integrating protection and conservation of natural and cultural assets and sites into recreation activity zones.
- Landscaping of coastal recreation zones.

Risk Management Criteria

Any recreation activities associated with the sea contain a high-risk component that needs to be managed. The following criteria should be considered in the development of a program of risk management:

- Identification of personal vulnerability and risk exposure from participation in specific recreation activities.
- Procedures for personal safety and equipment safety, for example, boat collisions and fuel spillage.
- Accident liability.
- Coastal hazard identification for recreation activities, e.g. physical coastal hazards such as rocks and cliffs.
- Potential damage by natural events such as major storms.
- Inundation and erosion.
- Climate changes.
- Establishment of an inventory of recreation facilities.
- Implementation of standards for building maintenance.
- Inspections of recreation equipment for wear and tear on a regular basis.
- Commercial competitive risks associated with recreation events and programs.
- Vulnerability to local, state and national economic downturns.

In an effective management plan, structures need to be established to actively manage risk rather than either denying its existence or endeavouring to eliminate all risk environments.

EXAMPLES OF GOOD COASTAL RECREATION PRACTICE

We can all learn from each other. Following are three very different examples of good management practice as distinct from 'best practice'. It is presumptuous to assume that these are the best, but they demonstrate elements of good practice that could be helpful to planners of coastal recreation.

Heysen Trail: A Lesson in Coastal Cooperation

This is one of the longest walking trails in Australia traversing the principal mountain ranges in South Australia between Cape Jervis on the coast and the Flinders Ranges in the north of the state.

It was originally developed to pass through government reserves and national parks where possible. In other areas, old government road reserves and agreements with land holders for right of access were negotiated. A change in land ownership and the lack of public land for a trail along the cliffs has excluded the public from a small section of the proposed trail route and therefore the opportunity to see and experience this unique section of the rugged Australian coast including views of West Island, Rosetta Head, the Pages and Kangaroo Island. There is also a lost opportunity to view seals, whales, dolphins, sea eagles, peregrine falcons, kangaroos, echidnas and other wildlife as well as diverse flora unique to this area from this closed section of the trail.

There is a resolve by a number of government agencies with an interest in the Heysen Trail to work with the local district councils to come to an arrangement to survey the area and provide an easement for pedestrian access along the cliffs.

The following important issues must be considered:

- High conservation value of the cliffs.

- Remedial strategies for soil erosion.
- Public demand for access to the cliffs and the rerouting of the Heysen Trail to take in these views.
- Safety fencing.
- Acquisition of the land and a determination of who pays.
- Management of this section of the Heysen Trail and deciding who provides the resources for the ongoing maintenance and supervision of what will become a popular section of the trail.
- Legal liability for walkers and the legal responsibility of adjacent landowners.
- Consultation with local landowners, taking into consideration their concerns about opening up this area for public use.
- Types of agreements such as Heritage Agreements, Land Management Agreements and other appropriate measures.
- Consultation with the local indigenous (Aboriginal) community.

Increasing pressures to open up unique areas of the coastline to the public will result in the need for cooperation between government agencies and the private landholders. The days of informal agreements and unclear management responsibilities for these areas are going fast and the South Australian situation is likely to be repeated in other areas along the Australian coast.

Marina: Environmental and Recreational Asset

Access to coastal waterways for recreational boating and other water activities led to the development of 'The Anchorage', a unique marina and resort combining an innovative waterfront development that balances commercial and environmental sustainability. The marina operation is now separate from the resort and it is this element that will be considered.

Three vital elements of the project are location, design and management. These ensure a marriage of good environmental practice with financial viability. As Ian McAndrew, director of the Anchorage points out, 'It is vital to ensure that the environment is protected and sustained as any degradation of the environment within the surrounding development will reduce its attractiveness and thus adversely affect its commercial potential.'[36]

Location

Location is all-important and the Anchorage is situated reasonably close to the large population centres of Sydney and Newcastle. Detailed feasibility and environmental studies confirmed the potential for a marina catering for boat owners that is linked to a hotel providing accommodation for land-based participants at the high end of the tourist market. It is interesting to note that a local residents' action group raised some issues that the developer was able to accept such as the discarding of the boat repair facilities.

During the late 1980s an environmental impact statement was prepared as a requirement under the NSW Environmental Planning Act of 1979. This EIS was comprehensive, addressing 119 different issues such as flushing and water quality, vehicular and pedestrian access, sewage and pump-out facilities, drainage, energy requirements, pollution control measures, navigation safety, fishing, landscaping noise and visual quality.

Design

Creative design features have been employed. These include a rock-walled harbour with a unique flushing system that provides excellent-quality water within the harbour by replacing the water every day. There is an abundance of fish and marine life in the clear harbour water that is in stark contrast to many marinas and harbours where a lack of flushing causes deterioration in the water quality. Consulting engineers were engaged to undertake some environmental studies and coastal investigations. They found that 'water quality within the harbour is comparable with that found anywhere within the port. Marine life is abundant within the new habitat formed by the rock walls, seagrasses are regenerating and the water quality is clear. The harbour walls have already become established as a good foreshore fishing spot within Port Stephens'.[37] This thoughtful and innovative design was at little cost with no ongoing running costs for pumps because tidal energy is used.

The design has integrated tourism accommodation with a range of recreational activities such as boating, fishing, surfing, water skiing, scuba diving, dolphin watch cruises, para gliding, hire boats, windsurfing and other land-based activities. This makes for excellent aquatic facilities in a creative landscape that is financially viable and environmentally acceptable.

Quality Management

Great emphasis is placed on the excellence of the customer service provided. A continuous improvement program is in place covering customer feedback, procedure reviews, environmental monitoring, industry analysis, operational reviews and property presentation and maintenance.

One of the strengths of this marina development is its management plan, which was required before development consent was approved. It is now a powerful management tool that has been expanded to cover such items as clear management objectives, tasks for staff training, safety, fire prevention, marina maintenance, disposal of waste procedures, noise, cyclone procedures and medical emergencies. Clear job descriptions and marina operations management procedures covering everything from berthing boats to fuel dock operations are covered. Staff are involved not only in providing quality service, but also in assisting to educate guests and visitors in maintaining safety and environmental standards that are the underlying reason for the high percentage of advanced seasonal bookings and return guest visits.

Boston Harbor: Public and Private Partnerships

Thirty islands in Boston Harbor, Massachusetts, USA, are designated a congressional national recreation area as part of the National Parks System. Of these, seventeen are owned by the State of Massachusetts as part of the Boston Harbor Island State Park. The others are owned by the City of Boston or by private owners.

The national park does not assume ownership of any of the islands, but it will contribute towards the islands' upkeep on the basis of one dollar for every three dollars raised by island owners or private contributors. Federal funds may pay for some capital projects such as construction or restoration of piers and sea walls.

A management plan is being developed comprising property owners; federal, state, and city agency representatives; and nongovernment organisations. The partnership was officially announced at a special community event at Long Wharf on Boston's waterfront.[38]

PRACTICAL STEPS FOR COASTAL PLANNERS

To summarise, there are certain key practical steps for planners involved with the provision of coastal infrastructure. These are at least a start to what for many planners is new territory.

- Do not underestimate the importance of coastal recreation and its potential growth, which must be effectively managed. You either face the recreation planning issues early or pick up the pieces when community pressures force expensive change.

- Introduce to your team competent recreation planners who know how to integrate recreation planning into other coastal planning activities.

- Be committed to accepting that recreation and sporting services and activities can be environmentally friendly.

- Work with and not in opposition to the providers of recreation activities, programs and commercial services in achieving sustainable coastal development of recreation development.

- Understand the underlying philosophy behind the objectives and principles for development of coastal recreation before considering specific projects.

- Take note of the range of recreational activities and their requirements for each project, then consider opportunities for creative design solutions.

- Consider your task as an educative one that involves both recreation providers and developers because we all need the outcomes resulting from careful planning and management of the coastal and marine environment.

- Introduce strong management practices including evaluation and monitoring mechanisms.

- Suggest good practice examples that can stimulate new solutions to challenging situations. None of us has the complete answers.

REFERENCES

1. Government of South Australia [1972] *Coast Protection Act*, Section 4. Government Printer.
2. Resource Assessment Commission [1993] *A National Coastal Action Plan.*
3. Bureau of Tourism Research [1996] *International Visitors Survey 1995.* Canberra.
4. Australian Bureau of Statistics [1993] *Involvement in Sport,* Cat. no. 6285.0., Canberra: AGPS.
5. Australian Bureau of Statistics [1997] *Participation in Sport and Physical Activities*, cat. no. 4177.0., Canberra: AGPS.
6. Australian Bureau of Statistics [1996–97] *Participation in Sport and Physical Activity,* cat. no. 4177.0. Canberra: Australian Government Printing Service.
7. Australian Bureau of Statistics [1997] *Labour Force Supplementary Survey of Work in Selected Culture/Leisure Activities,* cat. no. 6203.0. Canberra: AGPS.
8. Australian Bureau of Statistics [1998] *Employment in Sport and Recreation—Not Just a Game.* Office for Recreation and Sport, South Australia.
9. Australian Bureau of Statistics [1995] *Voluntary Work in Australia,* cat. no. 4441.0. Canberra: AGPS.
10. Gold Coast City Council [1997] *Draft Findings of the Economic Impact Assessment for the Northern Gold Coast Beach Protection Strategy—Executive Summary,.* Queensland.
11. Evans., M.D and Burgan., B.J [1993] *Economic Value of the Adelaide Metropolitan Beaches.* University of Adelaide, for the Coast Protection Board and SA Department of Environment and Land Management, p. 25.
12. New South Wales Government [1990] *Coastline Management Manual.* NSW: Government Printer.
13. Departments of Conservation and Land Management, Minerals and Energy, Fisheries and Resources Development [1994] *New Horizons in Marine Management.* Government of Western Australia, p. 9.
14. Environment Canada [1998] *Atlantic Coastal Action Plan.* Canadian Government.
15. Graham, Bob and Pitts, David [1997] *Good Practice for Integrated Coastal Planning.* Hawthorn, Victoria: Royal Australian Planning Institute.
16. Victorian Coastal Council [1997] *Victorian Coastal Strategy.* Melbourne: Department for Conservation and Land Management, p. 39.
17. Commonwealth Coastal Action Program [1997] *Coastal Tourism, A Manual for Sustainable Development.* Tourism Council Australia, Australian Local Government Association and Royal Australian Planning Institute.
18. Commonwealth Action Program [1997] *Coastal Tourism - A Manual for Sustainable Development.*
19. Government of South Australia [1994] *Harbours and Navigation Regulations, Regulation 139.* Adelaide: Government Printer.
20. Hilderbrand, Lawrence. P. & and Norenna, Edward J. [1992] *Approaches and Progress Toward Effective Integrated Coastal Zone Management,* in A National Coastal Action Plan, Resources Assessment Commission, Commonwealth of Australia, p. 3.
21. Brynes, Adam [1996] *Beach Safety: A Role for Coastal Planners.* Proceedings of the Australian Coastal Management Conference, Glenelg, South Australia, p. 5.
22. Australian Bureau of Statistics [1992] *Australian Population Census.* Table 8. Canberra: Australian Government Printing Service.
23. Recreational Fishing Advisory Committee [1997] *Fishing Code of Practice.* Fisheries of Western Australia. Perth: Government Printer.
24. Giles, Paul [1995] *Towards a National Water Safety Strategy.* Sydney: Royal Life Saving Society and Surf Life Saving Associations of Australia, p. 65.
25. Giles, Paul [1995] *Towards a National Water Safety Strategy,* p. 71.
26. Australian Bureau of Statistics [1997] *Participation in Sport and Physical Activities,* cat. no. 4177.0., Canberra: AGPS.
27. Coastal Studies Unit, University of Sydney [(1997]) *Surf Life Saving Association Australian Beach Safety Management Program.* Sydney: Surf Life Saving Association Australia.
28. Coastal Studies Unit, University of Sydney [1997] *Australian Beach Safety Management Program.* New South Wales: Surf Life Saving Association.
29. Information provided by John Woollatt, Administration and Development Officer, Yachting and Boardsailing South Australia.
30. Government of South Australia [1998] *Harbours and Navigation Act, 1993, Harbours and Navigation Regulations, 1994,. Schedule 10, Regulation 129.2.*

Adelaide: Government of South Australia.

31. Boating Industry Association SA [1998] *Personal Water Craft Code of Ethics,* Endorsed by the Boating Industry Association, Jet Sport Boating Association and Recreation Boating Council, South Australia.

32. Venning, Ivor, Member of Parliament [1998] *Establishment of Artificial Reefs.* Parliament of South Australia, p. 7.

33. City of Port Adelaide Enfield [1998] *Largs Bay Beach Area Dog Survey.* South Australia.

34. Department of Environment and Natural Resources [1998] *Recreation and Tourism Use of the Coorong and Lower Lakes Region, RAMSAR Management Plan.* South Australia, p. 6.

35. Australian Sports Commission [1998] *Volunteer Involvement Program (VIP) Resources.,* Canberra: Participation Unit.

36. McAndrew, Ian. A. [1995] *Understanding the Unique Characteristics of Waterfront and Marina Developments.* Paper given at the Indonesian Leisure Conference, Port Stephens, New South Wales, p. 8.

37. GeoMarine [1987] *Environmental Engineering Innovation.* Enmore, NSW.

38. *Gulf Marine Times,* vol. 1, no. 3 [1998] Boston, USA.

Example of a Recreation and Sport Consultancy Brief

1. Clients

The Council of _____ and the Office for Recreation and Sport.

2. Background

- [Enter in population trends and a brief physical description of the council area.]
- [Enter in any studies or reports that are relevant to the development of a Recreation and Sport Plan.]
- The Office for Recreation and Sport is a focus for recreation planning at state government level. In particular, efforts are being made to address recreation and sport planning among other urban councils.
- The Council of _____ is involved in provision of open space and recreation facilities and is interested in ensuring the most effective, efficient and equitable use of resources in the facilitation of recreation opportunities.

3. Objectives

3.1 Overall objective

To produce a Recreation and Sport Plan relevant to the needs of the people in the Council of _____ taking into account planning already undertaken by various departments within the council, including projects about to be initiated.

3.2 Specific Objectives

This plan will cover active and passive recreation, formal sports and unstructured recreation activities. The following are examples of specific objectives:

- Integrate the Recreation and Sport Plan into a regional planning process.
- Provide a variety of recreation activities at specified locations according to community needs ensuring equitable use for disadvantaged and disabled persons.
- Explore a variety of resource-sharing and joint-venture options with the aim of achieving maximum utility of recreation and sport facilities, e.g. community use of schools, joint/dual use of facilities by sporting and other community groups compatible with recreation and sport.
- Develop a council strategy for assisting recreation and sporting groups to more efficiently utilise facilities by considering dual/joint use of facilities and more efficient management that will result in financial viability.
- Identify playground needs, particularly to prioritise and make safe playground equipment within the council's area following a comprehensive consultative process.
- Develop a strategic plan for the management of a major facility, e.g. swimming pool, indoor recreation centre, major football ground.
- Introduce specific recreation and sports programs that will increase participation in active recreation.

4. Project Description

The major components to be addressed in this Recreation and Sport Plan can be summarised in a 'three-step planning process' as follows:

4.1 Analysis of Recreation and Sport Issues to Be Resolved by:

- Summarising and updating reports on studies that have already been undertaken by the Council of _____.
- Considering demographic information that will assist in predicting population growth.
- Considering recreation and sport demands and user preferences.
- Developing appropriate consulting techniques to clarify recreation and sport preferences, identify unmet needs and barriers to resident participation and identify nonusers and reasons for nonparticipation.
- Working closely with the various departments within the council to identify important recreation and sport issues.

4.2 Assessment of Guidelines and Policies

Having analysed and consulted as outlined in 4.1 above, the consultants will be required to prepare a 'Key Issues Paper', then assess particularly:

- Utilisation of recreation and sport open spaces.
- Recreation and sport facilities usage.
- Dual/joint community use of recreation and sport facilities.
- Cost of provision of recreation and sport.
- Maintenance issues.

The consultants will be expected to work closely with key community recreation and sport associations and clubs to make sure that their structures reflect the proposed guidelines and policies.

Consideration should be given to existing council guidelines and policies in the area of recreation and sport before identifying new guidelines and policies based on the results of the consultation process.

4.3 Implementation of the Recreation and Sport Plan

To ensure that the Recreation and Sport Plan becomes a reality and not just a theoretical exercise, the following implementation processes should be considered:

- Establishing realistic goals and objectives for recreation and sport open space provision and facility planning.
- Establishing clear policies for the development of recreation and sport in the Council of _____.

- Identifying priorities over a three- to five-year period for the implementation of the Recreation and Sport Plan.
- Preparing specific Action Plans for implementation.
- Recommending management structures for the development of the Recreation and Sport Plan. Note: The management structures should be in three parts:
  — for clubs and associations.
  — for major recreation and sporting facilities.
  — for the delivery of recreation and sport services within the council.
- Reviewing and evaluating procedures should be recommended for the implementation of the Recreation and Sport Plan.

5. Guidelines for Consultants

The following guidelines are set out to assist the consultants in understanding the nature and scope of the task:

5.1 Planning Principles

The successful consultant will be required to follow the planning principles as outlined above.

5.2 Collaboration

The consultant will need to have an understanding of community processes and possess strong negotiating skills, particularly with the ability to work with organised recreation and sporting groups in the community to help articulate their needs and identify problems.

5.3 Recommendations

The consultant will be required to recommend appropriate actions related to the objectives set out in section 3.2 above.

5.4 Access

The consultant will have access to expertise within the Office for Recreation and Sport particularly in the following areas:

- Recreation trails, including walking, cycling and horse riding.
- Playgrounds and play areas.
- Sport facility development advice (particularly swimming pools, sports playing surfaces and both indoor and outdoor facilities).
- Community sport programs such as Active Australia.

5.5 Resources

The Office for Recreation and Sport has a range of material available in its library.

5.6 Data Preparation

The consultant will be required to prepare data in such a way that it can be used in the GIS (Geographical Information System).

5.7 Consulting

The Council of _____ staff in the following departments have expertise in various areas and a responsibility for recreation planning. They should be consulted.

- Community Services
- Planning
- Engineering
- Administrative Services

5.8 Experience

The consultant will be expected to have particular strengths not only in recreation and sport physical planning, but in conflict resolution, community consultation and clarifying management structures.

6. Consultancy Timetable

The consultancy will commence in _____ and have a final report completed by _____.

7. Project Management

The Project Manager will be [name of title]. Overview of the project will be maintained by a Project Management Steering Committee consisting of [names of key people in council and community].

8. Copyright

The _____ Council and the Office for Recreation and Sport holds copyright on all material produced by the Plan. They also hold options on producing further copies of the report under the authorship of the consultants. The consultants may subsequently publish material obtained during the compilation of the report, but may not publish the final report without permission.

9. Contact Officer

For further information or clarification of the Brief, please contact:

Appendix

Relevant projects and detailed information relevant to the local council area such as the following should be included:

- Open space studies
- Facilities feasibility studies
- Youth, aged, and special interest studies
- Human services planning information
- Recreation and sport activities studies

Example of a Specific Project Planning Brief

CITY OF ELIZABETH PROPOSED RECREATION AND SPORTS HUB

1. Clients

The City of Elizabeth and the Office for Recreation and Sport.

2. Background

A number of strategic planning reports and proposals over the last twelve months have suggested that a regional recreation and sports hub be part of the Elizabeth City Centre.

2.1 One of the main proposals of the City of Elizabeth Recreation and Sport Plan suggested that the area surrounding the aquadome be consolidated with other built recreation and sport facilities as part of the city centre.

2.2 The Northern Metropolitan Recreation and Sport Strategy supported this concept and identified it as a high regional priority.

2.3 Also, the Elizabeth/Munno Para Social Justice Project highlighted the need for a major sports hub involving new and existing facilities relating to the regional centre at Elizabeth.

2.4 From the 2020 Vision came a broad direction for Northern Metropolitan Adelaide that suggested the further development of the Elizabeth Regional Centre. Building Better Cities funds have been allocated to an Elizabeth Regional Centre Urban Design Study. It is therefore important that this feasibility study is part of the overall design study.

2.5 In addition, the Central Districts Football Club has proposed the establishment of a Central Districts Sports and Recreation Association that includes a two-court indoor basketball facility, outdoor netball courts and a synthetic bowling rink to be developed on the Elizabeth Oval site. This feasibility study takes into consideration the Elizabeth Football Club proposals.

The Elizabeth City Council has required the Recreation and Sport Planning Unit to assist in undertaking a feasibility study as the first stage of providing regional recreation and sport facilities in the Elizabeth City Centre.

3. Objectives

Main objective: The main objective is to prepare a feasibility study that will lead to the establishment of an Elizabeth Recreation and Sports Hub that will provide regional recreation and sport facilities to serve the needs of the diverse and growing population of the northern area of Adelaide.

There are two specific objectives:

1. To prepare concept plans and a design that integrates the existing and proposed recreation and sport facilities with other City Centre planning being undertaken.

2. To create management and operation plans that will make the project economically viable.

4. Project Description

Part 1: Planning and Design

4.1.1 Evaluate and cost the design of the Recreation and Sports Hub that is detailed in the appendix in the City of Elizabeth Recreation and Sport Plan 1992–93.

4.1.2 Consider other planning and design alternatives that include the existing aquadome, the Central Districts Football Club Oval, an additional oval, a four-court indoor sport facility and additional facilities.

4.1.3 Consider the possibility of opening up the Elizabeth High School for community recreation and sports activities.

4.1.4 Other factors to be considered are accessibility to the transport interchange, pedestrian and cycle links to other facilities in the City Centre, access for the disabled to all indoor and outdoor recreation and sport facilities and parking for major regional recreation and sport events.

4.1.5 An open space should be produced that uses landscaping to encourage both formal and informal recreation and sport use of the area.

4.1.6 An important factor in the design of the facilities is their mix and scale in order to achieve efficiency of operations and economic viability.

4.1.7 A suggested phased development schedule should also be prepared.

Part 2: Management and Operations

It is important that the management and operations be aimed at providing the maximum use of the proposed recreation and sport facilities and services by the citizens of Elizabeth and people living in the surrounding regional areas.

4.2.1 An analysis of the Central Districts Football Club proposal should be undertaken.

4.2.2 The existing management structure for the aquadome should be evaluated for inclusion in a possible wider role.

4.2.3 Other management alternatives should be investigated, particularly, successful ones from interstate and overseas.

4.2.4 A major task is to prepare an operations budget including all overheads that will break even within three years.

4.2.5 An organisational structure should be prepared that clearly indicates lines of responsibility between the Elizabeth City Council and other organisations and operators.

4.2.6 A proposed staffing structure should be prepared.

5. Guidelines for Preparing the Brief

The following guidelines are set out to assist in understanding the nature and scope of the task.

5.1 Because this is a planning, design and management project that will require a wide range of skills, additional assistance may be required.

5.2 Particularly, strong negotiating skills and the ability to obtain cooperation from disparate recreation and sport interest groups are required.

5.3 There needs to be an awareness of the existing recreation and sport planning that is being undertaken in the north metropolitan region so that this project within can be placed in a regional context. Other regional strategies are also being developed, particularly concerning the Elizabeth Regional Centre.

5.4 Access to expertise within the Office for Recreation and Sport particularly in the following areas will be useful:

- Recreation and sport planning.
- Recreation and sport facility development (particularly aquatic centres, open space, indoor and outdoor facilities).
- Playgrounds and play areas.
- Advice on the provision of recreation and sport for people with disabilities, Aboriginals and women.

5.5 The Office for Recreation and Sport has a range of planning material available in its Resource Centre.

6. Project Management

A small team will be established to manage the feasibility study, including planning staff from the Office for Recreation and Sport, Elizabeth City Council and representatives for community recreation and sport organisations as appropriate.

7. Proposed Timetable

The proposed timetable is that the study commences in October 1993 and a final report is completed by the end of January 1994.

8. Contact Officer

For information or clarification on the brief, please contact:

Jim Daly
Manager
Recreation and Sport Planning
Phone: 61 8 8416 6732

Dimensions for Outdoor and Indoor Sport Facilities

The facilities featured in this appendix are appropriate for the following activities:

- American football
- Archery
- Athletics
- Australian football
- Badminton
- Baseball
- Basketball
- Beach volleyball
- Bowls
- Cricket
- Golf

- Hockey
- Lacrosse
- Netball
- Rugby league
- Rugby union
- Soccer
- Softball
- Tennis
- Touch
- Volleyball

A more comprehensive reference to dimensions of sports areas involving other sports is found in *Sports Dimensions for Playing Areas* (1998), produced by the Ministry of Western Australia. As with that publication, the author of this manual has no duty of care regarding the correctness of the dimensions. Persons reading this appendix acknowledge that no warranty or undertaking is given that the dimensions or other guidelines are safe or fit for the purpose for which they were intended to be used or that accidents and injuries will not occur. All liability and responsibility for losses, injuries, damages, costs or expenses, howsoever arising or incurred, are hereby disclaimed.

American Football

For flag football, length is 54.86 metres (minimum) to 91.44 metres (maximum) and width is 48.77 metres (maximum).

DIMENSIONS

Length: 109.73 metres

Width: 48.77 metres

Safety zone around the complete field:
3.66 metres

Height of goalposts:
9.14 metres

Cross bar: 3.05 metres above ground to top of bar

Space between goalposts:
5.64 metres

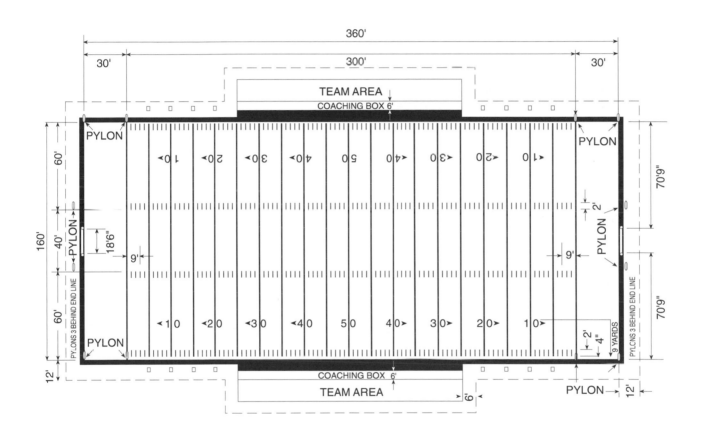

Archery

The field should lie north-south, with the targets placed at the southern end. For communal shooting, targets should be at least 3.658 metres apart.

OUTDOOR TARGET DIMENSIONS

Shooting distance:
90 metres (maximum)

Distance between shooting line and waiting line:
5 metres (minimum)

Width:
1 metre per archer per detail per target (minimum)

Safety zone behind targets:
50 metres (minimum)

Safety zone behind waiting line:
20 metres

Distance between fields:
20 metres (minimum)

INDOOR TARGET DIMENSIONS

Shooting distance:
30 metres (maximum) to 18 metres (minimum)

Distance between shooting line and waiting line:
3 metres (minimum);
5 metres (preferred)

Width:
0.8 metres per archer (minimum)

Height:
3 metres (minimum)

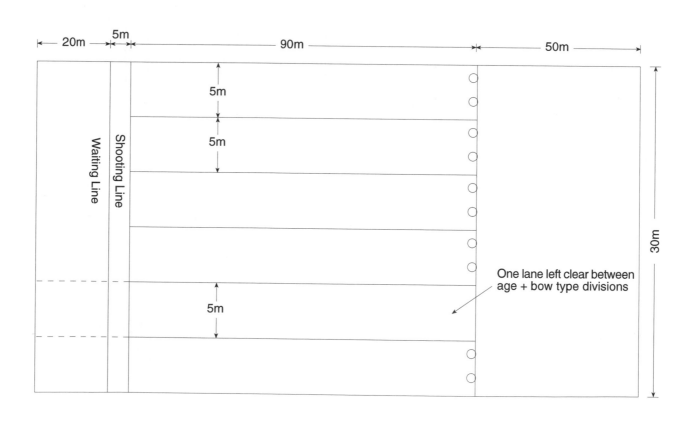

Athletics

The longitudinal axis of the facility should lie along the south-north axis. All markings are 0.05 metres wide.

FIELD DIMENSIONS

Length: 182.91 metres

Width: 112.52 metres

Safety zones: 1.0 metre (minimum) on the outside and inside of the track; 3.0 metres (minimum) at the start of the main straight; 17.0 metres (minimum) run-out at the end of the main straight

Width of lanes: 1.22 metres

Width of track: 9.76 metres

Bend radius: 36.50 metres

THROWING EVENTS

Discus: throwing circle diameter 2.50 metres; landing radius 80.0 metres

Hammer throw: throwing circle diameter 2.135 metres; landing radius 90.0 metres

Shot put: throwing circle diameter 2.135 metres; landing radius 25.0 metres

Javelin: runway length 30.0 metres (minimum) to 36.5 metres (maximum); width 4.0 metres; landing radius 100.0 metres

JUMPING EVENTS

Long jump: runway 40.0 metres × 1.22 metres; landing area 9.0 metres × 2.75 metres

Pole vault: runway 40.0 metres × 1.22 metres; landing area 6.50 metres × 5.0 metres

Triple jump: runway 40.0 metres × 1.22 metres; landing area 9.0 metres × 2.75 metres

High jump: semicircular runway 20.0-metre radius; landing area 5.0 metres × 3.0 metres

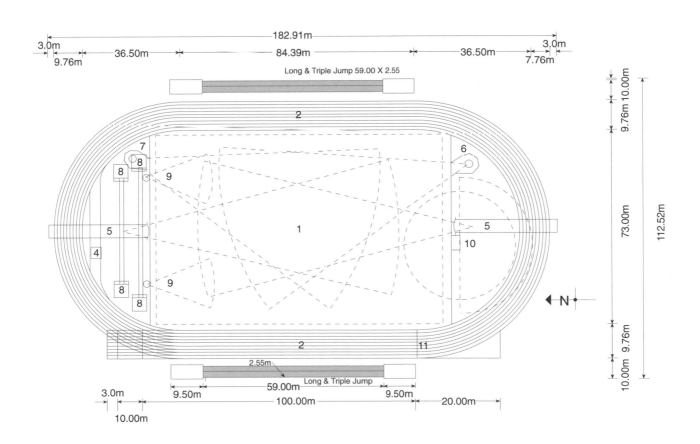

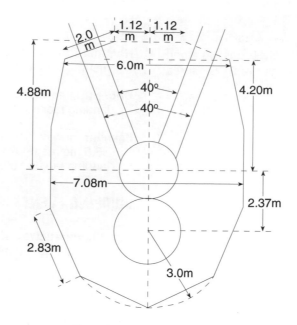

Cage for Hammer and Discus

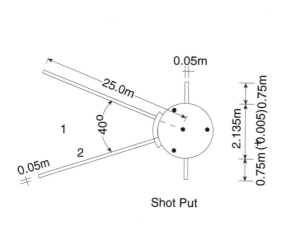

Shot Put

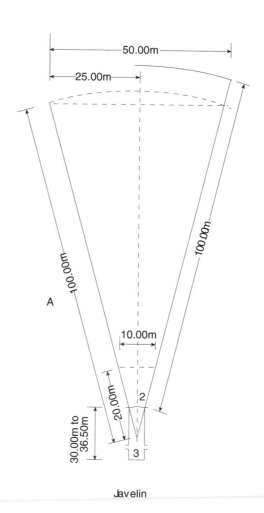

Javelin

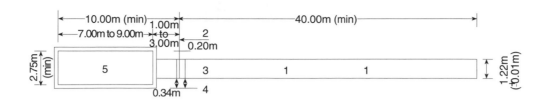

Long Jump

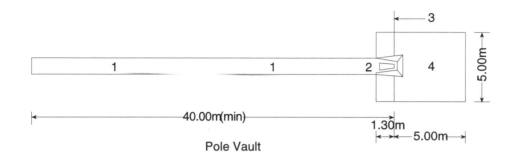

Pole Vault

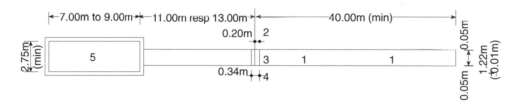

Triple Jump

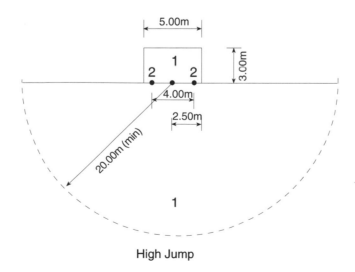

High Jump

Australian Football

The shape of the playing field is oval.

FULL-SIZE OVAL DIMENSIONS

Length: 185 metres (maximum) to 135 metres (minimum)

Width: 155 metres (maximum) to 110 metres (minimum)

Safety zone around the complete oval between the boundary line and spectator fence: 4 metres (minimum)

Centre circle: 1.5-metre radius

Centre square: 45 metres × 45 metres

Goal square: 9 metres × 6.4 metres

Goalposts: 6 metres (minimum height)

Behind posts: 3 metres (minimum height)

Space between inside edge of all goalposts: 6.40 metres

JUNIOR SIZE OVAL DIMENSIONS

16-18 Years Old: full-size oval can be used; recommended size 165 metres × 135 metres

13-15 Years Old: full-size oval can be used; recommended size 135 metres × 110 metres

11-12 Years Old: oval is two-thirds a senior oval including the centre square

9-10 Years Old: oval is half a senior oval including the centre square

All goalposts for juniors below the age of 12 should be 6 metres. Orientation of the oval should take into account the minimum impact of the sun being in the eyes of the players.

LAWS OF AUSTRALIAN FOOTBALL 1999

Playing field and playing positions

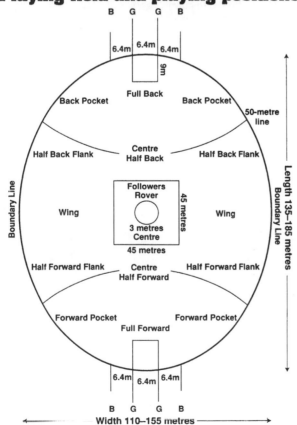

Badminton

Top of the net is 1.524 metres in height from the floor at the centre and 1.550 metres at the posts. Where courts are to be utilised by disabled persons, a 40 millimetre-wide line should be marked perpen-dicular to the side line for singles, 2.134 metres from the front of the short service line. Optional testing marks of which a shuttle of correct pace lands when tested can be included (see diagram).

DIMENSIONS

Length: 13.40 metres

Width (singles):   5.18 metres

Width (doubles):   6.10 metres

Line marking: 40 millimetres wide and coloured white or yellow

Safety zone behind the base line:
2.0 metres

Safety zone at the sides:
2.0 metres

Height: 12.0 metres (minimum)

Minimum distance between two parallel courts:
2.0 metres

INTERNATIONAL

Safety zone around the complete court:
2.0 metres

Safety zone behind the base line:
2.0 metres (minimum)

Safety zone at the sides:
2.0 metres (minimum)

Height: 12.0 metres (minimum)

POSTS AND NET

Posts: 1.55 metres high

At the net: 0.76 metres in depth

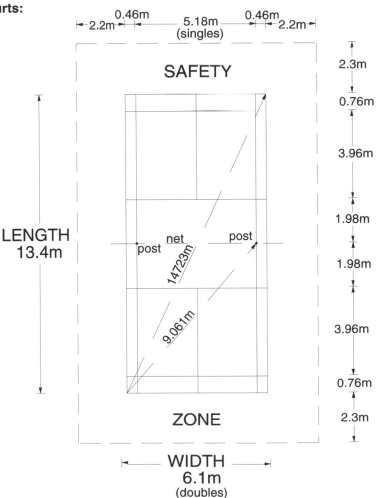

Baseball

INTERNATIONAL DIMENSIONS

Distance between bases:
27.44 metres

Distance home base to pitcher plate:
18.44 metres

Distance home base to centre field:
122.0 metres

Foul line length: 98.0 metres

Safety zone or extra foul area at home base:
18.3 metres (minimum)

NATIONAL DIMENSIONS

Distance between bases:
27.44 metres

Distance home base to pitcher plate:
18.44 metres

Distance home base to centre field:
114.30 metres

Foul line length: 91.50 metres

Safety zone or extra foul area at home base:
18.30 metres (minimum)

REGIONAL DIMENSIONS

Distance between bases:
27.44 metres

Distance home base to pitcher plate:
18.44 metres

Distance home base to centre field:
106.60 metres

Foul line length: 91.50 metres

Safety zone or extra foul area at home base:
13.70 metres (minimum)

JUNIOR DIMENSIONS

15–16 Years

Distance between bases:
27.44 metres

Distance home base to pitcher plate:
18.44 metres

Distance home base to centre field:
106.70 metres

Foul line length: 85.40 metres

Safety zone or extra foul area at home base:
18.30 metres (preferred);
13.70 metres (minimum)

13–14 Years

Distance between bases:
24.38 metres

Distance home base to pitcher plate:
16.46 metres

Distance home base to centre field:
96.10 metres

Foul line length: 76.30 metres

Safety zone or extra foul area at home base:
18.30 metres (preferred);
13.70 metres (minimum)

11–12 Years

Distance between bases:
18.29 metres

Distance home base to pitcher plate:
14.00 metres

Foul line length: 60.90 metres

Safety zone or extra foul area at home base:
13.70 metres (minimum)

9–10 Years

Distance between bases:
18.30 metres

Distance home base to pitcher plate:
13.10–14.00 metres

Foul line length: 61.00 metres

6–8 Years

Distance between bases:
15.20 metres

Distance home base to pitcher plate:
13.10 metres

Foul line length: 45.70 metres

Tee ball dimensions are the same as those used in 6–8 and 9–10 years competitions.

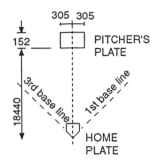

Layout at Home Plate

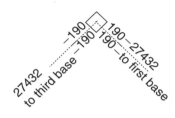

Layout at Second-Base Corner

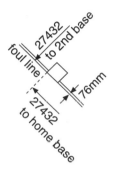

Layout at Third-Base Corner

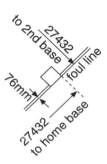

Layout at First-Base Corner

BASEBALL DIAMOND LAYOUT

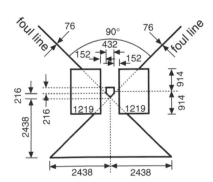

**Layout at Home-Base,
Batter's Box and Catcher's Box**

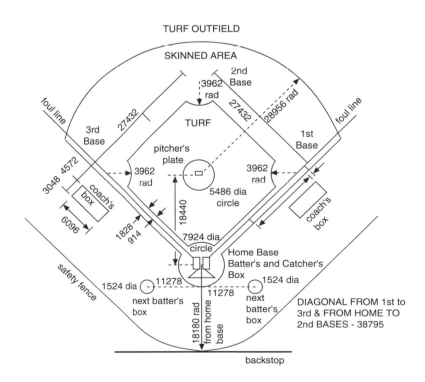

Basketball

Wheelchair basketball requires a clear space of 3 metres at either end of the court. Basketball supports should be well padded and placed outside this zone. Scorer's table and team benches should be at least 3 metres from side line. All line markings are 50 millimetres wide. The boundary lines are outside the playing zone. (Court dimensions are taken from inside boundary line.)

Width: 15.0 metres

Height: 7.0 metres (minimum)

Safety zone around complete court:
2 metres (minimum)

JUNIOR DIMENSIONS

U/10: basket height 2.59 metres

Miniball (10 Years and Under): court size same as seniors, but basket is lowered to 2.44 metres.

DIMENSIONS

Length: 28.0 metres

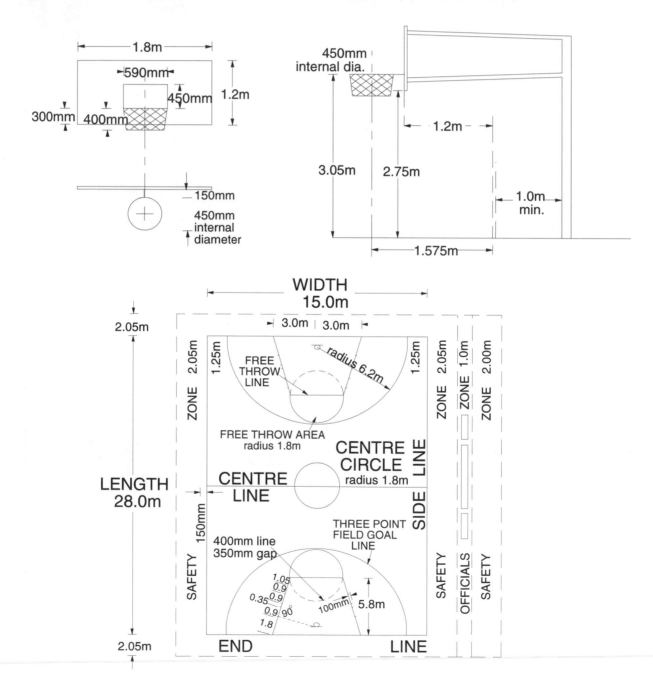

Beach Volleyball

For a permanent court, it is recommended to use Oregon posts 200 millimetres × 200 millimetres with a 1.0-metre piece of wood attached to each post for stabilisation.

COURT DIMENSIONS

Length: 18 metres

Width: 9 metres

Safety zone around entire court: 5 metres plus 3 metres on one side for officials

NET DIMENSIONS

Net height for men:
                2.43 metres

Net height for women:
                2.24 metres

JUNIOR DIMENSIONS

U/19: Net height 2.43 metres (boys) and 2.24 metres (girls)

U/17: net height 2.35 metres (boys) and 2.15 metres (girls)

U/15: net height 2.24 metres (boys) and 2.10 metres (girls)

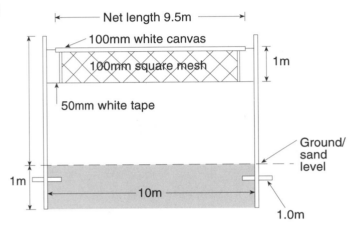

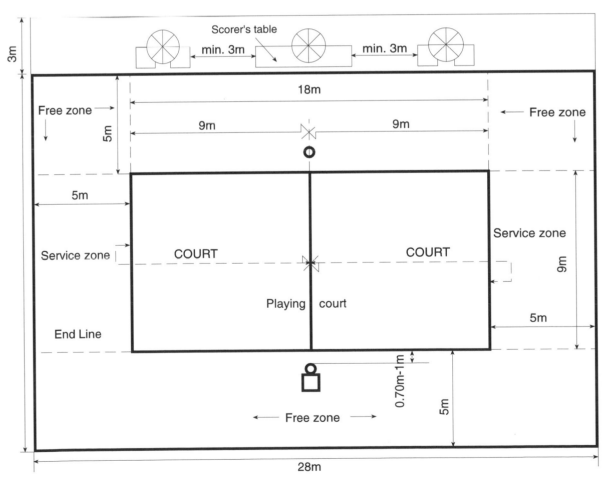

Bowls

The front of the mat is placed 2.0 metres from the rear ditch. The end of the rink is 2.0 metres from the front ditch. The green extends for a minimum of 0.6 metres beyond the side boundary of a rink.

LAWN DIMENSIONS (GREEN)

Length: 37 metres (minimum);
40 metres (maximum)

Width: 37 metres (minimum);
40 metres (maximum)

RINK

International width:
5.5 metres (minimum);
5.8 metres (maximum)

Club width: 4.3 metres (minimum);
5.8 metres (maximum)

INDOOR RINK

Length: 32.0 metres (minimum);
34.75 metres (maximum)

Width: 4.27 metres (minimum);
4.57 (maximum)

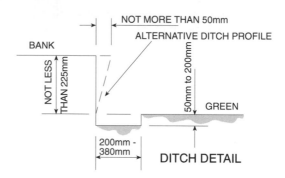

DITCH DETAIL

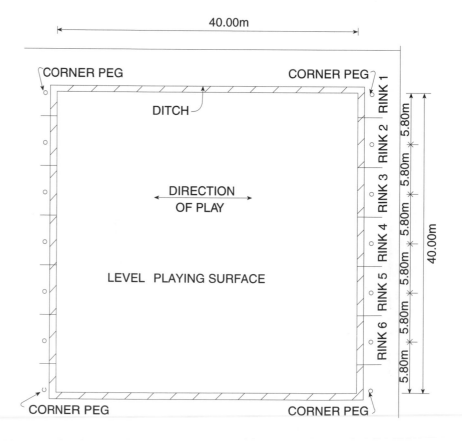

Cricket

PLAYING FIELD

In international play, the shape of the playing field is oval. There is no regulation governing the size of the actual oval. However, the controlling bodies for the sport have offered the following suggestions:

Senior men: 137.16 metres by 118.87 metres or a 64- to 68.6-metres radius measured from the centre stump at each end (minimum international width 64 metres).

Senior women: 75-metre radius measured from the centre stump.

U/21: 65-metre radius measured from the centre stump.

U/18: 60-metre radius measured from the centre stump.

PITCHES AND CREASES

Length of pitch: 20.12 metres measured between the two centre stumps.

Width of pitch: 1.52 metres either side of the centre line of the pitch.

Bowling crease: in line with the stumps; extends 1.32 metres either side of the centre line of the pitch.

Popping crease (batting crease): 1.22 metres in front of the stumps parallel to the bowling crease.

There is an unspecified length for the popping crease but is usually shown as a straight line 1.83 metres either side of the centre line of the pitch.

JUNIOR DIMENSIONS

In Kanga Cricket, boundary distance is variable but should be a maximum of 30–40 metres. Pitch length is 16 metres for U/10, 18 metres for U/12, and 20 metres for U/14.

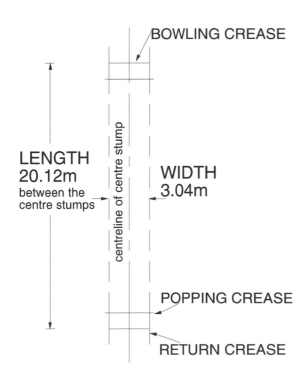

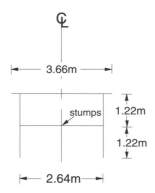

CREASE

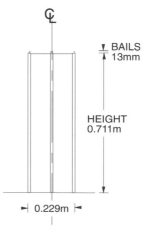

STUMPS & BAILS

Golf

TOTAL AREA REQUIRED

18 holes: 60 hectares

9 holes: 25 hectares

Par 3:   30 hectares

DIMENSIONS

Length: 5,500 metres (minimum);
6,100 metres (preferred)

Provision for back tees:
6,600 metres

Hole diameter: 108 millimetres

Hole depth: 102 millimetres (minimum)

REGULATION COURSE (18 HOLES, PAR 72)

Ten par 4 holes

Four par 3 holes

Four par 5 holes

   Distance of hole measured from the centre of the tee area to the centre of the putting green along the line of intended play.

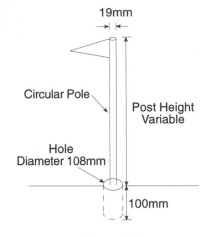

Flagstick

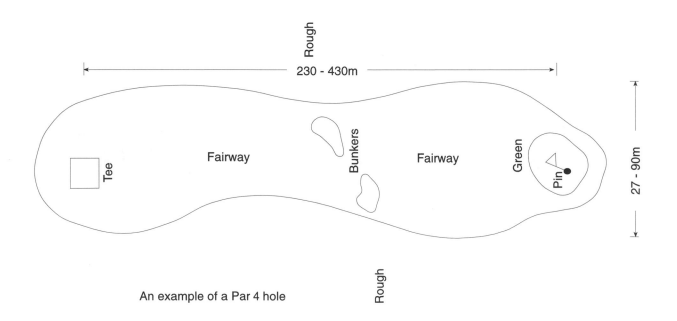

An example of a Par 4 hole

Hockey

Allow a minimum of 6.00 metres between adjoining hockey fields.

FULL-SIZE DIMENSIONS

Length: 91.44 metres

Width: 55.00 metres

Width of lines: 0.075 metres

Safety zone at the sides:
          3.00 metres (minimum)

Safety zone at the ends:
          4.50 metres (minimum)

GOAL DIMENSIONS

Length: 3.66 metres

Width: 1.20 metres (ground level);
          0.91 metres (top of goals)

JUNIOR FIELDS

U/12

Length: 55 metres

Width: 45 metres

Penalty spot: 6 metres inside goal line

Penalty corner mark on goal line:
          6 metres either side of
          goalpost

U/10

Length: 45 metres

Width: 27 metres

Penalty spot: 5 metres inside goal line

Defensive zone marked by flags 10 metres from goal line (line optional)

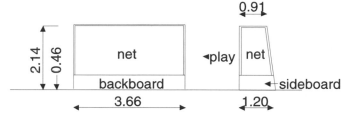

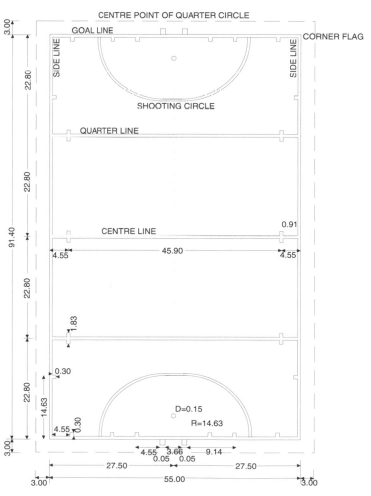

Lacrosse

DIMENSIONS: MENS

Length: 100.58 metres

Width: 54.86 metres

Distance between goals:
73.15 metres

Safety zone around the complete field:
3.0 metres (minimum)

Goalposts: 1.83 metres high to underside of crossbar

Space between goalposts:
1.83 metres

DIMENSIONS: WOMENS

Length: 114.0 metres

Width: 60.0 metres

Distance between goals:
92.0 metres

Safety zone around the complete field:
3.0 metres (minimum)

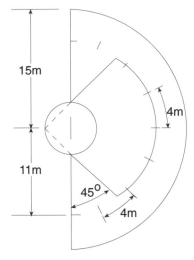

15m

11m

45°

4m

4m

Women's Goal Area

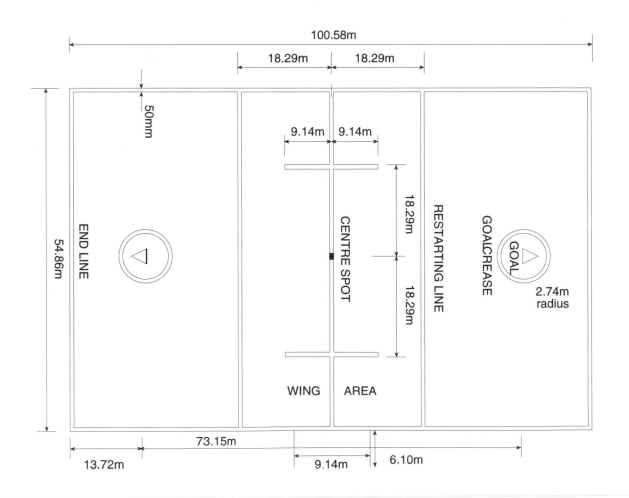

Netball

INTERNATIONAL DIMENSIONS

Length: 30.05 metres

Width: 15.25 metres

Height: 8.0 metres (minimum)

Safety zone at the sides:
3 metres (minimum)

Safety zone at the ends:
3 metres (minimum)

Team benches to be a minimum of 3 metres from the side line.

NATIONAL DIMENSIONS

Length: 30.05 metres

Width: 15.25 metres

Height: 8.0 metres (minimum)

Safety zone at the sides:
1.5 metres (minimum)

Safety zone at the ends:
2 metres (minimum)

Team benches to be a minimum of 1.5 metres from the side line.

RECREATIONAL DIMENSIONS

Length: 30.05 metres

Width: 15.25 metres

Height: 8.0 m (minimum)

Safety zone at the sides:
1.0 metre (minimum)

Safety zone at the ends:
1.2 metres (minimum)

Team benches to be a minimum of 1 metre from the side line.

JUNIORS

All juniors play on a full-size court but to modified rules. The height of the net for players under 10 years of age is set at 2.44 metres.

All line markings are 50 millimetres wide and included in areas of play.

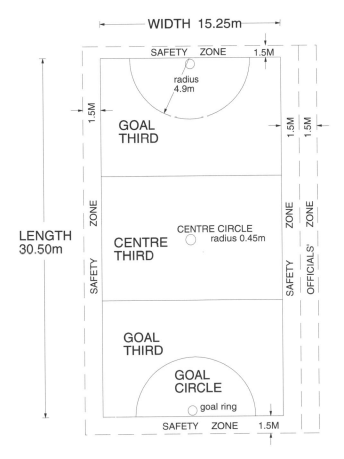

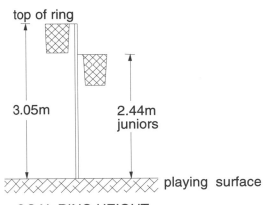

Rugby League

FULL-SIZE OVAL

Length: 100 metres (maximum)

Width: 68 metres (maximum)

Safety zone around the complete field:
4 metres (minimum);
6 metres (preferred)

Height of goalposts:
4 metres (minimum)

Crossbar: 3 metres above ground to
top of bar

Space between goalposts:
5.5 metres

JUNIOR SIZE OVAL

U/10

Pitch size: 70 metres by 30 metres with 2 quarter lines in each half of the pitch. In goal line minimum 6 metres and maximum 11 metres behind the goal line.

Height of goalposts:
3.1 metres

Crossbar: 2 metres above ground to
top of bar

Space between goalposts: 3 metres

U/12

Pitch size: 80 metres by 50 metres with 2 quarter lines in each half of the pitch. In goal line 10 metres behind the goal line.

It is recommended that the goalposts be padded up to a height of 2 metres.

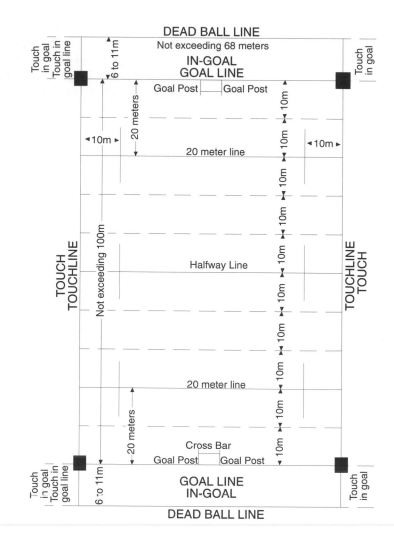

Rugby Union

FULL-SIZE OVAL

Length: 100 metres (maximum)

Width: 70 metres (maximum)

Safety zone around the complete field:
3 metres (minimum);
6 metres (preferred)

Height of goalposts:
3.4 metres (minimum)

Crossbar: 3 metres above ground to top of bar

Space between goalposts:
5.6 metres

Distance from goal line to dead ball line:
10 metres (minimum);
22 metres (maximum)

JUNIOR-SIZE OVAL

Length: 70 metres

Width: 50 metres

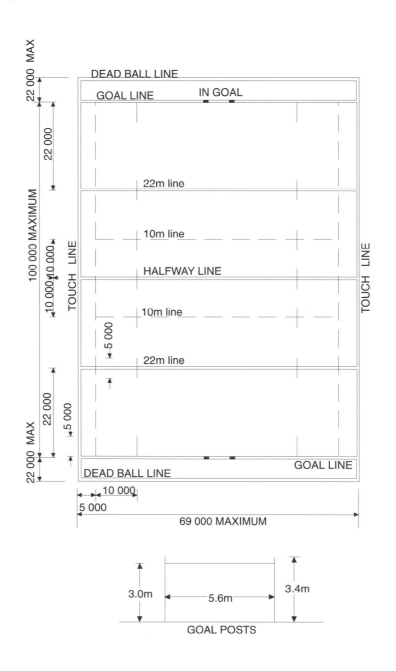

Soccer

FULL-SIZE PITCH

F.A. International: length 100–110 metres;
width 64–75 metres
(recommended 100 metres long
by 64 metres wide)

F.A. U.K. Matches: length 90–120 metres;
width 45–90 metres

Schoolboy International:
length 75 metres (minimum);
width 55 metres (minimum)

Safety zone at the sides:
6.0 metres

Safety zone at the ends:
9.0 metres

JUNIOR SOCCER

U/13 to U/17

Length: 90–120 metres

Width: 45–90 metres

U/10 to U/12

Length: 70 metres (minimum)

Width: 40 metres (minimum)

Penalty area: length 14 metres;
width 30 metres

Goal dimensions: height 2 metres;
width 6 metres

U/8 to U/9

Length: 50 metres

Width: 25 metres

Penalty area: length 10 metres;
width 20 metres

Goal dimensions: height 1.52 metres;
width 4.57 metres

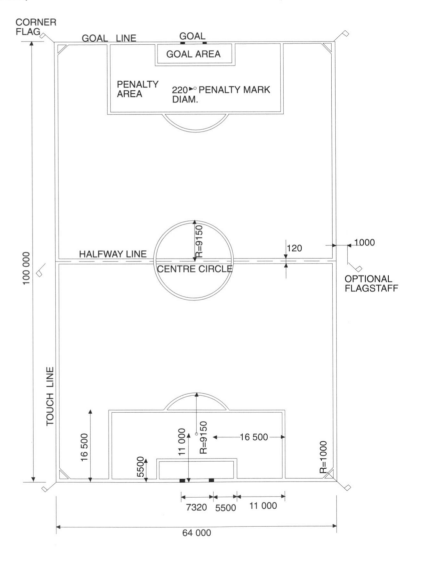

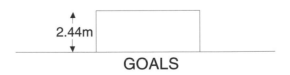

GOALS

Softball

Starting at midway between home plate and first base, the three-foot line is marked parallel to and 0.914 metres from the base line. The on-deck circle is 1.520 metres in diameter and is placed adjacent to the catcher's box.

DIMENSIONS

Official diamond: 18.288 metres

Diagonal between home plate and second base and first base and third base:
25.863 metres

Distance from home plate to back net:
7.62–9.10 metres

Home plate to fence distance radius:
60.90 metres (female fast pitch);
68.58 metres (male fast pitch);
76.20 metres (female slow pitch);
83.82 metres (male slow pitch)

Pitching distance:
14.02 metres (male fast or slow pitch);
12.19 metres (female fast pitch);
14.02 metres (female slow pitch)

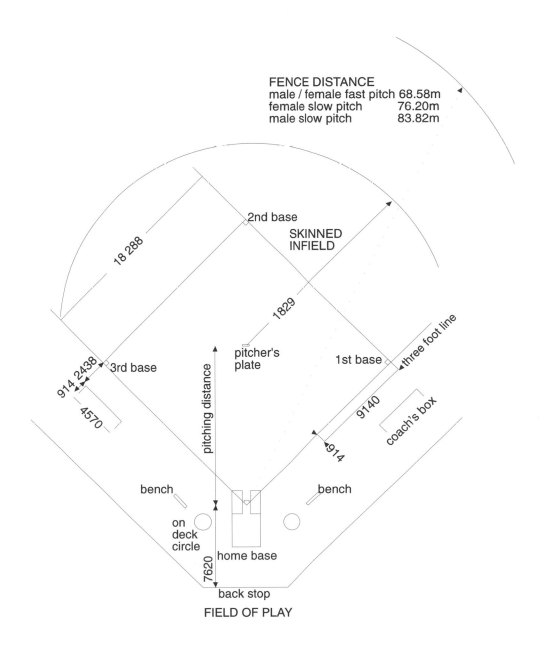

FENCE DISTANCE
male / female fast pitch 68.58m
female slow pitch   76.20m
male slow pitch   83.82m

2nd base

SKINNED
INFIELD

18 288

1829

pitcher's
plate

3rd base

914 2438

4570

1st base

three foot line

pitching distance

9140

914

coach's box

bench

bench

on
deck
circle

home base

7620

back stop

FIELD OF PLAY

JUNIOR SOFTBALL 10–12 YEARS

Distance between bases:
16.76 metres

Diagonal: 23.70 metres

Pitching distance:
9.10 metres

Distance from home plate to back net:
7.62 metres

TEE SOFTBALL

Distance between bases:
15.20 metres

Diagonal: 21.55 metres

Pitching distances:
9.10 metres

Distance from home plate to back net:
7.62 metres

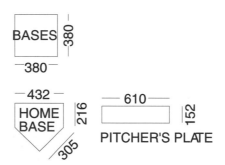

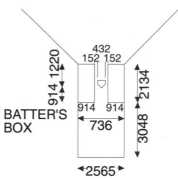

LAYOUT AT HOME BASE

Tennis

DIMENSIONS

Length: 23.77 metres

Width (doubles): 10.97 metres

Width (singles): 8.23 metres

Safety zone behind the base line:
6.4 metres (international and club);
5.49 metres (recreation)

Safety zone at the sides:
3.66 metres (international and club);
3.05 metres (recreation)

Officials' space all around court:
1.22 metres (international and club)

Height: 10.67 metres (international);
9.00 metres (club);
8.00 metres (recreation)

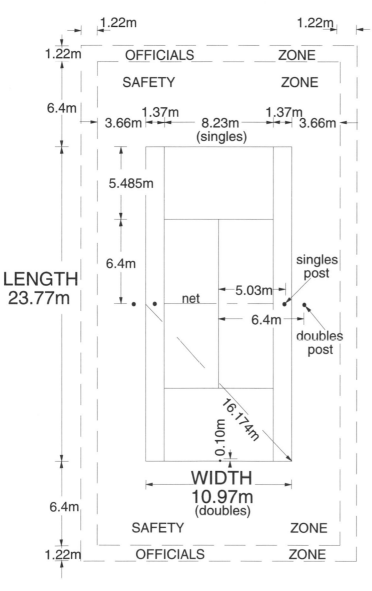

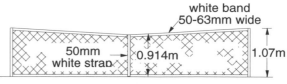

NET REQUIREMENTS

Touch

FULL-SIZE FIELD

Length: 70 metres

Width: 50 metres

Safety zone around the field:
3 metres (minimum)

The broken lines perpendicular to the score line and to the side lines are optional. The side line should be extended at a minimum of 10 metres; however, there is no dead ball line.

JUNIOR FIELD U/14

Length: 50 metres

Width: 35 metres

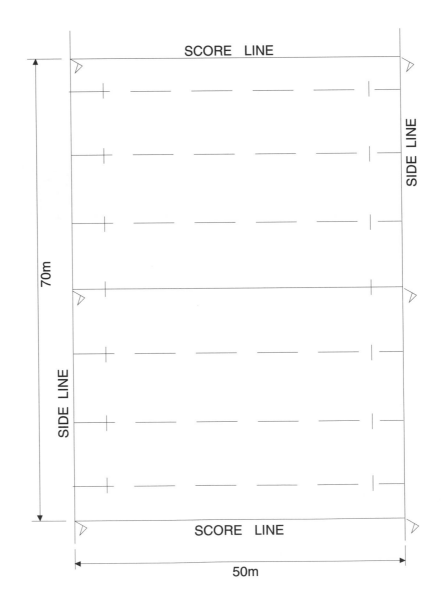

Volleyball

COURT DIMENSIONS

Length: 18 metres

Width: 9 metres

Safety zone behind base line: minimum 8 metres for service and play plus 3 metres for safety zone (international); minimum 3 metres for service and play plus 3 metres for safety zone (national/club); minimum 2 metres (recreational)

Safety zone at the sides: minimum 5 metres for play and referee plus 3 metres on one side for officials plus 3 metres on both sides for safety zone (international); minimum 2 metres on one side for officials plus 3 metres on both sides for safety zone (national/club); minimum 2 metres (recreational)

Height: 12.5 metres minimum (international); 9 metres minimum (national); 7 metres minimum (club); 7 metres minimum (recreational)

Net height: 2.43 metres (men);
2.24 metres (women)

JUNIOR DIMENSIONS

Mini Volleyball Court Size

Length: 13.4 metres

Width: 6.10 metres

Net height: 2.05 metres

Net Height

U/15:   2.24 metres (boys);
2.10 metres (girls)

U/17:   2.35 metres (boys);
2.15 metres (girls)

U/19:   2.43 metres (boys);
2.24 metres (girls)

Note: All line markings are 50 millimetres wide and are included in the area of play.

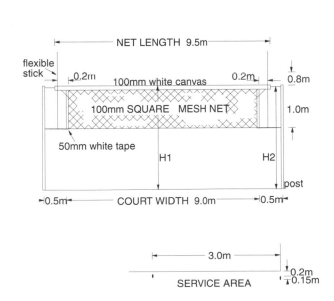

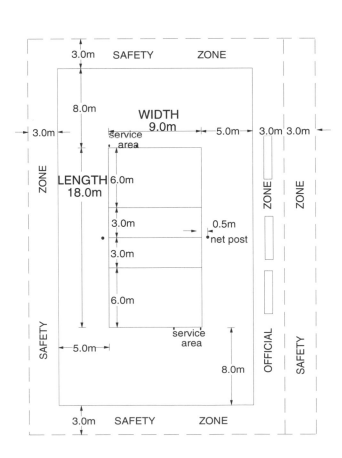

GIS Sporting Facility Inventory Questionnaire

Questionnaire: GIS Sporting Facility Inventory (International, National and State)

Prepared by Christina Gabrovsek, GIS Project Officer, Geographic Analysis and Research Unit, Planning SA.

Tick appropriate boxes unless specified. Additional information can be written in the "Other" category, found at the end of most sections.

Section I

1. Sport _____

2. Sport Information

      2.1 Sport association _____

      2.2 Contact person _____

      2.3 Address _____

      2.4 Phone number _____

      2.5 Fax number _____

      2.6 Email address _____

      2.7 Web site address _____

3. Sport level that can be played in South Australia

(Please circle)	International	National	State
Seniors **(please tick)**	☐	☐	☐
Facilities **(please list)**	_____	_____	_____
	_____	_____	_____
	_____	_____	_____
	_____	_____	_____
	_____	_____	_____
	_____	_____	_____
	_____	_____	_____
	_____	_____	_____

(Please circle)	International	National	State
Juniors **(please tick)**	☐	☐	☐
Facilities **(please list)**	_____	_____	_____
	_____	_____	_____
	_____	_____	_____
	_____	_____	_____
	_____	_____	_____
	_____	_____	_____
	_____	_____	_____
	_____	_____	_____
	_____	_____	_____

4. Accommodation

Does the **sport** provide athlete accommodation? (please circle)   Yes / No

If yes, provide details of the location, standard and how many athletes it can hold. _____

_____

_____

_____

_____

Section II

If there is more than any one facility type see attachments.

5. Facility information

5.1 Facility name _____

5.2 Is the facility known by any other name? _____

5.3 Street number name _____

5.4 Suburb _____

5.5 Postcode _____

5.6 Council _____

5.7 Facility contact name _____

5.8 Facility contact number _____

5.9 Facility fax number _____

5.10 Facility email address _____

5.11 Seating capacity _____

5.12 Title reference _____

6. Accommodation

Does the facility provide athlete accommodation? (please circle)   Yes / No

If yes, provide details of the location, standard and how many athletes it can hold. _____

_____

_____

_____

7. Facility description

Does the facility cater for other activities? _____

_____

_____

8. Facility access

    8.1 Access for people with disabilities ☐

    8.2 Fenced facility ☐

    8.3 Not fenced facility ☐

    8.4 Parking capacity _____

    8.5 Other _____

9. Facility amenities

    9.1 Medical facilities ☐

    9.2 Canteen facilities ☐

    9.3 Dining facilities ☐

    9.4 Conference facilities ☐

    9.5 Change rooms/toilets ☐

    9.6 Specialised training equipment ☐

    9.7 Equipment storage ☐

    9.8 Office administration ☐

    9.9 Warm-up areas ☐

    9.10 Laundry and dry cleaning ☐

    9.11 Recreational areas ☐

    9.12 Other _____

_____

_____

_____

10. Transport (to and from the venue)

    10.1 Bus ☐

    10.2 Train ☐

    10.3 Tram ☐

    10.4 Taxi ranks ☐

    10.5 Other _____

_____

11. Management of the facility

    11.1 Operational arrangements

        11.1.1 Who owns the facility? _____

        11.1.2 Who manages the facility? _____

        11.1.3 Provide information on the management arrangement, e.g. contracted out, leased, private or other _____

_____

11.2 Management structures

      11.2.1 Board of directors

      11.2.2 Management committee

      11.2.3 Other _____

_____

11.3 Facility operational information

      11.3.1 Strategic plan

      11.3.2 Annual business plan

      11.3.3 Marketing plan

      11.3.4 Operational review

      11.3.5 Facility audit

      11.3.6 Annual report

      11.3.7 Annual financial statement

      11.3.8 Policy documents

      11.3.9 Others (list) _____

12. Facility development plans

Briefly describe facility plans likely to occur over the next three (3) years. _____

_____

13. Facility plans

Can you supply layout/plans of the facility?   (please circle)   yes / no

Office for Recreation and Sport Only	
Sporting code from Sports Inventory	☐ ☐ ☐ ☐ ☐ ☐ ☐
Facility description from Facility Use Inventory	☐ ☐ ☐ ☐ ☐
Facility unique code	☐ ☐ ☐ ☐
Date surveyed	☐ ☐ ☐ ☐

Recreation, Sport Facilities and Open Space GIS Inventory

Recreation, Sport Facilities and Open Space GIS Inventory

Prepared jointly by Philip Freeman, Recreation Planner, Office for Recreation and Sport and Mark Mobbs, Project Officer, Open Space Development Unit, Planning SA.

Location Information

Facility/reserve code _____

Facility/reserve name _____

Street number _____

Street name _____

Suburb _____

Postcode _____

Council _____

Ownership _____

Standard (choose 1 only)   ☐

1. Local

2. Neighbourhood/district

3. Regional

4. State

5. National

6. International

7. School

Complete general description, linear reserve, and quality sections for open space and conservation only.

General description (choose 1 only)   ☐

0. Unusable/aesthetic

1. Useable

Linear reserve (choose 1 only)   ☐
0. No
1. Yes

Quality (not required for unuseable open space, conservation areas or vacant unimproved areas)
1. Poor   ☐
2. Good
3. Excellent

Date Inspected
Month / year   ☐☐ ☐☐☐☐

Facility description

Code	Indoor sport and recreation facility	Tick the box
IND_BA	Bowling alley	☐
IND_CC	Community centre/hall	☐
IND_EC	Entertainment centre	☐
IND_FH	Fitness and health centre	☐
IND_GF	Gymnastics	☐
IND_PL	Pool	☐
IND_RC	Recreation centre	☐
IND_SG	Showgrounds	☐
IND_SK	Skating	☐
IND_VD	Velodrome	☐

Code	Outdoor sport and recreation facility	Tick the box
OUT_AF	Airfield	☐
OUT_AR	Archery range	☐
OUT_AT	Athletics field	☐
OUT_CO	Coastal	☐
OUT_CT	Courts	☐
OUT_CY	Cycling track	☐
OUT_DF	Diamond field	☐
OUT_EF	Equestrian	☐
OUT_GC	Golf course	☐
OUT_GN	Greens	☐
OUT_MT	Motor racing track	☐
OUT_OR	Off-road vehicle area	☐
OUT_OV	Oval	☐
OUT_PL	Pool	☐
OUT_RC	Racecourse	☐
OUT_RF	Rectangular playing field	☐
OUT_RG	Rodeo ground	☐
OUT_SH	Shooting	☐
OUT_SK	Skatepark	☐

| OUT_TC | Triathlon course | ☐ |
| OUT_WF | Water based | ☐ |

Code	Reserve/open space	Tick the box
RES_GA	Formal gardens/cultural	☐
RES_GP	General park/reserve/open space	☐
RES_SW	Stormwater detention reserve	☐
RES_WC	Watercourse	☐

Code	Conservation	Tick the box
CON_CO	Coastal area (beach/dune/mangrove)	☐
CON_NA	Significant stand of native vegetation	☐
CON_WT	Wetland	☐

Index

About the Author

Jim Daly has worked in the area of recreation and sport planning for most of his working life—first with the YMCA for 18 years, then with the government of South Australia in recreation and sport. He is the manager for economic and industry development in the Office for Recreation and Sport, where he is responsible for the South Australian State Recreation and Sport Strategy Plan. In this capacity Mr. Daly has years of experience managing the development of projects that involve public and private sector planning consultants. He also has traveled widely to present papers and consult on recreation and sport projects in Asia, the Pacific Rim, England, Germany, Canada, and the United States.

Mr. Daly received his master's degree from the University of Adelaide in 1981. His master's thesis was the basis for his first book, *Decisions and Disasters—Alienation of the Adelaide Parklands*, which has been influential in preserving the integrity of these parklands during a period when there are very real threats to their retention.

In his spare time, Mr. Daly enjoys running, cycling, and reading. He also serves on the board of the Cairnmillar Institute, which provides counseling and teaches positive living skills to Adelaide communities, businesses, and schools.

OTHER BOOKS FROM HUMAN KINETICS

Recreational Sport Management

(Third Edition)
Richard F. Mull, MS, Kathryn G. Bayless, MS, Craig M. Ross, ReD, and Lynn M. Jamieson, ReD
1997 • Hardback • 344 pp • Item BMUL0808
ISBN 0-87322-808-1 • $40.00 ($59.95 Canadian)

This classic text and reference, formerly titled *Recreational Sports Programming*, has been updated and expanded to reflect current trends in sport management and recreational sport.

Human Resource Management in Sport and Recreation

Packianathan Chelladurai, PhD
1999 • Hardback • 312 pp • Item BCHE0973
ISBN 0-87322-973-8 • $39.00 ($58.50 Canadian)

This resource explains how to tailor human resource practices to fit each sport or recreation organization's particular goals, products, markets, and technologies.

Financing and Acquiring Park and Recreation Resources

John L. Crompton, PhD
1999 • Hardback • 552 pp • Item BCRO0806
ISBN 0-88011-806-7 • $49.00 ($73.50 Canadian)

Crompton has put every aspect of park and recreation financing into a comprehensive resource that will help today's and tomorrow's managers meet the daily challenge of "doing more with less."

Effective Leadership in Adventure Programming

Simon Priest, PhD, and Michael A. Gass, PhD
1997 • Hardback • 336 pp • Item BPRI0637
ISBN 0-87322-637-2 • $40.00 ($59.95 Canadian)

The authors' skillful approach to integrating all aspects of effective outdoor adventure leadership makes this book a valuable resource for entry-level outdoor leaders as well as for seasoned professionals.

To request more information or to order, U.S. customers call 1-800-747-4457, e-mail us at humank@hkusa.com, or visit our website at www.humankinetics.com. Persons outside the U.S. can contact us via our website or use the appropriate telephone number, postal address, or e-mail address shown in the front of this book.

HUMAN KINETICS
The Information Leader in Physical Activity
P.O. Box 5076, Champaign, IL 61825-5076

Code 2335